GOD'S
AND THE OCEAN

GOD'S WILL
AND
THE OCEAN

SUN MYUNG MOON

THE HOLY SPIRIT ASSOCIATION
FOR THE UNIFICATION OF WORLD CHRISTIANITY

Produced by HSA-UWC Ocean Church, 481 8th Avenue, New York, NY 10001

First Edition
Printed in the United States of America

Library of Congress Catalog Card Number: 87-80284
ISBN 0-910 621-52-7

Foreword

March, 1987 --- New York

Reverend Moon is a man with a vision. That vision, far reaching in its goals and comprehensive in its content, stems from the conviction that this world and especially the human beings who occupy it were created in order to share in a relationship with God. However, human history and current events show that we have fallen far short of becoming this kind of people. Rather than returning joy and glory to God and living with respect and love for one another, we have inherited and now participate in a history filled with selfish strife and stubborn ignorance.

It has not only been humankind who has suffered throughout human history. God, who created all things from the perspective and heart of a parent, has surely cried out in pain over each careless act that brought further misery into the lives of His children. How does one respond when he perceives this, the suffering of God and the plight of humankind? How does one face this endangered world and take up the task left by great prophets and religious leaders before him? How does one who hears the call, "Take up the cross and follow me," truly answer that call, and to the fullest extent, live out what that means?

From early on in his life, Reverend Moon has been patiently and painfully giving his full attention to these questions. Through years of scriptural study, ardent prayers and a daily life that rigorously tested every detail of his search, he discovered the answers. He realized that he could not just give words to bring solutions, but had to exemplify those words in his daily life. The arduous task which he began, of bringing a new and vitally needed message to this world, has been somewhat documented, but not fully as of yet.

The thirteen speeches and numerous excerpts contained in this volume are part of this man's vision. Indeed, they are a special part because they reveal the high hopes and practical plans of a man truly desiring to bring God back into the lives of men and women, and the world back into the bosom of God. Whenever Reverend Moon puts his hand and heart towards any project, large or small, he is always motivated by this singular desire. So it is with his vision of the ocean.

Reverend Moon recognizes that mankind has been greatly wounded by prolonged poverty and extensive violence. Our earthly environment has also suffered tremendous abuse through the centuries of unchecked and unwise use. Humankind has largely failed to develop an internal sensitivity, a spirituality, to guide its external technical advancements. Thus, we face a dilemma which threatens worldwide survival.

Reverend Moon perceives the task of healing this situation on both universal and individual scales. To have a good world, there must be good men and women within it. To have good men and women, there must first be good children, raised in good, God-centered families. From such families, good communities, societies and nations can grow and expand. In this way a good world can unfold, imbued with the spirit of God and built by the hands of mankind.

Tragically, we are often unaware of our precious value in front of God and fail to act accordingly. In other words, we are ignorant of and fail to manifest the full dignity of our human responsibilities. Young people today especially find it difficult to experience the presence of a loving God in a chaotic world that appears bent upon its own demise. Consequently, they give up and live out their despair in destructive acts such as drug abuse, immature and immoral love, and cynical lifestyles that pursue only self-fulfillment.

One of the cornerstones of Reverend Moon's message is that we are given life for a purpose; to experience and manifest God's very esssence, which is love. This purpose can be realized as each of us becomes attentive to and fulfills the fundamental responsibilities of human life. The first book of the Bible, Gensis, expresses this purpose as the three Great Blessings. These three blessings are the core of Reverend Moon's message, and his clear explanation of how they can be accomplished is providing inspiration and direction for people throughout the world.

The First Blessing calls us to the full realization of each individual as a true child and person in the image of God: "Be fruitful, . . ." The Second Blessing calls us to expand upon this through the attainment of mature and lasting love between a man and a woman expressed through marriage and family centered upon God: ". . . multiply, . . ." Therefore, children can be raised in a loving and secure environment which produces an ever-widening spiral linking God to people and people to God. Building upon the first two blessings, the Third Blessing exhorts humankind to take its proper position in the universe: ". . . and replenish the earth and subdue it and have dominion over the fish of the sea, and of the fowl of the air, and over every living thing that moves upon the earth." Thus humankind indeed becomes the God-centered caretaker of the world, empowered by the benevolent love of God rather than greed and selfishness. In essence, these are the responsibilities of humankind, and when respectively fulfilled, they become the wonderful blessings of life.

Reverend Moon came to America with this and much more in his mind and heart. He came with a special concern about the youth of this nation and the depth of this care is reflected in many of his speeches. Although he has begun an incredible array of projects, the central focus of his efforts has been to raise up the youth of this nation so that America's future and the future of the world can move in the direction of God's will -- towards the establishment of a heavenly kingdom on earth.

Ocean Church is one such project, for as Reverend Moon has often said, "Whoever is concerned about the future must look towards the ocean." Although he officially inaugurated Ocean Church in 1980, Reverend Moon had already spent more than a decade of active and intensive fishing upon the ocean. But it was not just for fish that he went to the ocean; he went there to pray and meditate. From those seasons of hard work in all kinds of severe conditions, he was able to lay the concrete plans which are now unfolding in the Ocean Church providence. The speeches herein outline the development of those ideas.

The ocean is the world's most vast resource. It is also the world's most delicate resource. To properly use the ocean, men and women must receive training so that they can become people of the highest caliber. If the ocean is utilized with anything less, it too will go the way of many other aspects of the Creation which have been, and still are, plundered and polluted to the point of no return.

One of Reverend Moon's desires is that ocean-going individuals and related communities and enterprises can be duly inspired to wisely integrate their approaches to the ocean. If we understand our position to be that of good stewards, we will want to use the ocean for the benefit of all. We will also be concerned to balance development of the ocean's resources with proper conservation and management. Many of Reverend Moon's speeches contain references to the potential of the ocean as well as the need to protect and take care of it. It is truly one of his greatest hopes that the resources of the ocean can be utilized in their full measure in order to better feed the world's hungry.

The solution of these and other related problems begins with dedicated individuals. In the following speeches, one will find that Reverend Moon regards every aspect of the ocean as a tool for teaching. No small detail lacks importance to this end. In training young men and women to take care of their boats, he asks them to do so with the spirit of taking care of the entire world. In discussing the minute procedures of catching a tuna, he asks them to accomplish what is often difficult and sometimes dangerous with the spirit of taking on bigger and bolder projects that yet lay ahead.

For Reverend Moon, the ocean is not only a classroom; it is also a cathedral. It is not only a place to learn daily realities; it is also a place where little exists that can close the mind and corrupt the heart. Out on the ocean, without the pressures and pretensions of modern life, a young person's heart can unfold naturally. At sea, the elements are much larger than the person. When the sun rises on the ocean, an entire horizon opens up and the mind can aspire to great thoughts. When wave upon wave rocks the boat, the rhythm of life itself begins to beat within the heart. One cannot help but feel part of a grand panorama that has pattern and power, beauty and abundance. There, the presence of God can be keenly felt and clearly known. Awe is a common experience, almost a daily event.

In the following speeches, one can see that Reverend Moon has experienced these things to the core of his being. Without hesitation, he has shared his experience in every possible way with those who have been with him and for those who will come after him. The ocean-going tradition is the tradition of the poetic heart that bears practical responsibility. It is in the spirit of that tradition that we commend this volume to you.

The Editor

Contents

xi

Contents

The Way of Tuna

July 13th, 1980 -- Belvedere

THE UNIFICATION Church is very special, with its understanding of the role of Abel. The world would never imagine that I spend a great deal of time on the ocean to catch tuna, so before I start on the main topic I want to talk a little about tuna. If you think some fish are beautiful, then you would have to consider the tuna to be the beauty queen of all fish. How many of you have ever seen tuna? Well, most of you haven't, so you may not know what I am talking about.

Tuna are completely streamlined for fast swimming and they are the only fish which can fold all their fins right next to their bodies when they are swimming really quickly. It is like the concept of the Concorde: for take-off the wings are spread out, but for cruising speed the wings are swept back. A tuna's side fins are completely hidden when it is speeding along, giving it a completely smooth surface. A tuna can swim up to ninety knots, like an airplane of the ocean! Water resistance is greater than air resistance, so airplane designers will have to study tuna when they want to come up with ideas for more efficient airplanes. The average cruising speed for tuna is thirty-five knots.

Tuna do not live in just one area, but swim in all five oceans. If the ocean were divided into sovereignties, then the tuna would be in trouble because it would need a visa. But tuna just fly through the water, in all five oceans of the world! Furthermore, tuna have solid meat which is good for eating. In the future, tuna will provide food for the world.

Tuna fishing is the king of sport fishing because it is so exciting and thrilling. Tuna fishing is really the ultimate goal of fishermen. I would like to generate world-wide interest in this apex of the sport by perfecting the skill of catching tuna. You have to outsmart a tuna in order to catch it because they are very smart fish. However, once you master the skill, you become an addict. Even when you think you will finally leave the fishing ground for the day, your attention is drawn back to the area and you are eager to return.

Tuna fishing requires a boat that is from twenty-five to fifty feet long. Getting a boat and all the necessary equipment, plus daily expenses for fishing, requires money that only more wealthy people can afford. Only people who have a strong interest in the ocean can concentrate on this kind of sport fishing. For this reason, people who can afford it always concentrate on tuna. Women of the world always dream of having diamonds, and sports-minded men always dream of catching tuna. Tuna fishing is more than just a sport or a hobby; it is really a battle, and this is why I like it; you must be ready to go after the goal and gain the victory.

A big tuna weighs over 1,000 pounds, which is six or seven times the weight of the average person, and is thirteen to fourteen feet long. When we pull a big tuna aboard the *New Hope*, it stretches diagonally across the whole boat, touching each side. Tunas are caught with a hook and long line, and great skill and knowledge are required to win the battle. After long, long hours of waiting, a tuna will strike and for that moment, you forget everything else. In Gloucester, three to five hundred boats gather for the tuna season. People sail for months from the West Coast and through the Panama Canal to come for tuna fishing in Gloucester. In some cases, boats come from South America. For that season, the richest and most famous boats assemble in Gloucester.

The fishermen are more proud of their boats than women are of their finest jewelry. These boats each need four crew members to go along. You can imagine that no one can afford to do that except wealthy people; they spend all that money and time to get there just for the excitement of catching tuna. Five hundred boats use about $50,000 worth of bait a day. Tuna season normally lasts seventy days, and the bait alone costs $3.5 million. If each boat is crewed by three people, that is 1,500 people in one area. If each boat spends $500 a day for seventy days, that is $1.5 million. This is the investment that they make in order to have a chance to catch a part of the quota of tuna that the government allows to be caught each year.

If the government allots 1,800 tuna and you sell each tuna for $1,000, that is only $1.8 million. In other words, tuna fishing is not a money-making investment. It is extraordinary to break even at tuna fishing; it is virtually impossible. When I see the enthusiasm these people have for tuna fishing, I think that if they loved America the way they do fishing, it would have become the Kingdom of Heaven a long time ago. I always think that if Americans have that kind of heart and soul, why not harness it for kingdom-building?

During the tedious wait for a tuna to strike, people may complain and fight, but when the tuna bites, they are instantly united as one. I have never seen such instant unification! That is the unification spirit I am trying to promote, so rather than just talk about it, I particularly want Unification people to come from all over the world and experience it.

The one thing men cannot say they have experienced is the pain of giving birth to a child. Only women know it through experience. However, tuna fishing is usually in the man's world, and it is difficult for women to understand it. The rugged tuna world is far apart from the world of make-up, manicures and jewelry. Fishermen usually wear nothing from the waist up, and they get deep tans.

I have experienced all kinds of sports in the man's world, yet I have never found any that was as exciting as the struggle with tuna. Do you have an appetitie for that? Not everyone can do it; you have to be born with the traits for it. However, women can be interested in it too. I am always studying how the American fishing industry can become prosperous once again, so whenever I am in Gloucester I am always planning how to interest American young people in the ocean.

Tuna season is like the Olympics of sport fishing, and I determined that I would be a record-breaking tuna fisherman. It took me twenty-two long days to catch my first tuna, however. There were many strikes during that time, but for lack of experience they were all lost. When a strike is so exciting, you can imagine how disappointing it is to lose the fish, but then you restore your spirit and resolve to go on. When the sun starts to sink at the end of the day, I feel like ordering the sun to stay up so I can stay out and get another strike. You really don't understand how I feel. If you have this kind of spirit when you attack any task or problem, there is nothing you cannot do. Though you lose the tuna, you just keep trying until you catch one. That's the way it goes.

When I first started out, people laughed at me as a novice. I thought, "They should watch me for three years and see what happens." All the professional fishermen were astonished that I broke record after record during those three years. Now they feel threatened by this "novice" who is having an impact on their world. They worry about what to do with the Moonies who are stealing all the honors. They can't stand to see us taking all the records, so they have started getting up earlier in the mornings in order to beat us. When they discovered that I was going out at four-thirty in the morning, they decided to go out one-half hour earlier. But, it didn't last; after the first day, only a few people came out at four. In the meantime, I started going out at three-thirty in the morning. When they resolved to go earlier than that, I started going out at two-thirty!

When you go out that early, you usually have to wait four hours because the tuna come to breakfast on time...their time. However, it was a war and I went out early. Now people are giving up trying to beat the Moonies; they know that for sheer consistency and hard work, they cannot compete with us. What is interesting is that even with all those boats anchored up and fishing, the first strike always comes to the *New Hope*. Yesterday when I went out, it only took four minutes for the first strike to come!

Do you have some interest in this? How about the women? If you are interested, you have to marry a tuna fisherman to enter that world. Those who don't know the taste of tuna fishing don't really know the taste of life. When the interest in tuna is so great, will the number of people getting involved start to shrink, or become greater? A person with a really masculine character who tastes the spirit of tuna fishing wants to go out each day, regardless of how rough the sea is. This is the fundamental attitude of the men of the ocean. When you know this thrill and excitement, even if you are seasick, you still go. Tuna fishing is the best way to learn about the fishing industry.

People begin fishing with smaller boats, but each year get bigger ones. They make it their goal to beat the best person of the previous year. In Gloucester, excitement starts to swell when tuna season comes, because they know the top champion always comes-- Reverend Moon in the *New Hope*. I feel it is good competition and young people will want to challenge that goal and record. If I set a goal for them to challenge, then the America fishing industry has some future.

Today, that industry has almost come to a halt because no one has that spirit. American women are not particularly fond of fish smells or the life of ocean-going men. It is an extraordinary woman who is interested in the ocean and its fish. When the battle starts with the tuna's strike, there is no time for courtesy or pleasantries. A team has to be organized and busy, and a fisherman would even yell at his own father at such a time. It is a rare woman who wouldn't mind being kicked by her own husband in the heat of a tuna battle. What about Unification Church women?

I am certainly not fishing for money. I already have the foundation to move in any direction. My goal is to break the record and demonstrate the sea-going spirit to the world. Year after year, I have set the record and people know now it is not happening by chance or coincidence, and that I have a special secret. People want to learn that secret, so they are trying to be nice to me. The other fishermen follow the *New Hope* with their binoculars, and when I get a strike, everyone's eyes are on me. Anyone in Gloucester who is interested in tuna fishing knows about the *New Hope*.

We want to establish something permanent in Gloucester, so we recently obtained a big estate there, which used to belong to the Catholic church. That house is being prepared to welcome people from all over the world. If anyone is invited up there to participate in our tuna fishing, they will not refuse. The mayor has been negative toward us, but let him come and see what we are doing. I see this house as an essential diplomatic base.

Gloucester is close to Boston, a major city in the world, and near Provincetown, where the Pilgrims once landed. The spirit of this nation was born in the New England area, so it is an important area. It is a cultural center of America, and well-known as a seaport. Thus, it is a strategic location to show the world my spirit.

Recently, we bought a marina that was up for auction and many people bid against us, but the price kept rising and soon everyone stopped bidding. Even the mayor was interested in that marina, and he was anxious to keep us from getting it because it was such choice water-front property. Many powerful corporations bid, but I never paid attention to them, and eventually, we bought it.

Now we have that marina, plus a dock and an estate, so Gloucester is being impacted by Moonies. Also the entire sport fishing industry is influenced by us, especially by our first opening of the world tuna tournament this year, offering the first prize of $100,000. Everyone was completely shocked when the announcement was made, but they became eager to see the Moonies come to their town. Gloucester citizens, the police chief and Coast Guard are all excited. Everyone's eyes popped at the thought of $100,000 and all of a sudden, they didn't mind the Moonies so much anymore. They say it is the most exciting event in a century in Gloucester. Boston, Gloucester and Provincetown are all bases for the tournament, so it is a topic in those cities as well. Everyone is talking about who will win the prizes, but I know who will win. However, since I am sponsoring the tournament, it would not be good for me to win first prize. I will, therefore, be the honorary chairman and compete, but I will not take the prize even if I do the best. Moonies can win, however.

The most important thing will not be who wins first prize, but which boat does it. I am determined that our people work the hardest for all three prizes. If they win, people will want to know which company made their boats, and then they will discover that I designed the boats and created the company that made them. I have planned down to the most minute detail what kind of boat would be best for tuna fishing, and yesterday I checked what our factory is doing, specifying what details must be changed. The people of the world will know these boats are my creation.

No one thinks I will build boats, but you will see that our boats will be 21st century boats. Once our boat is proven the best for tuna fishing in this contest, there will be a great market for them. I know the advantages and disadvantages of different styles, and through design, I compensated for all of those things. Mr. Henry Masters is our brother from England, and I have guided him directly in completing the plans. Our boats will win the prizes in the tuna tournament. You wait and see. The fact that we bought some property in Gloucester was world news, reported in the *Wall Street Journal* and the *New York Times*. *Time* magazine devoted almost an entire page to it. When the media finds out that Ocean Church boats win the world tuna tournament, that will really be news. They will wonder when a religious leader became such a fantastic boat designer.

Many thought it was just throwing money away to offer $100,000 for the tournament, but there are specific reasons. That prize brought more than $200,000 worth of publicity. The people who were anxious to get rid of the Moonies have seen the excitement build in Gloucester, and now they are embarrassed to be seen in public. The tournament will last seven days, and whoever does the best during that time will win.

This tournament is not just an exciting event in America, but in Japan as well. Japan is a great consumer of tuna, and the major Japanese tuna companies are represented in Gloucester. They will send their best people, and everyone will watch to see what happens. The major seafood companies will see that Reverend Moon's boats and people are winning, and they will know they can't help but deal with us in the future. The big Japanese companies are backed by their government, but we are backed by heaven. We will compete with them, and in the next few years we will beat them.

There are four major fishing areas in the world--one is in Norway, but the other three surround the United States. One is the Bering Sea, in Alaska; the other is the Gulf of Mexico, and the other is along the East Coast, especially in the Gloucester area. A few years ago, the American government set up a 200-mile limit for off-shore fishing by foreign boats. Foreign governments are trying all kinds of strategies to get inside that 200-mile limit to fish. There is a great deal of diplomatic pressure to use these fishing grounds which are monopolized by the American government.

However, we are not foreigners. The Japanese companies see that Reverend Moon has a base in the United States, and furthermore, has so many Japanese people working with him who are engaged to Americans. They realize that we are their only link to America. We are becoming the best bridge for Japan to trade in sea products with America, and vice versa.

The American and Japanese governments are fierce competitors, but by using our organization as a link, we can smooth out the bad feelings and work for the benefit of both countries. I am interested in marketing strategy. Mitsubishi and Marubeni have to use many middlemen, and each level needs to get some profit. My strategy is to send the product straight from the factory to the retailer, bypassing the middlemen. Then the product can be provided much more cheaply to the consumer. This is why I have created mobile seafood stores, which are converted vans fitted with refrigeration. We are good at preparing fish; the Japanese in particular know how to fix fish in many ways. Once we prepare the fish, all the people have to do is enjoy it at home. Many Americans don't know how to prepare fish, so we do it, and all they have to do is eat it. The lines will be blocks long outside our mobile stores. One van will be responsible for twelve home church areas, roving around, serving 4,380 homes. The vans will have special theme music and special signs so that people will get to know you when you come to their homes.

We will also cater and start seafood restaurant chains which will provide fresh, cooked fish for banquets. If you have the reputation that in a few hours you can provide good food for one or two hundred people, you will get an incredible amount of business. More and more the American diet will include seafood, because people are realizing that eating large amounts of red meat isn't healthy. Seafood provides much more healthy forms of protein.

My plan for marketing in Japan calls for 7,000 seafood vans to cover the whole country. Once they are in operation, they will make twice as much as the MFT fund raisers. When B and C members see how successful our A members are in the fish business, they will want to do it too, instead of their own jobs. Once we demonstrate reliable income, we can buy vans on credit, and when bankers see what the Moonies are doing, they will want our business. Whoever does well in this business will rise to ever higher levels in Japanese-American trade.

We have ordered 100 vans and thirty have arrived. Right now, three members are working in one van, but in six months they will branch out, with one person per van. I want to see it expand, from one van to three, then three to nine, and nine to twenty-seven, so that in three years, Japan will have 7,000 vans. If we have 800 by the end of one year, there can be far more than 7,000 by the end of three years. We will use exactly the same system in America.

Home church will be developing side by side with the marketing plan, so we will offer service to the people as well as income, and in this way, the home church providence will prosper. All the experts trained in this system in Japan will come to America and install their system here. At the same time, through a fellowship organization, we can make friends with wealthy people who are interested in tuna fishing. Through the tuna tournament we can organize them into a club and then expand it throughout the world. Tuna travel the world, so when the season ends in Gloucester it begins somewhere else. If we sponsor tournaments in five places around the world, that is $500,000 in prizes. That investment will lure tens of thousands of influential people. Their boats are capable of crossing the Atlantic or Pacific, going from one tournament to another. Once this plan has momentum, the government will have to be supportive, and they will organize all the necessary supplies. Also, since there are already many marine facilities around the world, we will create a system so that the major vessels can provide fuel to the sport fishermen. As the club's influence grows, these things can be arranged. People will certainly see that Reverend Moon is the king of the ocean, not only in generating healthy sea sport, but in generating trade and commerce as well as good food to benefit the people of the world. Eventually we will have our own capacity to supply our boats. The tournament fleet will be moving from one ocean to another, with an oil tanker accompanying it. The major corporations of the world will want to particpate because the worldwide publicity will be so great. Imagine tens of thousands of boats coming to Gloucester for the competition; they will bring tremendous prosperity to that small sea town. All those people will have to eat and sleep somewhere and get supplies, so the economic impact will be tremendous.

There are many resources that can be transported from one part of the world that is rich to another part where there is famine. This is why I created the International Relief Friendship Foundation. American companies sometimes have a surplus of products which become burdensome because they must be stored and, at the same time, the companies must pay taxes on them. Many times they cannot sell these old products for whatever reason, so they are in a dilemma. Often they are willing to give that material to some organization as a contribution, but even the churches today don't know what to do with so much material because they don't have the capacity to handle it. However, we have created a foundation which can receive surplus commodities, plus a fleet to transport them from one port to another, so we can meet that need.

This has tremendous implications. Any government that is interested in the welfare of its people will link up with us because we have so much ability to help them. To implement this, we need properly trained and skilled manpower. Where can we train people? I want to have 200 of our boats deployed along the American coast with three people on each boat, which means 600 people. Once we have continued for three years, three people won't be necessary; one person can do it. This kind of system can be expanded very quickly.

The young people who become experienced in small boats will want to handle bigger and bigger boats. In about sixteen years, everyone can be a trained, experienced captain of a big boat. We can get government loans and create more fishing boats, assigning an experienced captain to each one. Then, their mission will be to catch specific fish that are in demand.

Cold storage is the big problem in the fishing industry. Therefore, I am investigating advanced techniques of making dry fish powder that doesn't need cold storage. Millions of tons can be stored in bags in open air. We will develop powder for different fish and combine them, like multiple vitamins. This powder can be used in daily cooking, to supplement the overuse of flour and starch. You will be able to create new cuisine by using fish powder in nutritous cooking.

I will soon test fish powder bread versus wheat flour bread. Once people taste it, they won't have to be persuaded which is better. The best test will be giving it to children, who are very honest. I am sure they will all take the fish bread. There is already a fish powder company operating in Norway, and one of our members is researching that process in depth. The problem now is not in catching the fish, but in marketing the fish before they spoil. We are working on the solution to that.

Because we have a way to store the fish, we will catch as much as possible without hesitation. Already, we catch more tuna than anyone else. The fishermen will bring their catches to us because we will have no limit on how much we can buy. Therefore, we can provide a tremendous incentive for the fishing industry. I have the entire system worked out, starting with boat building. After we build the boats, we catch the fish and process them for market, and then have a distribution network. This is not just on the drawing board; I have already done it.

All these ideas I conceived many years ago, and I knew just where to start--with tuna fishing--because it is the essential way to train people in the fishing spirit. I have been doing that for seven years. Furthermore, another reason I have pursued this direction is that resources on land for feeding the world will soon be inadequate. There is a limited amount of land, and it gets poorer over the years, but the ocean is boundless. You cannot eat all the plants that grow on land, but everything that comes from the ocean can be eaten, and it is all good for the body.

Animal feed can be produced from the ocean; when seaweed is properly processed, there is tremendous nutrition there. In addition, we will not just harvest fish that grow wild, but will farm fish as well. Normally a calf cost one-fifth the price of a full grown cow. The tuna, however, has a tremendous capacity to multiply; one tuna lays

150,000 eggs. Would you have to pay one-fifth the price of a tuna for one little egg? Tuna farming is already in the experimental stage. Most baby tuna are eaten by other fish, but when they are protected they will grow quickly. There is great potential in tuna farming.

I am the founder of this gigantic spiritual movement, but I am also laying the foundation to solve future physical problems of the world. I know that all this is basic for future food production and solving hunger in the world. Some environmentalist might ask me, "Reverend Moon, why do you kill tuna all the time?" My answer is, "How can you worry about tuna when all the people may die? I want to prevent such a future from happening." In another way, I view a tuna as an offering, and I am in a position as a chief priest to offer it to God. I seldom eat the tuna I have caught because I see it as a sacrifice for the sake of mankind. In the Old Testament, the priests killed and burnt offerings on the altar, and blood was shed.

Another health food trend in the near future will be to eat raw foods like fish, grains and vegetables. It is medically true that raw foods give you more energy. Fish powder will solve many things because it will contain most of the nutrition you need. With a bag of fish powder you can travel anywhere in the world and eat wherever you are. The land has been fully exploited by man, but God preserved the ocean resources almost totally untouched. (There are even precious stones in the oceans).

This year, we have saved and numbered the tail fins of the tuna I have caught, and when they are preserved, each state center will have one. When people look at those fins, they can feel they are looking at the future food messiah who will solve the food problems of the world. Since I am so enthusiastic and have so many plans about the ocean, anyone who comes to the Unification Church cannot help but pay attention to the ocean. Would you like to go to sea? [Yes!] When did you become so enthusiastic about the ocean?

For seven years I have been going to the ocean and praying out there, early in the morning and late at night. As Unification Church members you cannot help but pay attention to the ocean. Did you think about the ocean before you joined the Unification Church? When you think of the ocean you think about the movie, *Jaws*, don't you? Now, instead of thinking a shark will use you as his food, you can think you will use the shark to feed the world. Not only men, but women will do it also. That is a long-standing goal of mine.

If there are any people who don't want to do this, raise your hands. From next year on, we will have ocean workshops lasting six months, and once you pass, you will go on a tuna tour around the world. You will even sail to Korea. We have radios, so I can command our worldwide fleet from one flagship, directing each ship around the world.

In the future when the Communist threat is ended, there will be no more war. Instead of being scrapped, all the government naval vessels can be utilized by us as mother ships for peaceful purposes. They can supply the fleets that are harvesting the resources of the ocean. An aircraft carrier is like a floating island and can travel thousands of miles with no problem. I will get one aircraft carrier for each ocean, or two for the big oceans. Then we can get airplanes, and they can use the carriers as airports. Would you want to join that fleet and become captains?

Usually Americans don't like the smell of fish, and when you talk about fish, you shake your heads. Now, you will be different. I am not just thinking about all these things, but have already started them. You sisters, show me your muscles! Oh, not very much. I have the ambition to train many women captains. You will still have your charming woman's smile, but will act strongly like a man. That will be very poetic. Our sisters will create literary masterpieces based on their experiences at sea. That is my thinking.

If your husband had this kind of dream, would you be a happy woman? To reach that goal, you will have to go through a great deal of misery because it is a tough process. You have to taste bitterness in order to appreciate sweetness. I would like to mobilize the spirited young men and women of the world and bring them to the horizon of this goal. I knew that governments and religions would persecute us, but I always had an alternate plan for building the kingdom of heaven on earth. I always thought that if people don't like me, I would build the kingdom on the ocean first and then bring it to land.

In the last ten days, I have become deeply tanned and my goal is to become darker than any black man in America. Then I want to see what white women will say. I am watching how Mother will react to having a black husband. I know that Mother will say, "Father, you are so handsome in your dark skin; I love you even more." She will have a black husband in the summer and a white husband in the winter.

My topic was supposed to have been the "Way of Abel," but instead it became the "Way of Tuna." Well then, when the way of tuna is followed properly, you will surely end up in Abel's role. I started with only my bare hands when I arrived in America, but in a few years I have truly created an empire. Do you know what is happening in Alaska? The most advanced seafood processing factory is being built there; even the state government is amazed. Now, people are asking my guidance for the Alaskan seafood industry because our factory is so exemplary. We have a shipyard in Alabama which can build boats up to 300 feet long, which is a gigantic boat. One of those would cost several million dollars. Wouldn't you like to go out as captain on one of those boats?

When transported to Japan, the tuna price is usually twenty times that in America. In order to do that, it must be fresh. For that reason, I researched how to transport tuna, and now that we can do that, we can utilize the same method for other fish as well. I have opened the door.

Anyone who has at least three spiritual children can come to Boston, though I think that maybe one-third of you will lose your enthusiasm after your first experiences on the ocean. You will spend more time in the bathroom, not sitting on the toilet, but leaning over it. Will you mind? It will be the world's most exciting drama and comedy. The interesting thing is that at sea you may be in the bathroom all the time, but as soon as you are back on solid ground, you feel fine and are truly hungry. In some cases, a person is so engrossed in throwing up out of his mouth that he doesn't notice that his bowel movement has come out the other end! The Unification Church is really somthing else. You are proud of it though, aren't you? Wouldn't you like to have dark skin like mine?

On the ocean you won't have good food like you do on land. You just have raw fish, but it will certainly be very fresh; just dip it in soy sauce and eat it. Now you know why I have been spending all my summers on the ocean these last seven years, and why tuna are so important. Now you know it is directly linked to the dispensation, so it can be a topic in your prayer.

It so happens that tuna season in Gloucester comes in the middle of vacation season, which means people from all over the world can come. The estate I bought is now tuna tournament headquarters. Would you want it to be an impressive place? There are thirty bedrooms there and this house will be used year round, not just in the summer. Famous professors will come for seminars there.

Our whole budget for the summer has been spent already, so I told our people that if they want to eat they can either have sand or go get tuna. Now the staff is fishing very hard to get tuna so they can go on. Tuna fishing is certainly not a vacation for me; it is a war and a battle, I sleep two or three hours at the most at night. The young people are always dozing off; my driver always sleeps in the car, but I never sleep on the boat. When God sees me, He cannot help but say I am something special because no one can keep up with me. Christian ministers are very interested in their honor and future, but I am crazy about the salvation of the world, how I can feed the world population, how I can help this nation. That is what I am thinking about day in and day out. In the summer your face should be tan and dark with the appearance of rugged men and women who are committed to the mission. Would you like this tough mission? Your "thank you" doesn't sound very strong! However, it is a beautiful day today, the best day for tuna fishing. Tuna is the Abel of the sea, so this wasn't too far from my original topic. From tuna, you have learned many things about my vision of the future and what fishing is all about. God bless you.

The Founding of
Ocean Church

October 1st, 1980 -- Morning Garden

SOMETIMES YOU might wonder about some of our church customs, such as bowing down. You might say to yourself, "Why do we do that?" Even though it has been a custom in many parts of the world for thousands of years, it becomes easier to understand why we also   practice the full bow if you hear a full explanation of it. First, it is a very symbolic act. You bow down with four limbs, meaning that you are standing on the four-position foundation. This bow also reflects the proper subject and object relationship, because, as you bow, you move from high to low, which symbolizes the vertical relationship between heaven and earth.

The Meaning of the Full Bow

To bow, you stand naturally, not in a stiff way, with one foot slightly ahead of the other. The right foot symbolizes man and the left foot symbolizes woman. The right foot should go slightly ahead of the left, symbolizing also the subject and object relationship between man and woman. Then, as you bow, all parts of the body come closer together, and this symbolizes how the four-position foundation becomes one.

The head symbolizes God, and both arms symbolize man and woman and the relationship that they have. The feet represent earth. So, when we raise our arms to touch our head, this shows the subject and object becoming one with each other and one with God, then coming down to be one with the earth. Even the face

16

symbolizes this whole relationship. The eyes symbolize God, the nose symbolizes man and woman--one but with two parts--and the mouth symbolizes earth. The eyes look out and see; this represents heaven. The torso, the body symbolizes the universe.

In other words, the universe stands on the foundation of the four-position relationship. It's very appropriate to greet and respect God, and those who represent God, in this way. In Korea, this custom has existed for thousands of years. However, we do it, not because of the Korean custom, but because it coincides with the Principle. This is the way children greet their parents every day, every morning.

When you see children, especially still within the womb, you see them clutching their fingers together and making a fist. Why? The thumb symbolizes God, and the fingers symbolize the four-position foundation which surrounds it. If you look at that and really notice how the body reflects everything in the universe, you can see that of all the greetings that are given in every country around the world, this one is the most comprehensive and most meaningful. It is the most proper way to show respect because it reminds us in a very meaningful way of who we truly are in front of God and in front of one another. In your own centers and where you work on your missions, do you keep the Sunday morning pledge service? This is also very important to do each week, each month and each year. At these times, the man and wife, if they are blessed, should bow down in an easterly direction, because that is where the sun rises and this too symbolizes God. The North is another direction you can bow towards because the highest point, the North Pole, is in that direction. Also, the North Star, which has been the guiding point for mankind throughout history, is in the northern sky.

The Original Seed of History

In history, there have been many civilizations. The civilization of the North is now communism. Do you understand? Now, communism is widespread throughout many nations and it is about to conquer the world. That has been the intention of the Communists and they have the ability to do it. This is the last of

Satan's work. However, when the springtime comes, even the farthest North Pole will have to melt down. What is unificationism? It is the beginning of a new civilization. Let me briefly explain. Ancient civilizations were in the tropical range, such as Egypt. The ancient civilizations started out in a hot climate. So, we can say they were "summer" civilizations. Today, we find the warm to cool climate civilizations which have risen from those times, such as Europe. These can be called the "autumn" civilizations. In autumn the leaves start to come down from the trees. In like manner, we see these civilizations coming down from their former greatness. The tree loses its leaves and the bare branches are all that is left. It's not utterly gone, but just the image of the tree remains and everything else comes down. Then, the cold winter civilization, from communism, from the North, will broaden out, and the autumn civilization be absorbed by it. It cannot remain as it used to be. The cold is merciless. Communism is merciless; it leaves nothing alone once it decides to intervene. It completely eliminates whatever is in its way. In these terms, we can certainly say that we have yet to see the "springtime" civilization. You should know that mankind was meant to start from the spring. We look back in history and see that there has never been a springtime in civilization. Mankind has never seen its flower truly bloom. So, perhaps this is now the beginning of true love and all the flourishing of the fruits of true love in its first bloom.

If we had started from the spring and then developed into summer, autumn and winter, the fruit would have blossomed from the original seed. However, no original seed was planted, thus when the winter came, nothing was left. If you have planted a seed, it goes deeper and deeper during the winter and comes out even more fully the next spring. However, without the original seed, the fruit will just die and there will be nothing left for the coming spring.

If you are going to live through the winter, through the severe cold and survive, you have to have the seed. The history of fallen mankind did not start from the original seed. God has to start a new history, this time with His seed implanted into it. So, what should this seed be like? It must be very strong and hard. If you are like that, you can be planted before the severest winter and the cold will not destroy you. You will not be cracked open by the cold and when spring comes, you will begin to blossom.

God created in such a scientific way; God is really the greatest scientist. Look at water. When water starts freezing, it also expands. Look at the pine seed that lies within the hard shell protecting it. The shell also has some moisture and when it becomes cold and freezes, this causes it to expand until after several times, it finally cracks.

Likewise, you Unification members have to be very strong, very tight and in one piece. Then, you have to go and confront communism, or what we can call, "winterism." And then, your outer shell will crack open and you will start growing. Finally, when spring really comes, you will start to grow and you will be able to meet the springtime in full. You will be like the flower that can open fully and spread all its leaves and its glory. This is what we are looking towards.

Then starts an eternal blossoming of a new civilization, the springtime civilization. This may have been loosely explained, the reasoning may not have been so exact, but nature is not that difficult to see and understand. You can see the logic of the seed in nature, and if this was God's way of beginning things in nature, it was also to be God's original point of beginning the history of mankind. Everything else was leading up to that point. When the original seed was lost, mankind had to go through a complete cycle again until the Second Advent could occur. This is the meaning of the Second Advent and from this, the eternal flourishing of mankind will begin. If communism is truly the winter civilization, it must precede the springtime civilization. Unificationism is that springtime civilization. It brings everything into oneness and harmony. For example, the hot weather of springtime is not too hot and the cold weather is not too cold. It is just like the temperature of the human being, thirty-five to thirty-eight degrees centigrade. In this temperature range, all the cells and life forms start to flourish. This is the Kingdom of Heaven or what we like to term, "The Ideal World." If you can understand this and give the correct image of it, you can give a full explanation of the entire human history--where it started and why, where it ends and how.

The Communists are typical of the cold weather. They will just storm against others, hit them and try to knock them down completely. But our way is to make peace everywhere and melt every-thing down, even the coldest ice. Even though everything melts, it will go on and on so that life will flourish.

That's idealism. Where should that idealism start? It must begin from man and woman. Unfortunately, in the original Garden of Eden, the original man and woman could not start the Ideal World. Isn't it wonderful and significant then, when we bow to the East? It reminds us of the original starting point for civilization, and denotes that man's destiny should be noble and eternal. East represents glory and North represents authority. The sun rises in the East, bringing glory to each day, and the North is the highest point, which is a point of honor and authority. When you bow in these directions, you are saying that man should have glory and authority.

Authority goes higher and higher, reaching for the highest point which is God. Glory moves from East to West, moving horizontally, so glory is always expanding. North is vertical and East is horizontal. These directions meet in man. However, the fall changed all these things. In the fall, man became one with woman, instead of woman becoming one with man. But now, we are going back and restoring the original positions, thus, the woman becomes one with man. When this happens, all the vertical and horizontal relationships can be restored. The husband and wife bow down together. That is the meaning of this.

Ideally, a couple bows down to Heaven and to each other. Then, the man sits down and the woman bows to the man. After that, they both sit down, side by side. In this, the woman is saying that she will not be a fallen Eve and the man is saying that he will not be a fallen Adam. Such is the meaning of the morning pledge service, especially in this way of bowing down. After that, all the children will come down and offer the same bow. The parents will sit in the parents position and receive their bow. In other words, the children express their relationship to their parents and to God. The children are saying that unlike Cain and Abel in the past, they are not going to be in conflict. Instead they will be in peace and harmony and will cooperate within the four-position foundation. When that is done, the whole family will come into unity and express their one heart.

The Meaning of the Pledge

We are not yet living in the Ideal World, but instead are living in the midst of an evil world; this is why we must recite the pledge. We pledge and say that we will fulfill the will of God. Without the family coming into unity, you cannot make this pledge. God does not want just the man to pledge, nor just the woman. God wants both the man and woman to pledge to Him after they first come into unity.

We have five sections in the pledge; the fifth section concludes all the first four. First we say that we are proud of one sovereignty. Although there are many governments in the world, we are proud of only one. Who is going to build that one sovereignty? We will make it, our family will make it. We have to have that understanding.

Who should have made the first sovereignty of mankind? Adam should have done that. Now, in place of Adam, you must restore that lost sovereignty. You must restore that first family unit. That is the first thing. We also recognize that we are proud of one people. That is, one people which come under Heaven. In the Kingdom of Heaven, there is no such thing as two or three different kinds of people. There is no such thing as white people, black people or yellow people. That kind of difference between people does not exist in the Kingdom of Heaven. That difference and separation has come about from the fall of man in the very beginning. However, the world of God has only one people.

Next we say that we are proud of the one land and one nation that comes under God. If God wants to visit from north to south, does He need a passport to go? If He doesn't, then why should His sons and daughters need a passport? There should be free passage everywhere and no boundaries. We are different in that respect. Satan is proud of many nations, many sovereignties and many peoples. But we are just proud of one sovereignty, one land, one nation, one people. This is really our pledge and strong determination against the divided world of Satan. The Satanic world is one long history of war. On the other hand, the history of God has been the hidden struggle to bring everything into unity and into oneness. Therefore, we have to recognize the problem of many different cultures. They have all developed from different origins and so, man has developed different styles and forms of behavior. This sets people apart from one another. This is also what is stopping and confusing the dispensation today. Satan uses this as his strong point. We want to do away with this painful problem, so we are proud of one culture.

We are proud of one culture and that one culture comes from one word, one language. Actually, language and culture are the same. Language is culture in essence. This means eventually you have to speak the same language that your parents speak. In the spiritual world, what is the language that you will use? The answer is simple. Whatever is the language of the parents, is also the language of the children.

Unfortunately, you don't understand the mother tongue. What is English? It is not the original tongue of God. Why are we teaching the young children in the nursery Korean? Because it is the first language that God could participate in. Of course, we also teach the children English because they could not survive in the world today without it, but at least the first words they learn are Korean. They can begin from the very earliest point in their life to learn the mother tongue and they can learn the English language after that. Is this carrying everything too far? No. It is really a very good beginning.

When you say that you are proud of one language and one culture, do you really feel it? Do you think, "Am I anywhere near comprehending the language and culture that I am proud of?" Have you ever stopped to think about that? So, when you come to that phrase, you must truly feel regret that you cannot have real pride in that one language and culture. You must be longing to participate in that original springtime culture.

It is not just any culture that we are looking for, but the original spring culture. There is no other "ism" in that culture except

"Adamism." Culture and civilization should have started from Adam and Adam's family. We should have one language. Many languages confuse and bring everything into division. There are many languages spoken here in America, and this can very easily bring about conflict.

What about us as Unification members at this time? We must learn the mother tongue that we are proud of within three generations. Within sixty years, we should be speaking the original mother tongue. I have never taught you this before, but this meeting brings me to speak about these things directly. What else are we proud of? Centering around one set of parents are all the children. When all the basic elements that we mentioned above are created, the children can then gather around their parents. Since there is one world, one nation, one family, there is also only one original set of parents. Isn't that true? You might wonder why the brotherhood of man must come before the one language and culture. Why is it in this sequence in our pledge? Without all people coming into one, we cannot create a world where we are all proud of becoming brothers and sisters. There is still a great war to be fought. Are you free to be proud of the parents now? No. You have no time to be proud because you are under constant attack by the world. You are always on the defense. You cannot proclaim to the world, "Let us follow our parents all together!" All of the things in the fifth pledge have to be fulfilled and then, after that, our pride can be freely expressed.

Then what comes? The tradition of mankind can begin to unfold. Only after you are proud of being able to have one original parent, can you create the world of one heart. And so, you can be proud of being the laborer who built that. There is no distinction there, no white, black, yellow or anything else. There is only one family, one tradition.

When your marriage is international or interracial, the children will all be different. Between an interracial couple, the children will not be the same. Some will be more like the mother and others more like the father. Will you discriminate between the children? Will the father say, "Oh, this child is more my color so I will favor this child?" When the heart dominates, there is no black or white.

If we carefully examine what we say in the pledge we can see everything from the correct perspective. Whenever I give a sermon, I see all these things in their proper order. I always have these things in mind. Do you think of these things? I conclude every sermon with, "Amen." When we conclude the pledge we say, "To accomplish all this, all five sections, we will give our very life." With such a conclusion you are saying that you cherish this pledge more than anything else, so you will fight even with your life to overcome the forces of evil and bring about the promises of the pledge. You are saying that you don't want to die without making the one world of the heart. Without doing this, if we go to the spiritual world, we have to do everything all over again once we arrive there. I have wondered why no one has ever asked any questions about the pledge. No one has ever asked why there was such a specific sequence in the pledge and what it means. No one has ever asked me why I wrote the pledge in this way.

The way we bow and what we say in pledge all comes into one meaning. Whatever we do, we have to do with the feeling that we are practicing how to do it in the Kingdom of Heaven. That time when we give pledge, the beginning of a brand new day, without any contamination or interference, is the moment when we make a deep intimate relationship with Heaven. Here we contemplate where we are and what we are trying to accomplish for the sake of mankind and Heaven. We should have those moments and those few hours and realize how meaningful they are. If we don't feel that and just waste the time, it is truly a pity.

When we eat fresh fruit, we should think, "I shall appreciate it as if I were in the Kingdom of Heaven." We should eat the things of creation with this kind of deep heart. We should consider every act as practice for living in the Ideal World. Bowing is like that as well. You should do it naturally, with sincerity and no one should need to prompt you. You should know when it is appropriate for you to bow.

I am telling you all these things because I am thinking about how our meeting started this morning. The moment that Mr. Kim shouted out, "Bow!" I wondered, "Why does he have to shout it out? Why doesn't everyone just naturally feel like doing that?" I feel unnatural from that kind of thing and I feel that it is strange for you too. However, once you know the meaning and have the full explanation of how and why, it's all up to you. You can express your feelings from deep within, in this significant way.

The Relationship between East and West

The Western way of greeting each other is horizontal. It is a friendly shaking of the hands, a lateral movement. It is saying, "You and I are equal, so let's get along together." But, the Oriental way has vertical relationships in mind. The vertical relationship is the first thing to come. You have to greet your superior first, and then care about your junior member. Both are necessary, but which comes first? The vertical relationship must be first established and then we can create a horizontal relationship.

In Western culture, there is even some pride to do away with all vertical relationships, but in reality this slows down real progress in relationships. Does this sound logical and reasonable to you? The way for human relationships to function smoothly is for the vertical to come first and the horizontal to come based upon the first. This shows the difference between Eastern and Western civilizations.

Western people are really looking for something new and they are looking to the East for new ideas. The East is not looking to the West for new ideas, but they are interested in finding out new ways of doing things. That is why they want to find out about technology and the more external customs of the West. In the Orient, people are tired of the old formal customs and narrow religious way of thinking. They are saying, "What do we get doing all of this?" They are interested in learning more practical ways of doing things. So, they come to America and study how to make things and build things and get things moving. This is actually very good. From the East can come a deeper way of thinking and from the West can come a good way of getting things done.

To you, such things may just be happening, but nothing "just happens." Once you know how the providence moves, you can see the reason behind everything. So, let's face it. Among Western men and Western women, the Western men don't prefer Western women, if they can help it. Men don't want to obey women and serve women, not if they can help it. If they don't have to do it, they don't want to do it. Something inside of them tells them, "I want to get away from here; this is meaningless."

The Oriental woman may not be so active. Their calm and serene nature seems to say a lot without any words. Once the Western man sees this, he is drawn to it. The Western woman is very talkative, whereas the Eastern woman doesn't speak so much. That's the general tendency, isn't it? However, the Oriental men sometimes think, "Our women don't express anything. What are they here for?" The Oriental woman just seems to sit there and do nothing. So, the Oriental man thinks, "If I marry an American woman, life will be very exciting."

In the depth of her heart, even American women want someone to dominate them in the right way. Someone like me. I am not always a gentle person. I can be very tough, very demanding. I can push and push and never give you an inch. Sometimes you like that. Sometimes you say, "I wish I had a man that consistent." Contrary to the popular belief that women like only soft people just like themselves, the chances are that they really like someone who is strong. The idea that men only like people who are masculine like themselves is not at all accurate either. It is not so much that one is better than the other; that is not what I am saying now. It is that men and women are made for each other by being different from each other. It is like boy and girl twins, not exactly alike, but from the same parent. And not that different once you get to know them from the inside. If you draw the line and split something in half, you have two things that are identical. Well, in somewhat the same way, men and women are the same thing, but they are also different too, in order that they can experience becoming one. That's the beauty of it. Do you understand?

Preparation for Pledge

I wonder about couples who may fight the night before pledge service. They shouldn't come to pledge with that kind of thing between them. It's hypocritical. They should pay some indemnity and repent. They should apologize to each other. If they do that, if one says, "I started the whole thing and I'm sorry," and the other replies, "Well, there was some fault in me too," they can then come and do pledge together. You don't want to come in front of Heaven with conflict in your hearts. The deep meaning of pledge is that it is the weekly, monthly and yearly opportunity to clear up your hearts.

So far, you have been doing pledge service in the early mornings and many times you say to yourself, "I wish Father would abolish this tradition of getting up so early to do pledge." I know that everyone of you has felt that way. Whoever has not felt this way raise your hands. Well, even I have felt that way sometimes; I am not always so excited to get up at 4:00 a.m. and then work a long day after that. But when we reflect upon ourselves, consider what we say in the pledge and compare where we are to that, we get better and better week by week. It takes time to perfect ourselves. We cannot just do it in a moment of magic. It takes many days, weeks, years, and we have to make consistent effort. To graduate from elementary school takes six years. If you are going to learn to go to Heaven can you do that overnight? You might look out and see a cloudy sky and say, "Oh, it might rain today, so I don't want to go to school; I don't want to go through that storm." Can you do that? Will you be excused? There were only a few days when you really wanted to go to school. There were mostly days when you were tired, or it was raining or snowing, or something else was going on, but you went to school every single day, didn't you? How about eating three meals a day. Don't you sometimes get tired of that? However, you do that three times a day, regardless of whatever goes on. What about going to the bathroom? If you hate to go to the bathroom because it isn't the nicest room in the place, do you refuse to go there when you really have to? Even though you may not want to use that room, you actually feel much better after you go there, don't you? Maybe you are really tired and don't even feel like doing it, but you feel much better afterwards and that is why you go ahead and do it.

When the pledge service comes, you have to shower or take a bath and clean yourself up. That is also the case spiritually. You have to think about what you did wrong the past week, and pray and get ready for the pledge service. Think about every part of your body. For example, if your hand did something wrong, pushed or struck someone, you have to really repent about that. You should repent if you thought badly towards others during the past week, month or year.

How good it is to have this time each week! You can truly clean yourself and prepare yourself. Then, for pledge you can bow down in the purest way. For at least a few moments, have a deep prayer before you bow down. The night before when you take a bath or shower, make it very significant. You are cleaning yourself, getting ready to face God again for pledge. Then, you can ask Heaven, "Since I am clean tonight, please stay close to me tonight and I will see you in the morning." You can even ask God to show you something good in your dreams that night. So, is pledge bad or good? You should change from now on. Don't be lenient or tired to do the pledge service. Instead, truly anticipate it and be joyful to do it. All year long, the very beginning of a brand new week is the very beginning of a brand new you. Think about yourself, your spouse, your children and if there is anything wrong in those relationships, clear it up. That is how serious pledge is. Feel to your bones the great privilege you have in doing pledge.

The Bible once warned us never to pledge, never to say an oath. That is because man did not have the condition to do so in front of God. But now, that foundation is laid and you can participate in the pledge. So, think about how great it is to come before God in this way. I am concerned that you have done pledge in a ritualistic way, that you didn't understand it, but have just done it like a habit. You should be very serious and solemn like the Jewish people when they go to the synagogue on the day of atonement, Yom Kippur. This ceremony is vitally important in order to build the Kingdom of Heaven in the family. Do you understand?

Understanding Oriental Culture

Now we know this important area. Since you are seminary

graduates and will be leaders in this movement, you must be serious to educate your members in this regard. You have to educate them well. So, are some of you learning Korean now? Even though I am improving my English, I will not speak English to you. Especially if I meet you in Korea, I will not speak any English. You have to speak Korean if you want to communicate with me.

It's not impossible to learn another language. I believe that everyone of the members ought to go to Korea for about two years. You should go to the rock bottom of society and move up through every level from there. Then, absolutely you would learn the language. I think that there isn't any one of you who doesn't want to do that. I feel that you will be ashamed if you go to spiritual world and cannot understand me when I am speaking. Do you think I am just saying this on a whim or is this really the way it is, especially in the spiritual world? So, by the year 2,000, which is only twenty years away, all of you should speak Korean. Up to now, there have been other things for you to do and I didn't emphasize it so much. From 1980 on we will concentrate more and more on points like this. We will even have a formal time to learn Korean. It's necessary. Don't you think so?

Some people say that the Korean language is difficult to learn, but that isn't so. It is logically composed. Your mind tends to think logically anyway. That is how you were made.The Korean language contains all the phonetic sounds. This is why, whenever Koreans learn another language, such as English, they learn it quickly and speak it very well. The Japanese can never learn English as well as the Koreans do. It is very difficult for them because Japanese is lacking in many sounds. When Koreans learn to speak Chinese and speak it well, the Chinese cannot even guess that these Koreans came from another country. It is the same when a Korean learns to speak Japanese very well. They can never guess that this person is originally Korean. The Korean language has that much spectrum of sound and pronunciation. Also, the adjectives in Korean are rich and varied, especially in religious terminology. There is much that is expressive of the internal realm, of heart and spirit. Korean is very close to the Principle in this way. Here, you might say, "slowly," but you have no way of saying, "slowly, slowly." Or you might say, "go fast," but you have no way of saying, "fast, fast." In Korean, you have words which can emphasize like this and can convey the idea that you have more clearly.

In Korea, they use a spoon and a pair of chopsticks. There is a strict rule in arranging your table in Korea, where the plate goes and the rice bowl and the tea cup. There is always a subject and object relationship for these placements. China brags about its being the oldest civilization and Japan brags about its own history, but they don't have many of the attributes that Korea has. I don't want you to look at China, Japan and Korea and think they are all the same. There is a world of difference between the cultures. I received a report about the book and the movie, "Shogun." You even pronounce it wrong. It is not "sho-gun," but rather "sho-guun." You see the "gun" and think of a gun and just say it like that, but it has no meaning when you say it like that. If you say, "sho-gun" it is like a gun show. I cannot help but relate it to that.

A shogun is a general, but a special kind of general. The shogun is the one who serves directly next to the emperor. Anyway, people are quite excited about this program. Fifty percent of the entire population watched that program. They thought they were learning about the Orient. However, I couldn't relate to it so much because there really wasn't a great deal there. You had only one or two interesting scenes, but you would need thousands of scenes before you even began to understand something about the Orient.

One interesting thing that I noticed was the ceremony of cutting your belly, which the Japanese call "seppuku." For them, that is the honorable way of paying indemnity. If you did not fulfill your responsibility, you would kill yourself rather than be fired. If you really meant business, then nothing came higher than that. You saw some scenes about that in the movie. In reality, in history that was a daily thing. In order to ease the pain, there was always someone there to cut cleanly through your neck so that you would end your life quickly and not suffer in agony. Who did that? The closest one to you, not your enemy. Your best friend or next of kin would be the one to cut off your head. There was that kind of honor put into one's task. There was such a seriousness linked to their life. Their life was always at stake. There is no similar concept at all in this country. Have you ever thought of doing such a thing if you failed to fulfill your responsibility? The Japanese have that sincerity and seriousness in the history of their Samurai. The Samurai was the warrior class and of course, the warrior was at his best during times of war.

Well, Japan is not at war, but they kept something of that Samurai spirit and that is why they have developed so quickly. In the economy of the world, they have achieved great things. They don't go about things in a lazy way. They really feel that their neck is at stake in their job. They still have some feeling that if they don't make their job a success, they will have to cut their own belly. The past few weeks, while watching this show, I have said to myself over and over, "Oh, that's one thing the American people will never understand. Not for a long time to come." However, if you really place yourself in a serious situation, it is not impossible to understand. Imagine that the closest one to you would cut off your head, and that it would take such love for him to do that. The whole thing expresses that it is more important to carry out an order than it is to care for one's life. The Japanese have that kind of background and feeling.

It says in the Bible that those who are willing to die will live. So, in the light of the dispensation, the Japanese will do the best because of that heritage. Once they understand about God's will, they will apply themselves towards their responsibility with that kind of intensity. You may find many faults in the Japanese, but that one point carries the Japanese over many obstacles, and they often go way beyond other nations. Should I continue or would you like to have breakfast now? Should we have breakfast, or should we not have breakfast? Breakfast is already cooked, but you don't seem to want it. Well, the ocean is close by and we can just dump it there. The fish would be very happy about that. You don't mind that? Sometimes you mind working, but you never mind eating. However, if you love your work as much and even more than you love eating, then your success is guaranteed. You will never fail by working and when it is finally so long between meals, your stomach will direct you.

What you heard this morning was not the primary talk today. After breakfast, there will be much more to say. However, this was for your daily life. You need it because it isn't just conceptual, but is really practical for your daily life. So, there is nothing to feel bad about. There is such a thing as a vertical way of greeting and a horizontal way of greeting. But, now that you know about the meaning of a vertical way of greeting, you have gained a lot.

I know about America, and probably more than most Americans know about themselves. I know a great deal about Western civilization. There are some very good points, such as getting things into action and bringing about results. Orientals have a lot to learn from you and we are going to adopt that. I know you can learn very quickly. I am encouraged even by the way you sit. When I first came here, you couldn't do that. But now, you can sit on the floor for hours without stretching your legs. When I came here I saw that Americans would put their legs up on the coffee table and watch television. Even the women did that. I am not yet accustomed to seeing that. You ought to know the Oriental customs since you are going to be people of the world. You have to be aware and sensitive to these points if you are ever going to visit or live there. Well, getting back to the Shogun program, in that show one of the actors talks about "six minds and three hearts." Such a saying really baffles the American person. You always expect an immediate reply to things and when it doesn't come you try to figure out what the Oriental person might be thinking. However, you Americans would never ever find out because they don't express it. This is one reason why, traditionally, the Chinese have been better diplomats than Westerners. The Western person expresses his mind immediately. You show what you have, whereas they never show what they have.

The Chinese may feel something inside, but goes all the way to the North Pole and does something completely different. There is no way of finding out why until a very long time later. If I spend three days with you, I will find out everything from you. On the other hand, the Oriental husband and wife may be married for years and still they take a long time to find out about each other. Even friends are like that.

There is a world of difference between the Oriental way of thinking and the Western way of expression. Even though you are Western people, you are about to set out into the world, and you have to care about how other people think and feel. So, I am sharing with you about the Eastern people, what they value and what they don't, what they think is bad manners and what is courtesy.

Korea is a small country. In the past, a large country could engulf a small country and there was nothing that could be done about it. It is just like a large fish swallowing up a small fish. There was simply nothing you could do about it. In this respect, Korea has been unique. It was small and could never win against an invasion. However, each time it reappeared. No one could completely engulf it--not China, Russia, Japan, not anyone. They quickly adapted to every situation, but still remained intact as Korean people and kept their Korean culture. Koreans learn very quickly because they had to survive so many things. Also, they are righteous in some ways, and they never want to depend upon anyone else; they quickly become independent. They observed the American way of life and quickly picked up all the good points about it. They have a viewpoint of the world and a clear idea about life. So, they estimate a situation and quickly make up their minds about it. If you look at schools like Harvard, you will see more and more Koreans attending and graduating from such places. In history, the Jewish people have usually been the ones to forge ahead in this way. The Korean people also have such qualities, and you will see them making an impact in many areas now that they have begun to come out into the world.

If the Koreans and Japanese had developed their nations together, they would have had a great influence over all of Asia. However, it didn't work out that way. Everything would have been led by these two nations, but this didn't happen. I am looking to the future now, and waiting to see what the offspring of Korean-American couples will do. I expect some unique qualities to emerge in these children.

I am not just a Korean man; however, I did inherit the basic characteristics of Korean history and culture. One of those basic qualities is that once I decide something, I will never give up. I am entirely consistent in this way. Korea is a very small and weak nation, but they have survived conquest over and over again. Also, Korea is a very religious nation. Almost everything in life is related to the basic meaning and concept of religion. Almost every Korean has had some kind of experience with the spiritual world. Many of them have had spiritual healings, and they understand very clearly about the interaction between the spiritual world and the physical world. They understand about their ancestors, and they know or sense how good actions influence the spiritual world.

Unity Through the Matching and Blessing

Those Americans who are matched to Koreans will have a very interesting life. Especially their offspring will be quite unusual. It is almost like a whole new race. How many of you are matched? When would you like to be married? There are so many couples now waiting, and if I were to bless all of you at once, the President should come and give his congratulations. Is it like that now? Could such a thing happen?

I am considering the whole nation. That is why I cannot just move in a simple way; I cannot just do things so easily. If I am going to hold a wedding ceremony here in America, I will have to bring many people from all the different countries. Would the American people welcome them or not? Is there a possibility or danger that someone would want to place a bomb in the wedding hall? Have you ever stopped to think about that? If I am going to officiate at your wedding, then it must be a fantastic wedding. I am very concerned that everything should go well and have a peaceful conclusion. I am thinking of where to have this wedding, in Korea or Japan, England or America.

The plane fare is quite a bit for someone to fly back and forth, but am I thinking about that or am I thinking more deeply? For years and years I have been telling you that the qualifications for gaining the Blessing are that you must at least witness to three people and raise them up to God. You are also responsible to witness to eighty-four people. Jesus struggled with twelve disciples and seventy-two elders. Because he couldn't bring these people into unity centered upon himself, he couldn't go forward and get the Blessing.

What is your ideal? Should you get married before you are successful in Home Church, or after you have gained success in Home Church? Have you all done Home Church now? Then, this means you will have to be blessed again before you go to the spiritual world. When the world comes to welcome you, I will have to bless you again, even though I have already blessed you. You have to receive the blessing from the church level, the national level and the world level. These three levels have to recognize you. When you come to think of that, a wedding ceremony is not that simple is it? Those who are married to Japanese members, raise your hands. Those American sisters who are matched to Japanese men, do you feel something quite different than if you had been matched to American men? You've got to study and come to understand the differences. These differences can become the advantage and merit of your relationship.

Even I did not dream that one day I would be involved with so many people in this way. Well, those who are not engaged, please raise your hands. Not so many of you. How do you feel about becoming engaged? Those who are engaged, if you feel unsatisfied with your spouse, and if you are thinking, "Of all people, why did Father match this one to me?" raise your hands. No one feels that way? Even in a minimum way? You will never know how you feel until you live together and have a child together. From among those of you who don't care so much for each other, may come the best children. What will you do then?

You may become the leader of a nation, or even beyond that a leader on the world-wide level. You have to go through that, and then you can assess your marriage. A typical example is President Kim, Young Whi Kim. When he was blessed he was troubled for more than three years. He wondered why I had given him such a wife. I said, "Just wait and you will come to understand." Then, after a few years, he came to respect and love his wife, and couldn't see how he could even carry on without her. So now, he is a woman worshiper. However, can a man become a woman worshiper when the woman is bad? If I am an expert in any area, I am at least an expert in studying about man and God. I have really researched about God's mind and man's mind. Actually, you don't have to say anything to me. When I see you I understand immediately how you feel towards your match. I can accurately foretell the spiritual outcome of a couple. When I match you, I don't match you on the same level that you are. Instead, my mind is looking down upon you from the very highest viewpoint.

My reputation for matchmaking is already very high in Korea. There is a Korean philosophy about matchmaking, which is a very consistent philosophy or system of study that has existed for a very long time. There are many matchmakers in Korea who have studied this art and have made many matches in their lifetime. Many times, members have gone to them and have shown them their match and they were very shocked by how good it was. These matchmakers admitted they could not have done any better.

There is a way in which you were born and I can understand about that. My matchmaking abilities didn't come late in life, but from very early on, people recognized my abilities. When I was very young I would see a couple and tell right away if it was a good couple or not. Soon, people started to come to me and show me pictures and ask me if it was a good match or not. For years and years I studied and practiced in this area of life. So far as matching goes, not just in numbers, but in quality, I am the champion of the whole world. So, if you are ever going to get matched or married, how are you going to do it? If you really know the value of it, and if the price is $100,000, what are you going to do? Would you say, "Well, I don't have that kind of money, so I'll just settle for something less than that."? No, you would go out and do anything to earn that money. You cannot judge your match so quickly. If you really understood the value of it, you would wait, and after three generations here on earth, you would begin to see. When you go to the spiritual world, you will know even more clearly. However, if you know something more than me, and if you do things better than me, you can come to me and complain. Some of you got someone you would never have even dreamed about. If there was such a person that would be the last one you would ever marry, that would be this person. Then I matched you to that kind of person. However, that couple is often the very best kind.

The quality of people is different. One is going on an upward curve and the other is going down. Someone may be at the very top of their own prosperity and they are going in a downward curve. Another person may be just starting to go up. This is just the natural way of life. You have to have the right kind of harmony. If one moves faster than the other, a spouse may be left behind and die. Marriage is a very important thing. No one knows this more than I do. It can lengthen someone's life or cut it short. What could be more serious than that?

The most important event in one's life is taking a spouse, getting married. In America, this most serious thing is taken in a foolish way. Some people meet each other and in the same day they are married. Some people don't even bother about marriage, but just freely come together and then never see each other again. This kind of thing produces a deep scar each time. I am so serious, however, and once you agree to a matching, you have to stay with it and make it successful. Do you feel that your match is a good match? If you truly feel that, then I am grateful. But please understand, even if you feel that way now, it doesn't always stay that way. Those of you who don't feel so good about your match, it will be quite different in a few years and you will feel very good about it.

Don't think, "Well, everybody is getting married and I am just one of them." That isn't so. The quality of your marriage is very different. Look at the ocean. There are many depths and colors in the ocean. Your marriages are like that. Each one is very unique. You have to feel that mystical quality towards your marriage. Think about how a man and woman who were once strangers now come to live together, and come to know each other as no one else. It is a very deep thing if you think about it. A very mysterious thing if you really stop to consider it.

So, all you men, do you need a woman? And you women, do you need a man? Some people choose the gay movement. The women live with the women and the men go and live with each other. They think they can live without marriage, but is this possible? Does life go on in this way? The basic structure of man and woman is a perfect match. It is as basic as the electrical system. To make a connection, there is an outlet and a plug. This seems simple, but many people are even confused about this basic point. All of creation is made in this way. It is a simple law of creation.

The Making of a Champion

Let us begin. What is it that you need now, and what is it that you need most? Do you need men or money? Which is more needed? Men or money? [Men]. Yes, we need manpower. Well, can any man do the job? There are all sorts of men. There are those who can teach, those who are technically skilled or those who sail the seas. There are all kinds of men. Which one is needed? You like the idea of being a sailor, but there are all kinds of sailors.

I didn't send you to the seminary to become sailors. My purpose wasn't to make sailors out of you. What I would like, what anyone would like in the church, is someone who is spiritually oriented and can be of service to other people, especially in a religious or spiritual way. That person would be able to function normally and correctly in every position that he is given. We need a person representing the spiritual world who is willing to work in a principled way on the earth.

Who is that person? He is the one who is willing and capable to draw out the people involved in the Satanic world and bring them to a Godly way of life. We need a champion who can do that. It takes a champion to make a champion out of someone else. For example, you know about the gymnasiums where there is a coach or trainer and young men come to train under him. After thoroughly training them, the coach sends them out to a contest. When they win the match or the title, they can bring the trophy back to the gym. The champion in the gym is always practicing, always fighting. In this way, he refines himself.

If he doesn't have men to train, he has to recruit them. Who will recruit them? The champion has to do that. Is there an administrator who will do that for him? No. This means that you have to become the champion before you can hope to bring in and make champions out of others. You have to have a gym and you have to have enough technique to be able to train people regularly. You have to have that capability before you can assemble people and do something with them.

If you are constantly training others, you have to be able to look at them eye to eye and be able to fight. If that person doesn't look directly into your eyes, you have to remind them to look straight up and keep their eyes focused. You have to show them how to use their hands and feet in exactly the right way. Sometimes you have to hit them and show them exactly how it has to be done. The champion is constantly showing others how to do each thing. He will never leave them alone, not for any single detail.

How many people have you trained like this? If you say that we need men more than we need money, you have to raise up those men. No one is going to bring you your men and say, "Here they are; they are already trained and you can use them." No one is going to do that for you. You will have to train them. However, before you can train anyone else, you have to be able to do every point by yourself. You have to pursue every detail by yourself. It is a desperate situation for you. If you need someone, you have to be clear. Don't just get anyone, but find the right person and then say, "Okay. I need him; I need that person." Then, you have to try your best for that person. You think about him, pray about him and do everything to bring him. That means you have to visit him and you have to work hard with him. The people surrounding him will oppose you, but you have to go again and again. You have to be persistent and determined to bring that person and nothing else will do.

Have you ever heard about one-sided love? You call it unrequited love. Once you have made up your mind, it doesn't matter what someone else thinks about you. What matters is what you think about them. You just go to serve that person, and if they oppose you, mistreat you, even knock you flat and make you bleed, still you will not give up. Instead, you will become excited by that and even more fervent to serve that person. By the time you do that, there is no such thing as a limit. That person will think, "Who am I to get this kind of attention from someone?"

When you are around many people, look and investigate who is the best one there. Determine who is the best man or woman that you want to bring over to God's side. Once you make up your mind, determine that you will never let go. Keep on working and praying until you win over that person's heart. Then, when you get to know him or her, express what you feel. Tell him how this nation is declining and how you are longing to meet someone who wants to stop that trend and turn this nation around. If he agrees with you, you can ask him to work with you.

You don't have to begin from the very first moment to talk about Divine Principle. He may not be interested in that right away. For example, if someone is good at fighting and takes pride in it, and you are a bit of a muscleman yourself, go to him and ask him to teach you a few things. Then, you can learn some points from him. If you have interest in something and that person has some skill in that area, you can approach him in this way. You can first learn from others.

When your relationship matures and you become more trusting of each other, you can say to him, "Well, so much for the muscle. In order to use the muscle right, you have to be able to use your head and be smart. Don't you notice that you don't always do with your body what your mind knows you should do?" Give your opinion of how you have to fight and why. You can explain about the Principle even in such a conversation. One thing you should never do is limit yourself. Don't ever say things like, "Oh, I can't sing. That's the last thing I'd ever do." There is no such thing as the "last thing" you can do. You should try anything and everything.

It's awkward in the beginning. Go to the extreme and try the things you cannot do. Do something that no one is expecting. Then, people will really begin to notice you and listen to you. I studied this for a long time and I practiced it. I have some limitations, but I learned to go beyond them, and you should be able to go beyond your limitations as well. What is my limitation? I am the leader of the Unification Church. I cannot do many things, even though I know how to do them. I am an expert in so many things, but I cannot always do them.

It's very simple. For you to become a champion in the ring, you have to train yourself. On what? On various techniques, not just one thing. There are hundreds of ways. There are ways to move your head and your hands, so that when your head goes down, your fist goes up. If you are serious and you have to fight, if you have to, you can do it. You can use your head, your hand, your hip. If you are a serious fighter and if you are in danger, you have to use such things. Are you a champion, or are you an on-looker? If you are a champion, what kind of champion are you? The one who is more interested than anyone else and the one who learns more moves than anyone else is the one who is going to be the best fighter. That is how a champion is made. You have to fully invest all your mind and your body.

There are all kinds of things that bring people together: hiking, jogging, music, whatever. I want you to be an interesting person to be with. Don't be like a piece of carved stone or a piece of wood, expressionless and motionless. You have to be interested in all kinds of things and get excited easily. Then, you can get along with people very quickly. That is one thing that I am. I am really filled with fun. It is exciting to be with me. One thing I will never do is bore you.

If I am hiking up the mountain, I go faster than anyone else. If you go out onto the field with me, I will run and jump more than anyone else. I am curious about everything, I am filled with enthusiasm to learn anything. When you want to become friends with someone, you have to be active in the same field. If you have nothing better to do with yourself, just go out and pick a fight with someone. That's far better than sitting and doing nothing in your home. At least you are doing something and can learn from it.

You are bound to get hit once in a while. Otherwise, you will never understand about life. Getting hit by another person is not that terrible. When you are hit, then you know what that feels like. It makes you think, and you have to be a fast thinker in this life. When you come into a situation, you have to be able to think fast and do something immediately. That's a champion. A champion has to be very active in any situation and decide things very quickly. He has to know whether to advance or retreat and then do it.

I am beyond sixty years of age, but when I talk about something and get excited, no one thinks I am that old. I am like a twenty-year-old and that's very attractive. You have to become a champion. If you are going to be gentle, you have to be rough first and then gentle. Experience the whole range of life. So, you need manpower don't you? What kind of people do you need? Perhaps God is worried about you. He is thinking, "If you go out and witness, you will just bring in the same kind of person that you are." Perhaps God is trying to protect that person from falling into your hands, because he doesn't want another person who will just sit around and do nothing. You have graduated from the seminary and you have a Masters diploma. What if someone comes and yells at you, but you don't yell back. You just sit there and take it. If you are going to go out on the ocean, you should know what happens all summer long. The fishermen bicker all the time. There are tense moments when lines get crossed up and boats get in each other's way. Then, you really have to shout and use very strong language. In that situation, there is nothing wrong with shouting because you have to protect your rights.

I am the first to shout out when something goes wrong. If they yell back at me, I just shout again in an even louder voice. They have to listen because I am right. Other members of the *New Hope*, such as Daikan, don't raise their voices so much. However, in some situations, it's far better to raise your voice and defend what is right. In the mountains you have a big voice and the mountain will at least echo, but some men don't even do what mountains do; they just sit there dumb. Mountains are natural. A man should be natural too. Even the rock responds to strength with strength. Aren't you better than rock and timber? I once had an experience that made me stay awake all night. I couldn't even wait for the sun to come up, and as soon as it did, I went to that person's house and kicked open the door. Then I said, "We have to discuss this problem right now." Well, I don't do this as my profession. However, when something bothers me and I know I am right, I cannot help but do something about it. Sometimes I feel sad about being a religious leader. I am an aggressive person, but I have to be patient for the sake of God.

However, sometimes, I even ask myself, "Why did I have to become a religious leader?"

To me, it's a mystery how anyone can just sit and sit, eating three meals a day for 365 days of the year and not do anything. It just makes me wonder, "What kind of man, or woman is he, or she?" Yet, whenever I call them, they have no trouble getting here. I wonder how they can respond so quickly to coming to a meeting, but don't go out and reach out to other people with the same kind of enthusiasm?

Winning the Respect and Friendship of Others

So then, what do you need? Men or money? You need men. Is there anyone who thinks, "Well, I won't do so much. I'll just sit tight and then I'll just wish for the children to be born." Do you ever think like that? You should first consider that you have to go out and find your spouse. Then, you have to go through the pains of labor which are almost beyond comprehension. And then, afterwards, the baby will often cry and you will be exhausted. Just think, you are trying to embrace the world. It is like trying to engulf a huge fish in just one swallow. Will that fish stay in your stomach? Do you have the power to digest it? First, you have to have determination. Then, you have to try and try. If you are trying to catch people, you have to invest all of yourself. Take that person out for lunch, then dinner, then again another day. Day after day, take care of him like that. Just go ahead and do that. Make friends.

If you run out of money, you can show your friends how to fundraise. They will be impressed that in thirty minutes you can make enough money to eat dinner and see the movies. Don't be limited by anything. Be able to do almost anything at anytime. That's the secret to real life. If there is a man and a woman, and the man says to the woman, "Stay right here; I'll raise enough money for us to have lunch." And then indeed, if he goes out and gets the money in ten minutes, the woman will be truly impressed by this.

You might be trying to get that money for lunch and see another gentleman standing on the street. You can talk to him in the following way, even though he might wonder about you at first. You just smile and say, "Were you ever in love?" He will look at you and remember one time when he was. Then you can ask him, "What would you have done if you had to take her to lunch and you didn't have any money?" If he understands your stituation in this way, he would gladly give you the money. I know one thing: if I was approached by an enterprising young man such as that, I would gladly give him a 100 dollar bill. The woman would be so impressed with him. If the woman is critical about all of this, then she doesn't deserve the young man. He should let her go and immediately find someone else.

There are ways to do things. Many ways. You have to be able to put up a show instantly without any planning. You can go up to a complete stranger and if you are sincere, you can say, "Oh, you are just like my sister. You really make me feel like my sister made me feel at home." If you are truly sincere, she will feel natural and she won't refuse to listen to you. You have to think always that you are in a drama. You are an actor at that moment. If you have an important enough reason, there is nothing that you cannot do.

If you have a noble idea, you can do almost anything. Your idea will guide your actions. There is almost nothing that I don't know about in the different ways of the world. I don't show it so much, but I know about hundreds and hundreds of things. If you are good at singing, you can sing out in the middle of the town. If you are good, eventually someone will be interested in you. He will come out and listen to you, because secretly he always wanted to do the same thing, but could never do it by himself. Then, he will start singing with you.

After a while he will feel close to you and ask you where you live. You can say where you are staying, but don't ask him anything. Then, he will ask you, "Why don't you stop by my house on your way home?" Well, that's what you wanted him to say to begin with, so you accept his invitation. If you linger three or four hours, it becomes dinner time. Why should you stop? That's how you can make friendships with people.

What upsets me is that you are a perfectly capable group of young people. Life is more than sitting around like a stone wall. You joke with your best friends, but I'm now telling you to extend that joke to a complete stranger. You joke all the time with close friends, however; if you want many people to work with you then you have to extend yourself and make new close friends. If you want to see the mayor, you don't have to make an appointment all the time. Just wait in the town hall for two or three days and stop him when he comes out. One day you can just walk in and say, "Are you the mayor? You aren't any better than me; you aren't any more handsome than me." You can tell him that you are more intelligent than he is. He will be offended and ask you, "What do you know that I don't know?" Then you can ask a fast question, "Did you ever see God? I can arrange that. You can see God." Or, you can bring some caramel and candy and offer him some. If he refuses you, then even in America, that is impolite. So you can say, "You aren't a quality mayor." If he is older, you can ask him, "How do you know that I won't be your son-in-law someday?" That might get his attention. After all, you never know what the future might have in store for you or him, so you can say that. If he treats you as if you are insane, you can tell him that you are offended.

I know how to make good friends with congressmen and senators. Don't do it in the normal way that everybody else does. Don't fall into the expected categories that everyone else does. Just go and kick the door in and say, "I want to see you!" He will be surprised and come out to investigate about you. Then you tell him why you came and why you want to talk with him. You have an important and urgent message. If the secretary gets in the way, just yell over her protests. You have to make a close relationship in the minimum amount of time.

There was one instance when I kept visiting someone, and that person said over and over that he didn't like me. I just kept on going until he changed his mind and began to like me. How many times do you think that I visited that man? I visited him for one year and six months. I went again and again. Finally the whole household came to the point where they were waiting and hoping for my visits.

If you need champions, then why aren't you going out to get

them? If I was a state leader I would go around the entire state in one week. You have to be constantly on the move. You have to always be like that before you can expect anything. You have to be on your feet all the time. Go out and visit and invite others to visit you. That has to be going on all the time.

Have you ever been out street witnessing? Do you know what kind of face you have out on the street? Do you know what you look like? You have to know about yourself. You have to know if your face or your character will interest others. If you just sit still, people will think you are half asleep. You have to study how to make your eyes move so that people will know you are alert. Your eyes have to scan quickly, and gestures will help. Don't sit still; your body should be moving along with your eyes. That is one of the basic things you can do to improve your appearance.

If you do that, people will think you are exciting. When I was a teenager I used a friend as a platform and gave an impromptu speech. Some friends went along with me, knowing what I was going to do. They liked me because of that. After I had finished speaking, another one said, "You want to do another speech? You want to climb up on me?" They didn't mind. If you really do things naturally, it's okay.

If you are the state leader and you find some nice woman, you can even stand on her back. She won't mind, as long as you feel very sincere and are natural about it. Surely, people will stop and listen to your speech. Someone might come up and protest to you about abusing women, and you can say, "Do you think you can do the same thing that I am doing? Then, try it. And if you can, what is your protest about?" When you really need some attention quickly, you should be able to do things like that. I have all kinds of friends. Wherever I went I had friends. In fact, there were too many friends and they insisted upon following me, but I was too busy to be friends with everyone. That is how I spent my days. That is why I know that no matter what, there is nothing you cannot do in order to get God's will done. Make your own story, make your own novel, then act it out. Become the hero of the novel. Follow your script and live out the drama in real action. Think that life is that. Figure out the course of action, how you will do something, how others will respond and then how you will move after that. Plan it and do it. I have that spirit and that is how I could come to America and visit some of the top officials and offices. I just walked in and that's how it went.

Try to imagine what I have to do. If I go to Africa, I won't be quiet, and that's not bad. I will stir things up and something nice will happen in that country when I go. How about you? How many stores would you want to manage someday? If you want to manage 100 stores, you have to raise that many people to at least run the stores while you manage the whole operation. Our members now operate many businesses. If I myself were to run each business, I know I could make it successful. There is no way that it would fail. I can understand how, in the very beginning, a member who has no experience in doing business before and is learning as he goes along, is bound to lose some money. That's understandable. For the first few years that's how it goes, but you should learn quickly and then you can begin to be successful.

If I were the lecturer, do you think people would come? Do you think I could persuade them and move their hearts? You might say to yourself, "Father, that's a good idea. Why don't you do that?" Why can't I do that? You know why. You know whose responsibility it is to do these things. I have already done all these things myself a long time ago. I am teaching you again, but I have already taught you how to accomplish in these areas. You must teach others. You know whose responsibility it is to hold banquets and visit the people day in and day out. You go ahead and do these things with all your heart. Go fervently to the homes and take care of the people. Then, their hearts will be moved by you. I cannot understand how the state leader can stay in his room the whole live-long day. Even the sisters who are graduating from the seminary, don't sit and wait for people to invite you. Just get up and go out. Invite yourself in with poise and charm.

You have to go after the people. Don't go after the small ones all the time. You have to grab onto the big guys in order to advance quickly. Do you want to become famous? Can you just sit tight? You'll never become famous if you just live like other people do.

You have to live differently and become greater than others. You have to do more things and make more effort than anyone else.

Are you the champion of the Unification Church, or are you a member of the Unification Church? There is no champion that doesn't use all his limbs, hands, arms, legs and feet. I am waiting and hoping that you will change. You have graduated from the seminary and I am really wondering when you will change. How many more years will it take for you to become different from what you have always been? When are you going to be different? It's a very serious question. If you are not going to do something first and yet expect to be put in a high position, you are just a swindler.

Creating the Foundation for Success

Did you hear that *New Hope* won first prize in a tuna tournament this summer? Well, what do you think? Did I win that prize by sitting here in Morning Garden and doing nothing? No. I went out every morning even before the sun came up. And then, did I just hold the lines all day knowing that the tuna had to bite? Is that how I got more tunas than anyone else and won the first prize? No. It never happens that way. One thing that no one said this year was, "How come the *New Hope* won first prize this season?" There wasn't a single soul who had that question. Everyone knew why the *New Hope* got first prize and when I got it, no one complained about it.

I went out so seriously every day for several years already. I developed a new technique for the hand line method and tested it over and over again. I proved it worked and there is no doubt that this method is really the best. So, I can now tell others to do the same. Those who follow the instructions precisely have caught more fish than anyone else.

People all around have become definitely impressed. They all thought that some miracle was going on. At any rate, many people came and asked questions and looked around. They know that I have gained real expertise in this area. They really want to find out about my method and some try to spy on the boats and find out what is going on. By now, if I were to announce a tuna seminar, I know that there are so many people interested in my method that they would certainly come and listen to me.

I have about ten hours of lecture contents. I can lecture at least ten hours about tuna fishing. Would you like to hear this lecture now? There is no question that I have the contents and the ability to give such a lecture, but I don't have time, so I won't give it today. Are you disappointed? If the tuna had ears to listen, they would be very interested in listening to my seminar. There is nothing that I didn't do. I did what all the fishermen did and then I went several steps beyond. If I didn't do something, it was something that wouldn't get the job done, so I naturally wouldn't do it. However, anything that would work, anything that would get the job done, I tried. I have the confidence to say that there is nothing I haven't done or tried. Many professionals come and they don't just catch two, three or four fish. It doesn't just happen like that. But here, we have people who never fished before and they come and get five, six, seven tuna. The one without experience used to try and if he caught one during the whole season, he was very lucky. I certainly understand all about that.

When I first started fishing, I went for weeks without catching one tuna and there were more tuna around then. Many professionals were catching fish around me. In the midst of them, I lost fifteen tuna in a row. That was the way I started. It wasn't easy in the beginning, but once I found the pattern, I caught fish over and over again. And now that I am teaching you, you can catch a fish without any experience at all. Five years ago, tuna was only five cents per pound. We have been working to gradually raise the tuna price. We aren't gaining money by doing that. Not yet. So far, we are even losing money. This year the price went up to $2.50. This means if you catch a large fish, you can make close to two thousand dollars. You should have seen how many boats came out this year. Hundreds of boats came out. Next year, we hope the price goes up to at least $3.50. This means one fish can make more than three thousand dollars. Can you imagine how many boats will come just to try it out? If you catch one fish, that's enough money for fifteen cows. So, on one line there are fifteen cows. That's some kind of fishing.

I have a real hope that someday a woman will catch a fish by herself--a solo effort. For now, at least in pairs, the women can catch tuna. I am truly looking forward to seeing women come out and fish amongst the men. So, you women, you aren't interested in this because you are women? "No!" Okay, I am going to assign a boat for the women too.

If you catch three fish, that is almost ten thousand dollars. This could cover one family's food expenses for an entire year. How many boats do you think will come out and compete for that kind of money? Who will prosper the most? The towns like Gloucester. There is the same number of fish to be caught, but there will be ten times the amount of boats coming out to fish. And those fishermen will spend money in the small, local town. The higher price is for their benefit as well.

We caught 165 fish this year. Isn't that incredible? That's a lot of fish. That's an increase of 150% from last year. Last year we caught 64 tuna and that was a lot of fish then, but this year we caught 100 more fish than that. Next year we can catch 500 or 600 tuna and that's only one-third of the quota. Imagine if we ever did that! Imagine if we ever caught one-half the quota! And yet, we can do that someday. I am sure of it.

Investing Yourself to Gain the Result

When I used to hunt in the mountains, there was quite some stir over that. I was more successful than anyone else. I had never used a gun before, so I first practiced with clay targets. I quickly got up to shooting eighteen out of twenty-five targets, which is pretty good. I have a very quick reflex. Well, the first time I went hunting, I took Colonel Pak with me. Colonel Pak served a long time in the Korean army where he was a rifle instructor for several years. However, I more than doubled his result. Do you think that I'm a capable person? If you are really following me, you should be like me. You have to at least mimic me. You have to show some sign of who you are. Let me ask you again, are you a champion yourself, or are you considering yourself a candidate to become a champion? You definitely need men don't you? Well, if you just sit tight, do you expect them to come to you? What should you do?

Pretend you are dying and when someone walks by you they will take sympathy on you. You have to start something and motivate something to happen. What do you smell with your nose, what do you hear with your ears, what do you touch with your hands? What do you do anyway? You have to smell for the sake of mankind, hear for the sake of mankind and touch for the sake of mankind.

Have you ever looked at a spider web? I am fascinated by the spider web, especially the king spider. Usually you think there is no spider in the web, that it's a dead web. However, if you throw something in there and it gets caught in the web, very soon the spider will come out. It never fails that the spider comes out. Well, do you have your spider web? If something gets entangled, do you come out to see what it is? Do you have such a sense about things? If you don't, it means you are not even up to the spider level. Whenever the spider moves to a new place it immediately starts making its web, its network.

The spider has to make his web precisely. He has to push himself from interval to interval just right, and in this way, the thread is connected to make the web. He does this thousands of times; he is completely an expert at it. He doesn't have to think about it. If you don't believe it, go to the spider web and see how he works. I tested it many times. I tossed in some flies or bugs and watched. The first thing the spider did was to wrap the bug up in the web. Before he examines it, the spider does that. Then, he takes a good look at it and starts to eat it. You should do things exactly the same way. Make a web and if something touches it, go out and catch it first. Then, look at it and see what you've got. Once it is in the web, don't take off for lunch or go to sleep. For example, if someone comes to listen to you, don't say, "Well, it's already twelve o'clock; let's go to bed and talk about it tomorrow." No, you have to stay up the entire night and talk to him. When he understands what you are conveying, you can give yourself a brief break, but go right on until he becomes your member.

Don't you see? If you don't even have the thinking of a spider, what can you become? So, you need manpower and what else? You need money. Well, if you have manpower, you will also have money. If you have money first, it does not mean that men will always follow you. However, if you have people first, then the money will surely follow.

If you decided to act now, which method would you take? Would you follow Tiger Park's method or Dr. Durst's? Why do you say Tiger Park? You are Americans. Now I am really curious. I coached Tiger Park closely and he has developed a fighting, championship spirit. Those who are not in CARP please raise your hands? Are you interested in CARP even though you are not members? Then, why don't you join CARP from now on? Maybe I will disguise myself and go around to the campuses and see what is going on directly. Don't make a scene if you recognize me. Just go on. Would you like to see me come to the campus in this way? If I appear like that, you will never notice me.

A New Beginning

Today is the first of October. October is the month of success. In this month, your fortune will open up to you, whatever you have sown for the year. From this first day of October, will you go forth and give all your effort? Would you like to go to the campus and work with CARP, or would you like to do what no one else is doing right now? Well, you've got to do something before you get old and die. Today may be a good day to start.

Years ago, we didn't have the science conference. No one was ready to do that, but I pushed them to go ahead and do it. If we hadn't done that, where would we be today? There would be no understanding from the scholar's world toward us. It would be downright miserable; no one would recognize or understand anything about what we have. But now, many people have been able to study and understand something of the message we have. It made quite some news that Unification members were educating the highest scholars in Western society. When people started to see that, it made them wonder about us. It was like lightning striking down into the culture.

The science conference is not attended by members; they are just staff members and coordinators. It is attended by the scholars in the different sciences. Through this they are all becoming educated about us. It is causing a chain reaction. In Germany there were only fifteen positions that could be opened for the conference, but over four hundred scholars applied to come. There are many more scholars who don't even know about the conference. When they find out, then thousands will be trying to come. However, the young professors won't even try to come. Only the famous ones, only the ones with experience, expertise and recognition in their field will be allowed to come.

What would happen if I stopped the science conference from now? Would you continue on with it? Who will do that? Last year the budget for the conference alone was 1.3 million dollars. Is that a small amount of money or a lot? If I bought lunch for seminary graduates with that kind of money, you would have lobster lunches all year long and still have plenty of money left over. Why don't I do that for you instead of spending all that amount in just one meeting? Is it more worthwhile to have the science conference than feed you lunch? If you just need money all the time, what do you expect to gain? You have to come to the place where you can give more money than you need to receive; everything increases from there.

The structure has now been made. We can bring all Europe into unity. It is taking visible shape. We are preparing the road, bringing all these scholars together. Technology and science can be guided by a deeper understanding of their purpose. I want to show the way in the technological areas, such as in Germany. I have already made good relationships with people in Germany who have a substantial role to play, particularly in the area of machine making. The standard has yet to be set and I want to pioneer that standard for the next century. I want to uplift technological standards in the East and go past the standard already set by Germany. In this way, Korea can go beyond the standards set by Japan. Why? So that Korea can better serve all of Asia and then the world. You cannot do anything for others if you are below or equal to their standard. You have to have something very great, something of the best quality to offer.

I have worked very hard in Europe for three years already. I have brought all the members together, centering in London and they are working together as if they came from one country, one nation. That is the way it should be. I performed a matching in Europe with all the European members. When you look at them, you can never tell which one is French or which is Italian or German. There really isn't that great of a distinction.

I was amazed after I matched them, because 90% of them were international matchings. I didn't plan it that way. I was just trying to put together the best match for each person, but almost all of them were from different nations. It was almost a completely international matching. The European Economic Market (EEC) has an ideal, but they have three big obstacles: the different languages; the boundaries between different nations; and the reluctance of people to marry between the different cultures. People are usually bound to marry someone from their own race or culture. However, through marriage, all these barriers break down. Let's face it. As long as these barriers exist, the EEC is only a nice dream. It will never work in a substantial way; there will always be friction and tension somewhere. They have no idea how to make their ideal come about. However, Reverend Moon, through matching and marriage, and teaching members how to live in a selfless way, can show them how to fulfill even more than their ideal. Now, the biggest headache that the EEC has is Japanese technology. The Japanese learned everything from them, copied it and then digested it, which means they improved it. Now the Japanese are ahead of the Europeans. This is what bothers the European nations. I want to make it so that the Europeans are competitive again with the Japanese. I have approached several people in Germany and they are all for the idea. I thought of this more than fifteen years ago. I already understood this problem and prepared for it. Now, it's incredible because no one thought the world would be like this, but I already predicted it years earlier.

Then, we can build the best machine making factory in Germany. How? Already members from Europe are working in Japanese factories. They are learning everything there. Then, in Germany we can hire people from all the different countries that really need the work. This is part of the EEC plan, so we will cooperate with that. You have to understand this world. You have to go into the world so that you can really turn it around. Always think very far ahead and on a very large scale. People don't really think like this so much. My plan in Europe will leave many of them scratching their heads. I have already begun with a prototype factory right here in America.

I thought of how to recycle automobiles. Once you have the machine making technology, you can buy old automobiles such as a Mercedes and fix it up completely new. Many people would want to buy such a quality automobile. In this country, there is so much wealth that it is a virtue to spend a lot of money, but it isn't a virtue to keep automobiles for years and years, even the very good ones. There is no need for this waste and the common philosophy of the people about buying and using things is changing.

We can overhaul the engine and completely recondition it. There is a good way to do it quickly and I have thought about it seriously. Now, they have to fix broken engines cylinder by cylinder, but there is a way to recondition the engine every 100,000 miles. In this way, the engine can last indefinitely. The engine is just a huge block of steel. There is no reason not to be able to fix it and make it run even better than new. If you have the technology to do it, it's no problem. We could recondition more engines than Ford produces in one year. However, the price will only be one-half to one-third of a new one. This is not just thinking. We are just on the verge of making such an enterprise come about. If you need a small engine for a fishing boat, you don't need to go out and buy a new one. There are so many broken engines that are easy to get. We can fix those engines, put them in the boat and there you have an inboard motor. The cost is almost nothing. Some engines are almost given away. What will they do with an engine without the body of a car? They will sell them for almost nothing.

We can remake those engines and they can run a boat the same as if a new engine were on it. We can send those kinds of boats and engines to Africa by the dozens. Some of the African countries don't even have one boat in their entire nation, and yet, the opportunities in fishing are vast. Can you now understand why I would think of machine making factories? Everything has a connection to the whole world. You have to have a mind like that.

Do you have the capability to implement these plans and run these operations? What will pave the way? The science conference will do that. They understand the problems such as in the EEC and in the American economy. They can make the plans and influence the politicians in order to make things happen. The whole basic outlook towards science has to be restructured. There has to be a whole new understanding of values and the application of science. There has been a longterm misunderstanding about these things.

The Time to Begin is Now

Four years ago, we bought fourteen acres of land right next to this house. We are one of the biggest landowners around here. Maybe that is why they are so excited. There is nothing wrong with what we are doing. We are going to make a marine college here and it's about time. The United States has needed one for a long time. They have nothing to say. Wait and see.

My mind is full of all the things that I have to take care of. Can you unload my mind? There is no boat that we cannot build. Steel boat? We have already done that. Wood boat? We have already done that. Fiberglass boat? We have already done that too. You name it, give us a few months and we will come up with it. The more factories that we start, the more people we need to run them. You are the ones who ought to do that. You have to start thinking like this. Make a plan and implement it: buy the factory, pay the people, make the thing work, bring the standard up beyond anything else around. I know it takes a long time. It's impractical for you to start out just like that. However, you won't sink. All you need to do is raise up the people around you. You don't have to find a genius to help you. Just find good people.

I have made all the foundations already. The foundation for you is already prepared. You don't have to bring the people in by the millions, but surely you can bring them in by the hundreds. After a few years, you can find the way to do that. If you aren't motivated, if you still have something which is holding you back and you don't move, should we then give up all these plans? Should we come down to the beginning level and witness like we did twenty years ago? Should I go back out and begin again myself?

Then, who will bring the people? One thing you cannot worry about now is your family. I am not denying you anything. Just think with me for a moment. If you are Blessed, within one year after you begin family living, many of you will have a baby. Within three years, many of you will have two babies. Within five years, many of you will have three babies. Many families will consist of five people: mother, father and two or three children. How are you going to feed them?

Don't you see? Don't you really see that you have to get on your feet now and start running? Don't worry about the whole national foundation, just do your part. You should start running in these next three to five years. At the same time, I will do my portion of work. If you bring more people, you will set the foundation, not only for your own family, but also for many, many families in the future. You have to see that.

If you have one or two babies, you can get along without too many changes, but after three babies, you really have to stop and consider things. You have to pay so many expenses, medical and otherwise. It just takes a lot to raise children; you have to support them. If your head has become so big because you have graduated from seminary, you won't go and dig a ditch, you won't do the humble job, then you might find yourself in an awkward situation.

Well then, shouldn't I chase you out? Shouldn't I say, "This is your area. You have to live or die with it."? Shouldn't I just push you and make you stick to it, even though you are in your early thirties? It's a good age. In ten years, more and more young people will come into the church and they will ask you what you did. How can you say, "Well, I graduated from UTS, but it was all too heavy for me, so I lingered behind the providence."? Can you say that?

My mind feels urgent. The more you linger, the more heavy you will become and finally you will not be able to move at all. Start moving now in the lowest place and don't be bothered by it. You will rise up quickly. Can you understand my feeling? Do you know why I called you here almost suddenly, at such short notice? Why did I call for all the seminary graduates? You were given the mission to witness and you found it very difficult to do that. Where will you apply yourself? In what position will you function? If you cannot do that, what can you do? I am thinking of giving you a new area. Do you want to keep going as you have been? If you keep going like that, if you sit long enough you will perish. Until now you haven't made any action. It has been a few years already and you may have tried, but nothing has improved.

So now, the only way is to try something which might work for you. If you hadn't gone to the seminary, but had instead gone out for two precious years of witnessing, how many members would you have increased? You have been dealing with the upper echelons of people, but there is so much more for you to do. Somehow, since you have graduated from the seminary, there must be some way to use all that knowledge.

If you get a new assignment, will you have a real objection? Why not decide that whatever you do, you will put your whole mind and heart into that, and make something of it? Our purpose is to raise up the standard, not only in America, but in missionary countries as well. We have to back up our ideas with some kind of substantial support.

I seriously thought about the recycling business; first, scrap metal, collecting it and reusing it. After that we would do the same with paper and other products. We would have to build a huge factory to recycle these things. However, after investigating this area, we found that it would be very, very difficult for us to enter into, as it is under a type of "mafia" control. You would have to sacrifice yourself unnecessarily and I didn't think that was a wise idea. We have something better than that to do.

The Plight of America's Fishing Industry

Then, we looked at the fishing industry. As you know, fishing used to be one of America's major industries. However, in the past twenty to thirty years it has steadily been declining. Now, it has gone down to such a level that it cannot rise up again on its own. On the other hand, are the fishing grounds in America lacking? No. In fact, America has three of the four best fishing grounds in the world.

There is a problem with the depletion of some species, but there are many, many species which are not utilized at all, and they are perfectly good to eat. The only problem with them is that they are not popular in the market. However, this can change. The government recognizes the situation, but they are at the point of throwing up their hands, especially if the fishermen just don't want to go out to sea anymore. What can they do? We can analyze the problem in a very simple way. Why are the fishermen reluctant to continue? They go out for several days and work very hard, but when they come back, they get almost nothing for their catch. There is no place for them to sell; there is no market for many of their fish. The wholesalers have been exploiting their situation for a long time; they force the fishermen to accept very low prices, knowing that if they don't sell their fish, their only choice is to throw them back in the water.

There is no steady income guaranteed in fishing. Sometimes the fishermen catch enough, but many times they don't. There is a limited number of fishermen. Not everyone can be a fisherman. It's a very tough life out on the sea. Once a fisherman goes out of business, he never returns to it. They will do anything else, but they won't return to it. It's just too much. Already, almost 50% have given up their boats and they will never come back to try again.

There is another problem with fishing: the wives. The fishermen go out for a week, two weeks or a month and this happens all year long. Many women just can't take that way of life, living alone for so much of the year, and they simply leave. This truly discourages the fishermen. It's a tough life to go out to sea; however, you can tolerate it if your family is intact.

Fishermen work hard to bring in the fish, but there is no guarantee that they will get a good price for them. Most storage for fish is inadequate, so if the market already has too much of a species, they won't get anything for it. Or, they may be able to catch a species, but it isn't popular on the market. This is especially true in America, where many kinds of fish aren't even known about. The market is completely unpredictable; some fish you can catch, but you cannot sell them. At the same time, they are not sure their family will remain intact while they are out working so hard. For many men, it's just too much.

For us, the solution is simple. If you can overcome these three problems, you can participate in a very wonderful business. Everyone knows that this is the case, but they cannot overcome these three problems. So, stretch your imagination. We will build our own boats. Then, we will catch the fish ourselves. Next, we will process and sell the fish by ourselves. Finally, we will export what is left over to foreign countries. Whatever we catch, we can sell directly. If this point is solved, then we can grow. You might worry that we will deplete the fisheries. However, scientists have studied this, and they know that a great deal can be taken from a species before it's depleted. In other words, there is a certain amount that you can take, and the species will be able to reproduce, year after year. There are still plenty of fish out there to be caught. We have to determine that we will become the best in fishing, processing, selling and exporting. This will become a merit to us.

Even though you might start up businesses in this area someday, the first thing is that you have to become familiar with the ocean. The business is secondary. The internal character needed to practice a good business comes first. You have not been out on the ocean for a long time, and some of you have never been on the ocean. Even if you are enthusiastic and like the idea, you have to get acquainted with the sea. You have to know what it is really like. That is the purpose of this summer training, of the seventy days out on the ocean. I myself pioneered and perfected this program. It took several years to build up a foundation for you to inherit. This year the method and procedure has been standardized. All you have to do is study it and practice it. It has been an exciting and rewarding process. From the beginning, I backed up this program by designing the boat that is most ideal for tuna catching. As you know, we first bought the boat that is considered in the market to be most ideal for tuna fishing, called the "Mako." However, I immediately saw that it was lacking many things. So, from scratch I designed and developed a much better boat than what now exists.

The Role of Tuna

In the last few years the fish price was so low, you wouldn't believe it. Sometimes they would just throw the fish right back into the water. The price had to go up just to stabilize the industry. We have been part of the push which has caused the price to go up from only ten cents a pound. When I came here five years ago, people didn't even bother with it; they just threw the fish back. Can you imagine that? Every year, the price has risen steadily until this year it is up to $2.50, and next year, we will see the price go to at least $3.50 per pound. We are paying out of our own resources, and we will have to pay more and more. This is a hard thing to do, but we have to do it for the sake of the future. We have an objective now. What is that? To catch tuna. All you need to do is catch tuna. It is good training for you, but more importantly, it benefits the fishermen.

The value of the tuna is in sushi. You have to deliver it fresh. As long as you deliver it in this way, no Japanese restaurant will refuse it. They will pay the best price for top quality fresh tuna. The Japanese understand the value of this fish. Fishermen shouldn't get a small amount of money for those tuna. Until I came out fishing, fishermen never got the benefit of the tuna price. That has changed now. Here, all the companies that deal with tuna have Japanese companies right behind them. In other words, the real buyers are in Japan; it's coming out of their pockets.

If we drive up the price, the Japanese will have to go back to Japan. Then they will tell everyone, "Well, because of Reverend Moon, we had to forget about buying tuna because the price went up so high." The news will spread overnight in Japan that Reverend Moon is taking over the entire fishing industry in Gloucester. It will have that kind of psychological impact. After all, the Japanese have no idea of what really goes on in Gloucester.

So long as our business can manage at $3.50 per pound and even more, we will buy and sell it. Then, we can begin to make a foundation. Do you understand? When the tuna price goes up and stabilizes, other fish prices will also go up. Years ago, whiting, herring and fish like that were only fifty or sixty cents per pound. That was when tuna prices were also next to nothing. But now, the price has been going up for tuna, and these fish should also go up in price. Presently we only pay ten cents per pound for fresh frozen herring.

The same thing can happen with these fish as with tuna. Why not raise the price back up to $1.50 per pound for these fish and sell them in the market? The tuna serves as a standard setter. By stabilizing the price of tuna, the general price of fish will go up. Whatever we catch, we have to be sure it is consumed, in other words, sold. When we are capable of this much, we can also sell what other fishermen bring in. In this way, we make the foundation from the bottom to the top.

Someday, the fishermen should say in unison that Reverend Moon really made a contribution to the fisherman, because he brought up the price and stabilized the market, and opened up a sales net to secure their future. They should be able to see their future become brighter and brighter.

Establishing a New Foundation

At this point, I feel that things have stabilized. From now on, there will be an increase in price. It is really up to us though. The question is, how fast can you build your own boat and how fast can you train yourself for fishing? We are going to produce 300 training boats to begin with. We will put them all around the three coasts of the United States. If you stay there all the time and go out every day for all the seasons, you will learn very quickly what goes on in that fishing area.

You can find enthusiastic young volunteers. They will be happy to learn about fishing. You can take them out and teach them. Then, you can also explain to them about Divine Principle while you are fishing. They won't mind. You can find young people like that, with a good nature and open mind. Whatever they catch with you they can keep. You can make friends with anyone this way.

If you witness to five people and bring them in, you will get a second boat. You will receive one boat for each five people that you bring. If you expand to ten boats, which is fifty people, you can graduate to a stern trawler. We have already built such boats and you will see one today. A boat like this, eighty to ninety feet, would cost you one-half to one-third of a million dollars. That's a regular stern trawler. You can catch almost anything with it. I want you to go through the training course and someday be able to take responsibility for such a boat.

We will build 300 "Good Go" boats which we developed for tuna fishing. It is also an all purpose speed boat. At the same time, we have already begun to build thirty stern trawlers. We will organize like this: ten regions will receive ten boats each. In each region we will train the personnel to do the basic maintenance of these boats. Then, you will use the boats just like a school, to teach young people about the ocean. Also, a trailer goes with each boat, and one van for each region in order to haul the boats and maintain them. That will be your basic equipment. Eventually, each region should receive one stern trawler.

Next summer, when the tuna season comes, we will have all these boats assembled and ready to begin fishing in Gloucester. Next year, we will go out and stay out. We will have a mother ship, a supply boat where you can get food and evening meals. Only if there is going to be a storm will we come back. After the storm, we will go right back out again. We will develop that kind of training program. Then, the people of America will start to get our message. They will see how serious we are.

One problem is how to get those boats produced within one year. We should have thirty centers with ten boats each. That's 300 boats all around America. Each Ocean Church center should function as a church, and each boat is also a church. So, we have "boat church." The center on land is the center for these boats. It is like the state center with the boats being smaller centers under its direction. Can you imagine starting off with all 300 boats up here in the bay?

Imagine the service we would have! Likewise in your local region, all ten boats should go out, and you should gather around and have morning service on the ocean. After that, go out fishing. Then, when you come back in the evening, you should have a worship service on land. Keep that schedule every day. As soon as our thirty centers are open, we will spread the news that more than 600,000 dollars worth of boats is being invested in this area, all for the sake of reviving the fishing port.

All those interested in such activities can receive great benefit from our various programs. We can teach them without asking anything for catching the fish. We can also teach Divine Principle workshops. If you can get fifty or sixty people interested, you can begin to manage a stern trawler. The *One Hope* boats are for your training, but the stern trawler is more serious.

With that, you can create your economic foundation. And, you will provide the livelihood for those young people whom you have trained. You can put the best people on the waiting list, and when we finish building the training boat for them, they can be responsible for it. I don't think fifty people in each center is a real problem. We can send you the boats you need within the year. Those who are really smart and the best in many different abilities can receive a training boat. You have to evaluate them and recommend them accordingly.

After training on the small boats, we can go out and fish from the stern trawlers. We can then sell the fish directly to the customers. In order for that to happen, we have to create a sales network. For the sisters who don't want to go way out on the ocean, they can sell fish to the homes directly. Just go out in the morning and come home in the evening.

Each region will have three trawlers; from those you can make your economic foundation. Catch the fish and sell the fish. You can do everything in your region. When your spiritual foundation is made, you can begin to make a substantial plan for your region, your local city and your own members.

Without a doubt, the fishing industry is declining. If the mayor and businessmen see such activities in their city, they will surely become interested in helping you. You have to make known to them what you are doing. Our small boats can be used for all kinds of things. We can offer ourselves as a supporting committee and use our boats to back up the work of the Coast Guard. We can offer these boats for many kinds of community service projects. If we continue like this we will develop real fishermen, something like the "heavenly marines."

We already have the small boats and we will develop thirty centers. Then, we will also build a sales network system. The business can help to support projects of the church, and through the business, you can support yourself. We will mobilize all our resources. We can sell the fish by van. Just do your job and bring in the people and train them and revitalize your community. This is the first phase.

Expanding the Foundation

So far, we have only discussed the primary industry. What about the secondary industry such as boat equipment? This means lines, nets, engine parts, electronics and whatever the boat requires to fish successfully. There is a whole area of secondary industries to support the primary one. All this has to be researched. We also have to develop all these areas. The government has been concerned about the declining fishing industry, but they haven't been able to do so much. Once they see us moving ahead and really making substantial progress in this area, they will want to help us as well. This is one thing that America must do right away. If they don't do something about it, there will be trouble from such nations as Russia, Norway, Japan and others who want to fish in the 200 mile limit. They see that America is not utilizing these fishing areas and they desperately want to use them for their markets. Eventually, there will be no way to keep these boats out of American waters. If we are catching the fish, we can respond to the pressure by selling large quantities of fish to them at a good price. Since they won't have to travel all the distance to get the fish that they need, they will be happy to buy it, and America makes a good profit. There is nothing wrong with that. However, if we don't catch the fish, they will keep coming in to fish and they will complain about not being able to feed their people. Their complaint against America will be right in that sense. However, with God's help, we shall go out and make this foundation. Then, great changes will occur in the fishing industry. We are not just thinking about it. It is all well underway, even as I am speaking to you. Once you get the feeling for the ocean, you will never want to give it up. That's the fastest way to get close to the heart of fishing. You have to just go out and do it. The tuna is the greatest of fish. The whale is actually much larger, but it is not a fish; it is entirely something else. But tuna is a fish, so we can say that it is the "king" of all fish.

In other parts of the world, we already have four long-range tuna boats in operation. These boats are fishing in Africa. They are about 150 feet long. Along with that, we are operating ten shrimp boats in South America. In their first year of operation they were able to regain their entire capital investment. Everyone down there is talking about us and calling it a miracle. And they are right.

Once you get accustomed to it, there is no reason why you should stick to the land. There is more opportunity on the ocean, more to be done and more to be made there than on the land. This is really the case. Would any of our wives leave because their husband stays out for six months? Or, would the husbands leave if their wives are out there? Nor will we be stuck with the fish if we bring them in, because we will have our own sales network. Likewise, the sales people won't be stuck if the fishermen come in and refuse to sell to them because they are Moonies. We will catch the fish, sell the fish and go on from there. First we need training.

We have members from all over the world. We can make branches in Germany, France, England, Japan and all over the world. We can process the fish so that it is really fresh and of good quality. Americans don't like herring and it's price is always at the bottom. However, in Germany the price begins at $1.00 per pound because they really like that species.

To produce 300 boats in one year is no small operation. It is likely that the Mako company doesn't produce that many boats in one year. In the future, if one of you is an enterprising person, you can open up your own branch boat building company. There is nothing to it. You start from the mold. Once you have the mold, you buy some fiberglass and resin and you apply it until you have the proper thickness. That becomes your hull. Then you have the deck. This is the same procedure. Finally, you assemble it together. It's not that difficult if you are quick to learn things.

Your church mission is one thing and you can be anything, CARP leader or state leader, while your business can be something else. So, why not build boats, or fish the trawler, or sell fish by van? Why not? If your state leader understands this, they will move the state center from the middle of the state to the sea shore.

How good a fishing boat is the Good Go? It is really very good. The number one fishermen amongst the members this year was Gerhard and he had *One Hope 1*. It's a pretty good boat. It's our first boat and he drove it. At first, Gerhard didn't think we were capable of building such a beautiful and strong boat. It's beautiful like a woman, isn't it? The difference between the *One Hope* boat and other boats is like night and day.

[Gerhard Peemoeller's Testimony of the *One Hope* Boat]

"This boat is very special. Father is the true man and this boat is very much like Father. I call this boat the 'messiah' boat. It is really like the true boat. When I saw the boat go in the water, I was very surprised. I first drove the boat at night time; I couldn't believe how well it handled. Compared to the Mako, which is a similar size, this boat is much more stable in the water.

"This boat is something else. When you are out on the ocean and the waves are coming to a small boat, you really hit into that wave and it's quite rough. But this boat is amazing. It goes into the wave and cuts into the wave. The water splashes way out away from the boat. It almost doesn't hit into the wave at all, but just cuts smooth and soft through it. This boat is about 2,000 pounds heavier than the Mako. That means it is 2,000 pounds more stable and solid. Considering that, and then knowing it has the same engine as the Mako has and yet doesn't burn any more fuel than the Mako, makes you wonder what the secret is.

"Even though this boat is twice as heavy as the Mako and has the same engine, it doesn't burn twice as much gas. It burns a little bit more, but not so much. It is almost the same. There is something special about this boat; the way it is designed has a certain impact. On or out of the water, people look at it and they really know it is a very remarkable boat. Driving the boat in water is a wonderful experience. It is much more stable than anything comparable.

"This boat cannot be compared to any other boat in its class and size right now. It's stable in the water. Anyone who has ever been out in the water in a Mako or something comparable can immediately find out the difference. The entire boat itself, how it is designed and how it fits together is just a total experience. Many fishermen have been coming around and looking at it and asking if they could buy it. These boats could be sold so easily. It is really the 'true' boat."

When I hear Gerhard talk about the *One Hope* boat, it reminds me of the expression, "love at first sight." Once you see this boat you will understand this. Especially when it is running, it presents such a beautiful profile. There is no question as to what a beautiful boat it is. Imagine, this fiberglass boat will last and last. No boat has lasted long enough. In the future, the lower the number is, the more valuable it will be. *One Hope* 4 or 10 will be far more valuable than *One Hope* 3,000. So, if you take good care of your boat, in forty or fifty years it will be extremely valuable. It will be the pride of your entire state. People will look at this boat and you won't have to tell them to believe in Unification Church. They will just believe it by themselves. Do you understand how that could happen? Every house would want to buy one of these boats. Living in a house that has such a boat will be more pride than living in any mansion. You should sleep and live right on the boat, and create a wonderful history for it.

Every Unification family should buy one of these boats. That is how historical and precious they are. Those who want to own a boat like that, raise your hands. If you are persuaded simply by my talking to you and Gerhard's introduction of it, then wait until you see it with your own eyes. Wait until we produce everything, the boat, the trailer, the van, the engines, everything with our own hands. Do you believe it? Those who feel really excited by the whole idea and want to go into it with all your effort, raise your hands.

The Ocean Church Mission

The reason I called the seminary graduates is because I want you to become leaders for each of the thirty centers. You are the ones to become regular fishermen. You are the ones that have to educate fisherman. You have to teach them Divine Principle and Victory Over Communism, and eventually Unification Thought. You have to educate them so they understand God's will and purpose. That is how you will equip them to enter into the future. Otherwise, they will decline into the past.

You have to be able to teach them from the very beginning. Perhaps, I will get a helicopter and visit all the boats. I will let you know when I am coming. Maybe I will meet you out on the ocean and eat lunch with you. Isn't that a wonderful idea? We can eat the fresh fish that you just caught. Wouldn't you like that? Now you know why I called you. If you really implement this plan, don't you think Unification Church will grow? We will have 300 churches very soon from the original thirty centers.

Imagine driving this Good Go, this fast and beautiful boat. It is unsinkable. It does not sink because it is foam-filled. It takes water up to the brim and still stays afloat. When there is a big storm, it will not sink. As long as you have a life-line you can tie yourself to it and you will be all right. Maybe the fish will die from the storm, but you won't. It's a sport boat, but it is also a safe boat.

Later on, we will build similar boats for the commercial market. If you want, you can become a sales representative and sell those boats. This will also help your economic foundation. Look at it this way. If you become rich, then the Unification Church will become rich. However, if you sell that boat and donate the money to Africa, it's even better. Would you say "no" or "yes" to this idea? Then, who profits if you are successful? Success can be a very good thing, if you are willing to invest it in others. This is why I want to train you. It is your job to make these thirty centers a success. If you do that, the initial investment will not be lost. If you extend your success to others, it will never be lost.

The Role of America and Japan

When you talk about the fishing business in general, you cannot leave the Japanese out of it. The reason is this: the way they process fish and sort it out; the way they package fish and sell it. No one can even come close to Japan in these areas. Japan is truly envious of the fishing grounds in America. They cannot get along without fish; they must have fish in their diet. They cannot catch enough in their own waters, so they are dying to have a connection with the fishing grounds here in America.

America is aware of that too. The American fisheries would never continue without the market that exists in Japan. They have so much fish, but where are they going to send it? American people simply don't eat that much fish. However, thanks to the Japanese almost every bit of fish that is caught here is bought (by the Japanese) at a reasonable price.

However, the Japanese are almost over-extended now. There are no large Japanese companies working here in America without some support from Japan. The Americans don't want the Japanese to go beyond what they can handle, because the American companies want to continue to sell to Japan, and the American government understands this. Today, some Japanese companies are buying the fish in America and then selling the fish to another company in Japan.

The American companies are saying, "Let us buy the fish from our own fishing grounds and sell them to you in Japan. You go back to Japan and buy from us there." They would much rather do that. Japan is looking for, and needs a company here which is American, but focused upon the Japanese market. They want to be able to trust that company fully and know that it would sell the fish to Japan. It is just like the American companies in Japan. They have Japanese representatives there, but in essence the company is always considering the American market. So then, how shall we meet that qualification? All the American members married to Japanese spouses will form a company. Which is it, an American company or a Japanese company? Well, it is an American company. The Japanese can look at it, however, and feel quite confident that it is also a Japanese company. Then, the Japanese will want to invest in this company. This is truly possible and is quite practical, isn't it? We will prove this out.

We will even let Middle East entrepreneurs invest their oil dollars in this effort. The desert countries have never invested very much in fishing because many of them don't have coastal waters, or their fishing grounds are not so good. They drill for oil and live off of that, not fishing. However, when they start to eat fish, they will find out how good it is for their appetite and their health. From that point, we should try to develop a good relationship with them. Then, there will be a boom effect. Good things could happen. New international relationships could be built.

Think about yourself. Where are you going to be ten years from now if you invest yourself and work towards this goal? You will have security for your family. There are already large Japanese companies working very strongly here in America, but we will have our own sales network here in America, as well as back in Japan. When we have a good wholesale and retail net, we can move forward with confidence.

We cannot use other wholesalers because they will just pay us the cheapest price, and then make the most money by increasing the price to the consumer. That is why fish is close to $2.00 or more per pound once it gets to the consumer's table. We have to make our own foundation, from catching fish to processing it to retailing it. Actually, we should eliminate the need for the middle man. This just adds extra cost to the consumer. Why should the people pay for a wholesaler if the fish can come directly from the processor to the retailer? This is where we can truly make an impact on the market and everyone will benefit. Even though we have such a plan, there are problems. Fish resources will be depleted by overfishing in some areas, especially certain fish which are already popular as table fish. These species, like the striped bass, which are already very expensive, won't be available anymore. If too many are caught, the supply will be exhausted. For that reason, we have to go into fish farming; we have to go into it as soon as possible. The tuna is one example. They lay close to a million eggs. However, out of a million eggs, only two or three fish will ever get to full size, over 600 pounds. We have to devise a way to hatch those eggs and protect them. Look at the salmon. They have been coming back, largely due to salmon hatcheries. We have to make a plan to do the same for the tuna. If you can hatch and protect them to a certain size and then let it go into the water, there will be a tremendous increase in the amount of tuna available.

Tuna is an excellent source of protein for human consumption. One tuna has more meat than two or three cows. However, no one has been thinking about that. Instead of letting cows eat up all the grain, people could eat that grain. Why not catch tunas instead? It is a much healthier protein to eat as well.

Accepting a New Assignment

Maybe you haven't thought about the fishing industry so much, but based upon what you have heard, you have come to have some new perspective on it. What do you think? Are you thinking that this could really work? When you were carp fishing in Barrytown, you were already starting on this providence. You didn't know it then, but you certainly were. Those who made the nets with me remember going late into the night and even the next morning without any sleep. That was not unrelated; it was actually part of your initiation.

So, you might as well take it, because I am planning that each Unification Church leader should spend eighteen months on the boat as training. We have a saying in Korean which goes, "The one who gets the first punishment gets away the easiest." It means, if you get the task the first time, it is not as hard as when you get it later on. Are you interested? Are you starting to dream of fish already? You should be dreaming of something because it is already late into the day, and I am sure you are hungry by now. Are you at least imagining lobsters or fish? Those who listened intensely, did you connect with lobsters? If you have done so, then you have certainly listened. You won't have to be convinced.

The lobsters must be cooking and cooking for you and they might be worried that the customers have turned them down, making their effort meaningless. Should we make the assignments now or should we eat first? We now have our own seafood restaurant. Should we eat first or decide later? Let's eat first and when you go to the restaurant, look at the Good Go boat. Look at *One Hope 4* and you can see what I have been talking about all morning long.

You have had a long time to enjoy your reunion, and after our meeting tonight, you can spend another night here. Then, the conference is over, and you can leave tomorrow. Did you take the tour, go around and see the castle? Do you like Morning Garden? Is it a good place? We will buy many places like this around all the coastal areas. We will use them for training centers, research centers, and centers for the fishermen to come back, rest and recuperate. Did you see the Good Go? That's our pride. A boat is the pride of any American family. They really take care of their boats and go to the lakes or the ocean with them. Are you ready to order a boat now and apply for it?

The members of the boat building factory always want to do things like other companies. However, when I look at the list of things there is so much that we don't need to do. Many factories operate with a great deal of waste. Then, I advise the members to use just what they absolutely need to use. There is always plenty of room to save costs and yet not affect the quality of the boats. It just takes an alert mind.

Getting back to the original question and explanation that I have given to you, should we position these boats all around the coastal waters? It's easy to say, "Yes", but do you consider all that it means to you, the change in life-style that you will have to make? Once you assume the position, will you really determine to work there for three or four years and not run away? Certainly you wouldn't say in front of me, "Oh, yes Father, I will run away." However, just to say "Yes" in front of me is not right either. You have to consider what you are saying. It will be your foundation. It will be America's foundation. That is a real and eternal foundation. It will not fade away.

The Foundation for Africa and South America

I cannot stay here all the time. I have to go to all the different countries. If I stayed in this country all the time, what would happen to the other countries? They would blame me for not coming to them. The African countries and South America, especially Brazil, are really asking for me. The members know that so much more could happen and develop in their countries and they are really eager for me to come there.

I am thinking seriously about establishing machine factories in countries like Zaire to make farm machinery. People are farming with ox carts and hoes there. However, we can make farming machines that will work there and we will teach them how to fix the machines when they break down. It's incredible. White people occupied Africa and made colonies there, but they never educated the people. They just took everything for their own use. They didn't show them how to make farms and they didn't tell them how to reap crops, vegetables or fruit. They never introduced anything, not even how to make bread. They are still eating the bare minimum of staple foods in Africa, like the wild potato. There are just a few kinds of food and for every meal they eat almost the same thing. No one ever educated them. They received very little education, even at the grammar school level. They cannot read or write and they cannot begin to understand the modern world. How can they hope to survive? All these wrongdoings were made by white people. If the white people don't try to solve these things, it may be that the yellow people will go there and correct them.

In Africa, we spend only 10% of what we spend here in America, but it is enough to get a whole movement going in one country. A little bit has a tremendous impact in Africa. Don't you think we should do that? We should show them everything, how to grow and harvest vegetables and fruit, how to produce crops and bake bread. One problem in the past was that when they received education, they chased the white people away. The white people responded with, "Why even bother to educate them?"

Finally, a few Africans would get to go to London or somewhere in Europe, and you can imagine how they felt when they came to those continental countries. They saw the difference between the living standards in the Western world and their life back in Africa. This caused a lot of anguish and anger. Even though there have been some reforms, this racial concept is still there. White people don't like people with color; they don't like black people.

What happens is that the communists use this as a vulnerable point. They agitate the people and say, "Look what the white people have done to you and look what they think about you. They don't care about you, they are only using you." Then, the communists tell them that their only hope is communism, where they will live in the laborer's kingdom, the common people's kingdom. It has always been proven to be a lie, but if you don't really know about communism, it is very sweet talk. This is how the communists start racial wars. If you have doubts about it, you have to study more. It's very clear to see their strategy. Before such things happen, the white people of the Unification Church should go to Africa and pay indemnity for the wrongdoings of white ancestry and make things more even. Then, they will begin to trust you.

Most recently in Zaire there has been a spiritual church which the white people have massacred. It was a new Christian denomination and this awful thing is now history. No one tells this story in public. They just want to put a lid on it and forget about it. But the black people will never forget about it. We will have to open that up and indemnify it. Someone will have to pay for it and ease their hearts.

When I bring these things out in the open, am I cruel or just trying to find fault with white people? Do you think that it's good for me to bring this out? It's good because it's the only way to make things even and start things new. We have to be sure about that. We cannot hide the things that we did. I want to go right now and help them, but I cannot go to them with empty hands. My first priority is to get you on a solid foundation.

Creating Your Own Foundation

It is not my credibility that concerns me. It is your credibility that I want you to build. You have to accomplish something. I want to start some foundation for you so that in the future you will have some protection. Otherwise; the persecution will be too severe if I were to leave. This is why I am hastening so much. It is why I go through so many sleepless nights and compact three years of effort into one.

Many people say, "Father why don't we take a little longer to do this project?" When the fishing industry becomes prosperous, I want to donate hundreds of boats and give them away for all kinds of good programs. The point is, how to make a good quality boat without a great deal of expense. Once we do that, the American people will work hard and give the boats away. You might like the idea, but don't want to work so hard.

I understand this about you. You don't want to work hard if you can get away with it, but this is the only way for you to get results. I have to push you, but you get the results, you get the benefit. Each boat cost twenty-five thousand at the minimum. If we were to sell them, the retail price would be around thirty thousand. The material alone costs sixteen thousand, while the rest of the cost is labor. These first boats are for you to use for your programs. So we need to make the boats just as good, but cheaper. One thing that we can do is make many of the parts ourselves. The parts we have to buy, we can buy in large quantity. This brings down the cost. If you really keep a close check on everything and buy everything at the time when its more of a bargain, you can reduce the cost by two or three thousand dollars. With the extra, you can give benefits to the members making the boats.

We will have to put at least twenty million into this project. If you were to deposit that into the bank, you would get three million dollars every year without doing anything. That's only two or three percent interest: it is not much, but it adds up. I know that when you first invest money like this, you will lose in the first few years. We might lose up to one-third of the original investment. I know that we will lose this good money, but that is how it is when you start a new venture. The typical way of working in a factory is that you work for a few hours then take a break. Then you work a little bit more and then you have to have some coffee. By the time you have four or five breaks, it's time to quit. I don't think about work that way. I like to work twenty-four hours around the clock in order to finish more quickly. Time to eat doesn't take an hour, it only takes half of that time. The fastest way to eat is just to pick up the food with your hands. I have trained myself how to eat fast. I can eat one meal in one minute. You can put all your food into the soup bowl and just drink it down. Can you imagine it? You might be thinking, "What kind of a lifestyle is that?" That's the lifestyle to make the foundation. That's what kind of lifestyle that is.

If you have a choice, if you really want to establish the foundation for the Kingdom of Heaven on earth, then you cannot go about it in the old way of doing things. Just forget about that. You have to devise a whole new way to make things happen. I have worked to the point that when it came to dusk I wasn't even sure if it was morning and the sun was rising or if it was evening and the sun was setting. When I was eating something, I wondered if it was breakfast or dinner. You might hear this and think it is just a story, but I have lived through this. This is exactly how things happened.

I have a record in Korea. We built the Il Hwa factory, three stories, a steel reinforced and concrete foundation building. This was a regular building and usually it would have taken two or more years to build it. To plan it would take six months, preparation takes another six months, and then it takes at least a year to build it. Our factory only took three months from start to finish. We poured the concrete for twenty-four hours, using lights and two different shifts. We did it like that. The training center we built in just twenty-eight days. One man went away for a few days and came back to find a whole building there. He thought he was lost. We built another training center which is not as large, but just as substantial, in only seven days. Can you imagine building a permanent house, including the foundation, in just seven days?

The tempo that you work at really upsets me. I don't even want to come look at it. You do things so slowly, dragging them on and on. The garden lies in front of you, and you can make it in just a few days. You've gone on and on for two months now and you aren't even beginning. I am studying Americans now and learning about you. I am now thinking of how to lay everything out for you and show you how to accomplish really fast and efficient production. That's for your sake.

You have to investigate how to improve the speed of production. Invent a machine if you have to. The leader has to take responsibility. If he cannot do it, then someone else has to come in and do it. You cannot do it the easy way. No other factory would ever try to push this hard. Well, we have to be reasonable, but as much as we can, we will try to bring the costs down for these 300 boats. We can bring the costs down, of that we are sure. How about you? Don't you think this is the best way? Then, would you want to work slowly and get only a little bit of benefit, or work very hard and get a great deal of benefit? One is easier, but the other is more sure in the long run. This will be your foundation.

No one is thinking this way and it just baffles me. Anyway, we can put everything together for less than twenty thousand dollars. I am sure of that, including all the parts and the trailer, everything. Mako is now twenty-two thousand dollars without a trailer. You have now seen our boat. It's a handsome boat isn't it? The Mako boat, speaking honestly, is one class lower. Our boat can still run in twenty-five knot winds. From twenty-five to thrity-three knots is small craft advisory conditions, but our boat can still run. It is as stable as a mid-sized boat. The boat will be produced; there is no question about that. We may have to build it in Alabama where things cost less and the weather is better so that we can build it in an almost open space. Now then, the question of building 300 boats is settled.

The New Assignment

At this time thirty people will be assigned to manage centers. Initially, let's begin with volunteers. Those who want to take this new mission, stand up. From the way you look, I think you will all get sea sick when you first go out. "Soft bones," is the term I am thinking of. If you don't get sea sick, raise your hands.

I want to select first those who can get along with the ocean. Some people are born in such a way that the fish will follow along with them. Just like some people are born to make money in business, some are born to make money in fishing. I will first go around and pick those who are best suited for this life. It is like a matching ceremony isn't it? Then, let's begin. After you are picked, please register your names.

With these members I feel that I have more than enough to create the ocean kingdom. What about you? You have to be very flexible and you have to be able to make very quick decisions, especially when the sea is rough. You must always be thinking that the ocean is dangerous. You have to be able to handle that. You have to have a body which can handle the harsh weather and hard work. Can you understand that? Well, I have picked twenty-four members, and this will be it to begin with. Six more members will come later on.

We need good lecturers as well. Education doesn't exactly need a big person. Those who are state leaders already, please raise your hands. You should come to Ocean Church, but not just yet. Seminary graduates are directly responsible to me. They don't go automatically to HSA or to CARP or anywhere else. No one can just reassign them at will. Since they were especially trained at the seminary, they are under my responsibility. Now, it is pretty much understood. For you new center leaders, the boats are still in production. This means that twelve of you will receive your assignments tomorrow. The other twelve will be temporarily assigned as a state leader. However, when the new boats come out, you will be assigned a boat and you will go to your new mission. Until the first twenty-four boats are produced, you will go in this order. It will take about two months. Daikan is the one who is advising Ocean Church and I trust him to pick the first twelve leaders from you.

This is not a separate organization that I am starting. It is very much a part of our movement. Tiger Park will come to visit you and Reverend Kwak will help you organize your lecture programs. You are very much a part of the movement. In a real way, you are just like a state leader, especially in your region of Ocean Church. Don't settle down, but keep moving and visit all the ports in your region. We have to reorganize quickly and leave no blanks. As you see, many people have been recruited to be state leaders and new leaders for Ocean Church. Now, those left will have to work twice as hard.

First Instructions

Then, God bless you. If you new Ocean Church leaders do well, you will develop faster than the inland churches, including the state centers on the coastal lines. You have more motivation to create something. When you go to your assigned area, first visit with the Coast Guard chiefs, the Police chiefs and the mayor. Introduce yourself and explain what you are going to do. Let them know that your interest is to revive the fishing industry in America, and that you will train many young people to work hard and live sacrificially for the sake of the seaport. Tell them that boats, trailers and vans will be coming into their area. Assure them that you will do your best to reverse the trend of young people, from living in a decadent way to a constructive and creative way. You will quickly have to form a lecture program, and when there are enough people assembled, give them a lecture. In this way, explain to them all these things.

There are a few crucial ports to which you will first be assigned. You are in the position of director for that port and/or that region. A few boats and a few members will come under you. They will be notified that you are coming. Since you haven't had any experience this summer, and those who are assigned to you have already had some amount of substantial experience, you can learn from them. You have to let them know that you want to catch up and close the gap quickly. Many of them will be European members and they will be happy for you to be the director there because you can link them to America.

Your main task is to lecture and educate the young people in the region. While you are doing that, you can take them out to sea and fish together. Lecture in the boat and train them as you are fishing.

All these things are done at the same time. I have already directed you how to bring them along. After they go through a period of training, let them apply for a boat. The boat that comes to Gloucester during the summer can fish the East coast. It is best for this boat to go to Norfolk first and the crew can get their experience there. Fish there and you will learn what you need to know. During the tuna season, we need a tender boat; this boat can come up from Norfolk and provide chum for the boats and buy tuna.

There will be many boats assigned to Alaska, trawlers as well as small boats. A plan to organize and supervise the boats, especially training captains, has to be made. Each boat has to have a good captain and a trained crew. The members who go to Alaska cannot become isolated. Allan Hokanson should go there and help to organize these things. He should live with them and try to train them day by day.

All the fishing vessel captains must come through Alaska. They have to go through Allan, or the person who is in that position. The boat operations and the training of the crews are under him. Whoever is in that position cannot care about himself so much, but has to really care about training others. Allan has a high standard and that is why I am putting him up as an example. He has to go with the others on their boats and be on board with them. He has to educate them and then branch out, training many other groups after the first one. He will have to become something like a "mother hen" up there.

This is a good type of activity for him and if he establishes himself in a good way there, he can become anything. He is the testing case. If he can establish himself with the captains in Alaska and gain their respect, he can then move forward. There will be a leader who works on land with the business and Allan should establish himself on the ocean. These two must work together. The motto for the business manager on land and the captains on the ocean, especially Allan, is "To Be One." Allan should captain one of the new boats and compare it with the *Green Hope*. How many boats are needed in Alaska? What is the optimum? We have to consider how to keep our expenses down, especially mechanics expenses and food expenses. We have to train our members about mechanics. Also, if we eat fish a lot, we can cut down on the really expensive costs of meat. If you spend without consideration, there is no end to it.

On the longline fishing vessels which are our commercial boats, we pay the crew members a salary and a food allowance. Do you know what they eat? They eat rice and vegetables and the fish which they catch from the ocean. They fry it, bake it and fix it in all kinds of ways. In this way, they can save their food allowance and add it to their salary.

We too can train that way. You have to find the way to do that. If you spend and spend, you will never be able to save. You should always think how to economize on the boat, including the cost of repairs. As you will soon find, you have to make sure every member is trained in engine maintenance. You are the leader and director, but you also have to be a first class mechanic. If you don't know something, you cannot teach others. You have to be a first class mechanic: there is no other way around it. Start with an engine book and just learn. You have to know the engine inside and out, and be able to take the engine apart and put it back together. To qualify yourself as the director of your region, you have to be the expert on the boat.

When I come to visit you, I want to see you taking that boat out. You are the leader and director of the sailors, fishermen and oceangoing people. You are not administrative directors. You have to be busy, directing the spiritual education of your area. At the same time, you have to learn the business side; you have to find out how to sell fish. Sometimes you may catch a great deal of fish, but you don't know where to sell it. That's part of your training. After you understand how to be self supporting, it's guaranteed that someone will buy whatever fish you catch. Each region should work together in a smooth manner. You have to know how to work in all the departments: witnessing, fishing, education and also, business and fish sales. Then, we will expand and move forward and we will fulfill the purpose of the church. The first thing you need to do is go and make friends. Ask them questions and find out as much as you can. Then, get a book about the local area and study the fishing there.

For at least half a year you have to do that. Around the coastline, we can set up various factories such as a net making factory and a boat making factory. If those factories are in your region, you have to manage them as well.

If you manage things well, work really hard and move around quickly from project to project, your foundation will be set. It is your foundation. You can even someday run for congressman or senator, representing the fishermen in your region. This will be to your credit. The whole town will notice your existence. You have to be welcomed by the people. I believe there will be a substantial number of good people who will come around you and ask for your guidance. Then, educate them and inspire them to work for the sake of the country.

You must learn quickly, each to your ability. A very good person to inherit from is Daikan. One thing that Daikan never did: complain. Six o'clock is the quitting time, and I always say, "Bring the lines in," but Daikan would always linger on for five more minutes because the tuna might strike at any minute. At least three times the tuna struck at that last moment. I wouldn't be happy if at the end of the day when I said, "Let's go!" everyone would be so happy and just jump to bring the lines in. Daikan goes very slowly because he is hoping the tuna will bite at the very last moment. You never know.

From next season onward we will charge participants a minimum fee for the training program. They should at least pay for three meals a day. It takes one or two hours to go out to the tuna grounds. If you can stay out there and keep fishing, it makes a big difference. We will place a big boat in the center and you can moor around it at night. You can go back and forth to the big boat from your anchor spot. Other people argue about their anchor spots because it makes a big difference where you are, whether or not you will get the tuna to bite.

Those who have been out tuna catching in any season, raise your hands. Those who have fishing experience, the European and American members, have to help the new leaders.

Questions and Answers

Do any of you have questions right now?

Member: "If some of us don't get boats right away, can we go on a commercial boat to get some training?"

Well, not here because it is getting too cold, but you could get on a boat fishing for bottom fish. If you want to fish here for one day tomorrow, you can at least do that. Anyway, for twelve of you, the boat is already waiting. We are short of trailers and vans. We will first have to tow your boat to your location, put it in the water, leave it there and use the van to tow another boat. Soon, each boat will have a trailer and three to five boats will have one van. That will be the standard.

Member: "What is our priority? Fishing, selling fish, training, lecturing?"

Before you get your boat, you can do public relations. This is first. You start out that way; you are the main force. However, CARP members should also help and the state leaders should assist you. First you have to make a foundation. Then, you can branch out from there. We haven't done that yet, because we aren't planning to go commercial at first. We ourselves need 300 boats which we don't intend to sell. These are for training. Eventually we will sell other boats similar to the *One Hope* boats. They will be a Good Go, but not a *One Hope*. The *One Hope* boats are special. However, when people see these boats, they will want one. It's already happening. People want to buy the *One Hope* boats now, but we are not selling them.

The First Priority

You should go directly to your states from here and become active. For example, Dr. Durst has to go out often to the states. I would like to see him go around to all fifty states at least once a month. That means he would be on the road all the time. However, if Dr. Durst talks to an audience of 100 people, how long would he take to reach the entire population of America? If he did that every day, how long would it take him? It would take ten thousand years.

Instead, if he concentrates on New York and can reach 7,000 people and bring them into the Home Church activity, it is much faster. If he gives banquets and public talks for five years in the same area among those 7,000 people, and does this over and over again for five years, it will bring a much better result. When New York starts to understand and get our message, then so will the entire United States. The whole nation can turn around very quickly if that happens.

In this way, Home Church is a more direct restoration. More people can be restored more quickly, so he is concentrating on this. Instead of inviting people to headquarters, he should go out into the Home Church area and make two or three tours all around there. He shouldn't do so many banquets then, but have meetings instead where he can give lectures. He should do that two or three times each day. One or two hours at one place and then move on to another place and spend a few hours there. Those people are there to stay. They won't go away. It's the same way in which I approached the people when I first came to the United States. It's the fastest way. I know. Through the revival meeting, the banquet meeting, these kinds of meetings, you set a very good atmosphere for people. State leaders should operate like that. And you should operate like that. Then, with his experience, Dr. Durst will know what needs to be done. He will visit your center and work with you. You can call on him for that.

Tomorrow, you will all go to your new assignments or back to your old ones. May God bless you in your work. Let us give three "Manseis" for the victory of Ocean Church.

Colonel Han's Prayer

"Heavenly Father, we are thankful to have shared this time with

Father. Time is moving, and on this particular day we find a great transition occurring. Not yet within America, but within ourselves. Heavenly Father, help us to change in the most dramatic way, because we have to catch up and fill in the gap between what you expect and need of us, and where we are at this particular moment. Heavenly Father, help us to overcome all our self-imposed limitations.

We want to inherit the tradition that Father has set up in Korea, Japan and now in America. We know that tradition has been so painfully established. We pledge to quickly change and inherit your tradition, to work selflessly for the sake of mankind and for the sake of you, Heavenly Father. At this moment, we are deciding within ourselves to work with all our might according to the examples you have given to us. We are about to begin Ocean Church. It is a historical development in this country.

Later, in history, all of America will witness to this day. Let us pray deeply about the next years to come. True Parents have already put in so much sweat and tears, and they have invested so much in the seminary so that the students could come to this one day. Many are working in CARP and many have become state leaders, and today many were assigned as Ocean Church leaders. Their success depends on their hard work.

When this becomes successful, we know that America will have hope. If we do not act according to the standard, then this country will still have to go through more turbulence, more indemnity and more misery and the results of that will not be guaranteed. So then Heavenly Father, taking your pattern, let us dedicate all of ourselves to you. Live or die, we will do your will. If we live, we will do your will here on earth and if we die, we will continue to do your will in the spirit world. Heavenly Father, help us to remain on earth as long as we can to complete this historical task. We are so grateful to have the privilege to do your work along with True Parents. We are the happiest people on earth, even though there is hard work waiting for us. Even though there is no luxury in our lives, we are the happiest people in history since we have True Parents. Heavenly Father, we are so thankful for all that they have done already for this world and for America. Protect them and their family because we could never replace them. We want to someday take over their burdens and pledge to carry on until you have educated us properly how to do so.

We pray all these things in the name of True Parents. Amen."

Ocean Church
and
America

August 28th, 1982 -- Provincetown

SINCE WE cannot go out to sea today, I called you here. Would you prefer to go out to sea or come here? As you know we have Morning Garden in Gloucester, a very nice place which we prepared some years ago, however, because of a pending court case we cannot use the center there right now. Whenever you start a new religion there is always the path of persecution that must be followed. Not because there is anything bad or wrong with the religion, but when something new grows out of the old tradition, the new movement always has to pay indemnity. This is historical fact.

The Goal of History

The goal of history is to come to final fruition. When we look at this point, it is only natural that we go through such a process. Just as it is for fruit, which stems from a big tree, so the process to final maturity is not easy. The seasons come and go, some of the branches may be broken off by the wind, but the fruits which unite together and hang onto the branch will complete the process. It is the same with human history. That is why we cannot judge until we look back at the total process, until all has taken place. Persecution is part of the process towards that final growth. Therefore, it is not something we can escape; we have to go through it.

You are young men and women. You all live in America, but your backgrounds are very different. What is the purpose of American youth? We have to make that clear. They would like to

88

have something of value and do something worthwhile with their lives. They would like to have these nice boats and go out to sea; it is something that almost every young man dreams about. What about you? Is that why you are here, to go out every day on a boat?

Let me ask you then, why did you join and stay in the Unification Church? You see the final fruit in the future don't you? That is why you can stay in the Unification Church, even though you have been working many years, going on and on. The history of mankind and the history within the Unification Church have many parallels. History started with a certain goal and people have come and gone, starting something, then complaining about it and leaving, then some joining again and others leaving.

Within Unification Church too, the same pattern exists. Human history and Unification history go through this struggle. It is the struggle against selfish desire and for the will of God. Within this group, I see three kinds of members. There are those who try to go forward, those who try to maintain and those who try to pull others down. Human history is the same. American history is also the same. Some people envision a better future and try to create it. Others just try to keep what they have in life, and then there are those who want to go back to the good old days.

Who will take responsibility for the future of America? Certainly the group which wants to pull others back is not the group to take this responsibility. Certainly not the group which wants to maintain what it has, that wants to keep the good life they already enjoy. This group might be good for the current national interest, but not for the world, not for the sake of human history. History always has to go beyond just normal human interest. History has always been led by the people who have an ideal and actively pursue that goal.

Look at Provincetown where so many youth come to use drugs and gay people gather together. They might become the people who lead America. Their lifestyle goes against universal law. Why was man or woman born? Man was born for woman and woman was born for man. Man was not born for man and woman was not born for woman. We are born for each other. Even in the insect world there isn't any mix-up in that standard. Even in the animal kingdom there is no such confusion in their natural setting. No other group in creation has this problem. Just mankind. This indicates to us that the final days are here when mankind must decide between future prosperity or its own destruction. We have to ask, why did Adam need Eve and vice versa? We have to understand clearly that they were made for each other in order to bear children. Children represent the future. They would have produced better people than themselves. Just as a tree produces better fruit, the desire of man and woman is to produce better children than themselves. For the sake of a better future, that is why man and woman need each other.

Why do you want to get married? Just to love each other? Actually you want to bear better fruit than yourself. Why do you love your children? Why do you love your wife? Because you can love the generations to come through her. The future is centered on you. You have to prepare the love that you have for your wife and for your children. You have the responsibility to connect the past, present and future. Each one of you has that responsibility. Therefore it is shameful for America that so many young people are destroying their bodies with drugs and also destroying their future by indulging in homosexual relationships. They are not the hope of America. History really needs a group which can lead young people into the future. The world needs that group, America needs such a group. Even God himself needs that kind of group.

Whoever goes and pioneers this new era for America, for mankind and for God is the kind of group that all of history has been waiting for. It will be the age of true man and true woman, of true men and women. I am always looking at the work of the Unification Church. I am always thinking of every detail, always thinking of you, of the future. Daytime and nighttime I am thinking of what kind of people you need to become. You should look at yourself and examine yourself. How much have you changed since you joined the church? Do you think selfishly about yourself all the time or do you now think more for the public purpose? You used to be only concerned for "me, me, me." But now you are thinking, "what can I do for the sake of God, for mankind, for others?" You used to try to find value in life with a self-centered scope, but since you joined the church you now look for value in a much greater sense. Your future has broadened. Where you stand today is not limited to yourself; rather, it is limitless. You used to have a limited future, but now your future is without any limits.

Before you used to think at least about your own nation, but now you think about the entire world and even beyond. This kind of interest will only benefit America in the long range. So at some point, America will welcome such people as you. In the past, all your sweat and tears and hard work were only for yourself, but now all that same effort is for the sake of mankind. This is really the beginning of a new era, a new history for yourself and for your nation. It is really the new beginning for the world. You young people can start an entirely new world.

I want you to realize that this is our motivation; this is the direction of our work. If you look at what we are doing this summer, everything looks as if it is for no gain. We are going out to fish for tuna, but we are losing so much money in the process. You don't like to go out everyday like that do you? It's really hard to get up so early and stay out so long. Why are we doing this kind of work and why do we make so much effort? I am not thinking of what we do just today; I am thinking of the future goal. Why do we spend so much money just to catch tuna? It doesn't even seem to pay for itself and it takes thousands of dollars to train you. We do this for the same reason that we do all our projects. For example, why do we want to construct a highway in Asia? Why build such a super highway? Usually companies that build highways try to make money from their effort, but we are raising money to build that highway and we will give it to the world, for the sake of mankind.

It is the generations to come that will look at what we have done and those people will truly look up to you. It is for those people that we are living today. Therefore, our work has to have a vision of the future. We have to create a tradition that thousands of others can respect and follow for generations to come. So, today our purpose has to be for that better future. We must become a victor, not a loser for the sake of those to come. All of my life has been like this. While I was working in the early years, everyone came against me;

everyone misunderstood me. But now, as some look back and see what I have done, they admit that I was right. The same is for you. Sixty years from now, people will look back at your life. People looked at my projects with such a small eye at first, but as I continued, their eyes got bigger and bigger. My work didn't stop in Korea; it went out to America, South America and Africa and beyond. I am somewhat of a mystery to others. However, within myself, I have a crystal clear plan; the goal is very exact.

The Ocean and A New Way of Life

In ten years, you will see why I am doing this program, why I am putting so much effort into it now. The Ocean Church movement then, that's what we are talking about today. Is it a good movement? You are shouting that it is a "great movement," but why is it a great movement? What we are doing is great, that's true. Think about the meaning of "great" in history. What has it usually meant? It meant to control everything. But no one likes that, so why is this Ocean Church movement great? If you look at the fishing towns in America, most of the young people are leaving, they are even cursing their home town. However, you young people are coming to these towns and creating a new movement. You don't even know that yet. People will see this new movement in each Ocean Church city and they will begin to think, "Reverend Moon is a great man."

Let me ask you something. Since you came here, did you like the strong winds or did you hate them? Did you feel on a windy day just like you do when you are meeting your fiancee or wife? No? Why are you laughing? In the start of the morning when you see a windy day did you say, "Today there will be something great out there waiting for me!" Did you feel like that? You have to cultivate your interest in life, even beyond the windy day. You have to see through it. Every young man is afraid of a storm. Have you ever studied why? Do you really feel stimulated and interested when some big wave comes over the bow into your boat? Do you see any hope there? Are you interested in that big wave? A man of the sea really tries to find hope in something like that. A small boat going through the wave is so dramatic. When you see your boat going through a wave, crashing over onto the other side, you really have to think, "Ah, here is hope for the future."

Don't hate the waves. You will only become like them. We have to accept everything, cold water and stormy skies. Always welcome the water with your hands, your feet, everything of your body. Do you do that every day? On the flat calm day look at yourself in the mirror of the ocean and realize the power of the water. On a calm day that flat mirror looks so peaceful, but the next day it could tower above you like a twenty foot mountain. It is only taking a rest on those calm days, but its power remains constant.

Man is the same as well. You can be highly excited and stimulated, but then you calm down and your heart maintains a humble, quiet, appreciative standard. It is also the same within women. You can see your face reflected in the peaceful water, even so, the ocean is always moving. It has to for the sake of the fish. The wind moves the water and this movement allows for the oxygen that the fish need to live. God gave life to the ocean and this is how they live.

If you look at a drop of water, it has no color. But if you gather more water, a beautiful color begins to emerge. How beautiful it is. In the water are so many species of fish; the ocean contains all kinds of fish and life. Water is life-giving; more than 70% of man's body is made of water. When the water hits your face, it scratches your eyes because it's so salty. How do you feel at that moment? You spit it out, don't you, and try to shut your eyes? Ocean water has a basic taste, it is the natural taste of life. So when you go out again, you will feel and taste the water differently won't you?

After working all day your hands will be dry and salty. Then you can taste them. That is a wonderful moment. That is the beauty of the sea. You can even write a poem about the salt of the ocean. Any great art and literature comes from this kind of intimate exchange with life. Those who hate all the natural things of life cannot create such art and literature, but those who really love life to its bottom core can create such beautiful and inspiring art and literature.

You look out there on a calm day and suddenly a fish jumps up out of the water, just like a man would. The whale makes a huge leap and then it looks around. It seems as if he is looking for the future. Just look at yourself. When your mind and body are calm, your spirit wants to jump up and look for something good. So look upon the ocean in this way, and then life itself will be revealed to you.

When you express something in literature about the sun and the moon it is too simple, but if you talk about the moving waves, the dancing waves, it is more beautiful. If you look at the sun, you can talk about the smiling face of your father and the sun is more beautiful than just a shining ball. You have to experience the sun in that way. You have to experience everything more deeply like that. From that kind of deep experience you gain unlimited inspiration for your conscience.

One time we caught a lot of rotten, dark fish. The smell was like ammonia. I seldom feel seasick, but when I smelled that my stomach began to turn. I first thought, "I'm no good, because I'm feeling so bad over this fish." Then I began to think differently and said, "I have to pay indemnity." When I realized that, the sickness disappeared, because I could love that smell. It meant I could pay indemnity for something, for someone. I could have a sense of gratitude for that smell and with that, I overcame any feeling of sickness.

When I come back with that fish smell, that chum smell, Mother sometimes says something about my clothes, but I tell her, "You don't have to do the laundry for these yet, they are still good." Mother does them anyway. Some of you wear the same fish smelling clothes for the entire month. You shouldn't apologize. We have to learn how to digest things like this in our life, every day of our life. We do this for the sake of the future. Look at me. I am going out every day and certainly I am tired, but I never say, "I am so tired; I cannot go out." When I think of the fisherman who has to go out every day and take care of his family, I cannot think of being tired. I have often said to Mother, over and over, "today I'll get the striper," but it's very difficult to actually do that. I think of the fisherman who promises his wife and family every day that he will make the catch.

He has got to catch those fish. I think about that kind of life very seriously.

Who is more desperate? Am I, who promises Mother I will catch the striped bass, or the fisherman who has to catch fish in order to feed his family? Which is the more difficult feeling? Is it me when I have to apologize to Mother for not catching the fish, or the fisherman whose family will starve if he doesn't catch something, anything? When I think about those fishermen, I don't ever feel tired and going out is no problem. We need to develop that kind of thinking. We must believe, "I am doing this for the sake of all mankind, I am leaving something behind for mankind."

With that kind of spirit we have to go out. Through this activity, I can see that mankind will someday have hope. In the future what we do here will bring great benefit to all of mankind. I want to really make you men and women of the sea. If you men grow a beard, I want you to touch your beard and say, "I am a man and I must work harder always for the sake of mankind." Do you have that spirit? You should say, "since I have a beard, I want to get to the fishing grounds faster than anyone else." You have to prepare to go out. You have to have a good engine, bait, gasoline, everything. This is basic. I am always prepared before leaving. Yesterday I received a report that the eel bait we were going to use was ready the night before. However, in the morning, I found out that the eel wasn't fixed right. That's no good. You shouldn't wait until the morning to find out these things. Everything should be ready and finished the night before.

When I look at you in this basic area, you are still almost at zero. Is your spirit looking forward, always getting ready for tomorrow? If your spirit isn't like that, then you will be accused by the fisherman working so hard. I may look humble now, but my vision is crystal clear for the future. I am preparing the foundation now for a great future. How about you?

A New Future for the Ocean

There are many religious groups in America, but no one is doing anything like this. God has a great hope in Ocean Church. From this point of view, do you feel that Ocean Church is bad or good? You like to shout that it's great. However, let's look at the word "good". God has how many O's? Just one. How many O's does good have? It has two O's. So, good is really double God. Spirit world is good and the physical world is good. Together they are double God, they are good. That's the meaning of good. Double God has a subject and an object, a spiritual world and a physical world. Also, there is land and ocean. We can't be a mountain man all the time, nor can we be an ocean man always. We have to go to both and love both. In Korea, we had a boat and just one captain of that boat. In the very beginning I had to be that captain. It was just one boat, but I saw the future and it was much more than just one boat.

Are you like that? Look at yourself. In Gloucester you have to sleep on the boats. Sometimes you are out fishing for several days and there is no shower, no toilet, and you have to use a bucket. It's a hard life. You may be looking for a place to die and cannot even find that. I look at that and think, "that's good." When I see that, I can see a great future. People don't think beyond the point of their daily life, but we think way beyond. With that, we begin the way towards a new life. I want to restore everything for God. Gloucester and Provincetown are two places where we can make our foundation. We have to think that we are great men; we are catching the giant tuna in one of the best fishing grounds in the world. With these boats you now understand how to catch tuna. I want to catch the striped bass next. However, *New Hope* hasn't caught enough tuna yet. Soon, during this summer we will expand the foundation. Why are we doing this? We are offering all this for the sake of mankind. I never ate any of my own catch until last year. I have fished for seven years, but never ate my own catch. It was always offered for the sake of others. The fish are hoping to be caught by us. Many of them will just be eaten by other fish, but it is far better to be eaten by man. The fish wants to reach the highest degree of life by becoming part of man. The same way that the fish think towards man, we must think towards God. We want to become part of the highest degree, we want to become part of God. A large part of the economy in the future will come from the ocean. I would like to spend that money overseas. There are over twenty million people starving each year. You can't imagine it because the American way of life is so luxurious. When I am with the members, they are asking every minute, "Father, don't you want something to drink, don't you want something to eat?" Instead, I am thinking that it's better to conserve even the Coca-Cola and find some way to give that to the rest of mankind. We have to have the concept of conservation in every aspect of our life. If we don't have that, then God's blessing will go away. However, we can inherit God's blessing if we are always thinking of how to conserve things for the sake of others, for the sake of mankind and for the future. God's spirit will always penetrate us if we do all things with this kind of sincerity. If we simply want to find the best fishing spot and if we are doing more for God than anyone else, then God will help us, providing us with greater insight towards that goal. Do you understand? Those who graduated from UTS, please raise your hands. You are responsible for a boat during this summer season. Do any of you think your spouse might be against you coming to Ocean Church at this time? They have to realize and you have to know that I would have never started Ocean Church if I had not had any interest in the future of the ocean. Two-thirds of this world is ocean. Who will take care of the world in the future? God is the master of the universe, but who will rule and take care of the world? The children of God have to inherit the world. Then certainly they have to inherit the ocean. That is why I am interested in the ocean.

Many people are leaving the ocean behind. Why? Because a new age for the ocean is coming. Even some nations have left the ocean behind. Why? Because the time has come for the true caretakers of the ocean to come. That is why we have a great hope for the ocean. In the past the ocean served many bad purposes for mankind. Even today, drugs are smuggled on the ocean, but the purpose has to be made heavenly. We have to change the purpose of man's use of the ocean. That is why we have Ocean Church. We have to cultivate a courageous spirit. We have to have more daring and courage than the pirates of the past.

Preparing Mind and Body for the Future

Ocean Church is the primary movement for developing that kind of spirit. The secondary movement to raise up the standard in young people is a martial arts movement. For a healthy spirit and body few things are better than martial arts. If you prepare for martial arts with a good spirit, no evil power can attack you. Martial arts have often been used for a great purpose in history. Unfortunately, it has also been used with an evil intent. Martial arts, if left to themselves will most often be used for an evil purpose. However, with a religious movement, martial arts can be used for a constructive, good purpose. That is the point. If someone comes to martial arts with an arrogant manner, we have to teach them a higher meaning for its use. We have to know that it is necessary to prepare a unifying martial arts movement throughout the world. We have to defend all aspects of our life. We are now organizing a martial arts group worldwide, and preparing to make this martial arts part of the Olympic games. Most seminaries don't teach any martial arts or even physical education, but our seminary teaches martial arts so that our students are not only prepared intellectually, but also spiritually and physically. We are preparing a world movement for God and everything should come together under that. We are even preparing for a religious Olympic association. The top religious leaders of the world, prominent theologians and scholars will come together and open these games once every two years. The Olympic games have a standard of coming together every four years, but we want to go beyond that standard by meeting every two years. More importantly, we want to go beyond that standard by having a higher purpose for coming together.

Everyone needs a good system of give and take for their body. The body, just like the mind or the spirit, needs to be balanced and have a good flow of energy. If you have pain in your stomach, it is because there isn't a good flow of energy between your stomach and other body functions. When I come home after working hard all day, I exercise every night. This is one reason why I don't get tired even though I am competing with you, a younger generation.

For a sound body, you have to exercise; for a sound spirit, you also have to exercise. For the spirit, this means a religious way of life. We have to embrace the land, the sea and encompass all the arts. These areas we need to cover. Then, centered around these things, the new world will begin. At the core, we are religious, but our goal is to establish the Kingdom of God on earth. A sound body develops through external practice; a sound spirit develops through internal practice. Literature, music, poetry, art, all these areas we have to develop ourselves. I have learned how to do well in all these areas and so should you.

No one ever dreamed that I would come to Provincetown and fish like this, but now I have done it for ten years. The public doesn't understand why I initiated many of the things which we do. They cannot see our motivation, so it is natural that they come to oppose us. As time passes, those who oppose and those who try to help us will move a greater and greater distance apart. One side will eventually disappear and the other side will eventually be embraced by God. Thus, a new era will be created.

The Formula for Pioneering Ocean Church

Will you inherit my spirit and carry on when I have gone to the spiritual world? You are shouting a loud and clear "Yes." If indeed you carry on my tradition, then, Ocean Church is wonderful, it is good. It is double God. One god is land god and one god is sea god. Ocean Church is both; we live on the land, but we go out to sea. So that is double God. Ocean Church is really good then, isn't it? Now you are receiving persecution; this means your future will be great. No one can understand you now, but they will later on and they will respect you twice as much. They will respect you for your perseverance when they misunderstood you and for your compassion towards them when they finally do understand.

Would you like to take care of an ocean city? There is a basic formula for how to develop each city. When you plan to take care of a city, to be a leader in that community, you have to think about it. When you come to a city your first question is, "What should I do?"

Taking a boat out and catching fish is not the beginning and end of it. When you show up with a *One Hope* boat in the city, people will recognize it as a Moonie boat. They will start to oppose you, persecute you and test you. They will start talking about Moonies, about how you are good or bad. The tendency of any community is to test a newcomer.

Therefore, the short-cut for us is to find a way to make unity with the major leaders of that city. Then you don't have to be tested by the entire community. The key point is how to meet the established leaders, the mayor, the police chief, the coast guard commander, the fishermen's union leader and other business leaders in the community. Just a few people have to understand and unite with you and each other. The key point is how you can help them understand why you are there and what you are doing for the future of their city.

I myself followed this very same pattern when I came to America. I started many different aspects to our movement such as IOWC and CARP, Home Church and Ocean Church. From the first moment that I arrived in America I met with the leaders of America, the city officials, the congressmen and senators. Whenever I met those leaders I explained what I was going to do in America. They had a difficult time believing me then, but now many of them recognize what I meant.

In that way I could see what kind of movement was needed in America in order to mobilize the national leadership. I even prepared the newspaper media and six years ago started publishing. Those who came to the *Washington Times* didn't come just because we started that newspaper; they came because a foundation had already been laid. They came because they could understand our vision.

Although the *Washington Times* has only been three months in publication, it has already gone above the national standard. The conservative groups usually fight amongst themselves, but they all concurred that this newspaper is a great asset for America. One conservative group is centered on Christianity while another one is based on the business community in America. There is a new group rising in the intellectual community and the fourth group is mostly patriotic in nature.

At one time or another, each group has made a stand against me, against our movement, but through the *Washington Times*, we have been able to unite all four groups. Even though I am now preparing for the court case, we are moving ahead all the time. It is like a dream to see all that we have accomplished. It is hard to tell the whole story about it. One small example: President Reagan made a summit conference and took with him the correspondence chiefs from only four American newspapers. In America there are 1,753 newspaper companies, but Reagan took only four representatives. One of them was the *Washington Times*. This happened only five days after we started! Why was this *Washington Times* correspondent chief selected to attend? It was because people already recognized the excellent quality of this newspaper and its courageous stand, and they didn't want to ignore it.

This is only one part of the plan. From this foundation, we will begin to publish a nationwide newspaper. The time will come when the major television news media will frequently and constantly quote from the *Washington Times*. Then the basic trend of the media in America can be changed. Many conservative business leaders want to invest in the *Washington Times* because they believe it will make it, that it will be successful. The "times" indeed have changed. I am explaining this to you because I want you to see that the foundation for the future of this nation is already being prepared for you.

Why did we put so much effort into the movie *Inchon*? No matter what the result, the motivation was for people to understand about MacArthur. I wanted to show how MacArthur loved God and loved people. MacArthur came to Japan after World War II and put the nation back together. He really respected and loved the people. He also loved God very much and fought with great strength against tyranny and communism. That is what I want the people to understand. We must love God and we must love people. Communism destroys both, and so we should hate that. All these projects and activities make me extremely busy. When you are finished you just come back here and rest, but I have to stay up almost all night listening to reports and giving new directions. I am busy day and night. There is almost no time for coming here to fish like this. Why then have I done this for at least ten years? I have been going on and on every year, never getting tired. When I look at you, just going out for a few days and then getting tired, I feel ashamed for you.

Already I have seen many members run away from the ocean. This season we can only catch one tuna per week. Many people thought we wouldn't come. Anyway, we came and many people were shocked. They were certain that I wouldn't come, but our reason for fishing is not just economic. We have to fish, we have to continue on. We have to set the tradition.

I want to leave behind at least ten "Reverend Moons" so that the tradition will go on. I am wondering who has the desire to go out to an ocean city and restore it within ten years? How many of you have that idea and desire? Within ten years, if each one of you became a top fishing leader in your ocean city and could expand that foundation to at least 100 ocean cities, I would feel I had left something of value behind.

If we have 100 cities, we have a foundation for this nation. Once you become a well-known and established person in a city, you can start a fish company or a related business and be in charge of that. You have to make your foundation quickly. In other words, once you go to your ocean city, you have to meet the top leaders and give them something of value for the future of their city. You have to be able to work with the young people. You have to solve two problems. Manpower and money. How can you make money and how can you raise young people so they can someday be responsible for that city? Those are big problems. If you can solve them you can start a big company, anything. No problem. The problems are how to make good members and how to make a good economic foundation. If you can solve those problems then everything else comes. First, you make a good relationship with the major leaders in your city. Then, you make friends with the major fishing leaders and the major business leaders. Pick up their knowledge and experience, and from that point, you can make the foundation to someday be the leader of your own company. First, you have to solve those two problems.

You have to train yourself. Centered on you, these problems will be solved. You can do that. You can accomplish these points. You have to work hard, day and night. Then, great things will happen.

The Ocean Providence and the Fishing Industry

When I came here almost ten years ago, tuna was only ten cents a pound. I asked myself, "how can I make the price of tuna go up?" I want to see the price go to $4.00 this summer. People used to come to catch tuna as a sport only. They came here from all over the world, but the fishermen themselves couldn't fish for tuna because they would lose so much money going out every day just for tuna. There was a great opportunity there for them, but they couldn't participate in it.

I saw one boat come in several years ago and there wasn't even a price for the tuna that day, so they lost their money on expenses. This was really sad for me to see. Last year we pushed the price up to $2.50 per pound. This year the price started at $1.65. Why? Last year the price ended higher, but the habit of exploiting the fishermen is deep set. You have to keep pushing the standard, raising it higher. They don't like the Moonies, but they welcome me coming every year now. They persecuted us so much when we first started coming, but now they really want to be our friends. You now know the fishing grounds and you see mostly small boats out there. Before there were only the expensive sport fishing boats, but now even the little fisherman can try to make money by catching tuna. Think about it. If the price goes up to $4.00, which is my hope for this year, then a fisherman who catches one tuna weighing more than 1,000 pounds will earn $4,000. He can earn that much from just one day's work. That's amazing. So now, many small fishing boats are out there, going for the tuna. Anyone can own a small boat at least. Why not a thousand boats at the tuna grounds? Every day there will be a great competition to catch the tuna. That's not bad; it's good actually.

Now that the price is going up, everyone is interested in coming here to fish for tuna. We can bring people here and they can experience the ocean. Some of them will be rich, but have no vision for their money. When they see the potential of the ocean, they will want to invest their money in it. There are all kinds of good projects which could benefit.

We are preparing the foundation in each part of the important coastal areas of America. As you know, in the Gulf of Mexico we have a shrimp business, and in Alabama we have a ship building business. In Alaska we have a plant which can process 400,000 pounds of fish each day. The question is, how can we manage such enterprises? I am hoping that the Ocean Church centers will train young people who can quickly mature and provide that kind of leadership. We start with only thirty centers, but eventually we have to create up to 3,000 centers on the coastal waters.

I have this large vision for America. Why? Because the fish are here in American waters. I have seen many other areas of the world, but here you can just drop a line off the fishing pier and catch a fish. However, no one is guiding America to realize its potential in fishing. You have to be the ones to do that. Over three years ago, we started thirty shrimp boats in Surinam. They are also tuna fishing. These boats are quite large. Somehow, the Americas should be connected. The ocean provides a way for that to happen. The ocean connects all the major fishing countries in the world. Eventually we can improve prices for all fishermen and also feed more people.

In Japan we have already prepared every aspect of the fishing industry. We made a famous fish-selling team. Their logo is a picture of a fish-selling boy with a band on his head. Every fish-selling person wears that band on their head whenever they go out to sell throughout Japan. We are now preparing similar fish selling techniques here in America. Those with a Japanese husband or wife will participate one way or another in the fishing providence future.

How about it? Wouldn't it be great for every couple to have their own boat? They can fish with it and live on it and even make their babies on the boat. You can start with the *One Hope* training boat. If you do well and mature as a fisherman, then you can earn a big boat like the ones they make in Alabama. Some people have to spend twenty-one years to reach that state, but if you really apply yourself, you can reach it in only seven years time.

In Japan, when the members fundraised, they always experienced the spiritual world guiding them to the right person to make the sale. The same experience is waiting for you. When you go out to the ocean you will find the spiritual world helping you to find where the fish are and you can catch tons of fish. You don't think so? I think so. You have to find out for yourself.

Many people complain, "Oh, Ocean Church is so difficult; I don't like it." However, once the foundation is laid, the next steps are no problem. It only took a few months for us to come up with the *Washington Times*, which is now so prestigious. With that ability and capacity, it is no problem to build the right kind of trawler and bring it to this area. You can become a good captain of a large boat. Then, you will automatically be able to meet the leaders of your city. You will come to know the president of the fish processing company and other businessmen. If you make one phone call from your office, you can connect all over the world. Whatever I say I mean with utmost sincerity. It will come to pass. Do you believe that?

Leadership Training on the Ocean

I spend a great deal of time, precious time out here on the ocean. It is because I have such a vision for the future. I see that you are not disciplined yet. How can you inherit this vision? I am thinking of sending you one by one, or two by two, to the Surinam shrimping boats for a period of time. It would be good training for you. Once you go there you won't come back for two or four months. That's how long one trip is. I should also send you to Alaska. How about if I send you there in the winter time? You should be able to change back and forth. You should go easily from the land to the ocean. Those who have been out to sea for a while should go back and re-invest in the land. You will have more strength and enthusiasm for it. It works the other way around too; after a while on land, you should go out to sea.

The formula course for Unification members has been that for three and one-half years you fundraise as basic training. The economic foundation represents creation and this restores your relationship with all things. This should be changed to two years of fundraising and eighteen months of ocean duty.

I am educating you here so kindly, but how about if you are hired to go out on the ocean in a large boat? If you go out with a rough captain on a big trawler, he will just throw you around. In that way, the captain gives you training. I myself would like to start out like that with you, but I know that if I start like that, no one will be left to finish. That's why I am giving you a nice introduction. Actually, we haven't really started yet. Anyway, all church members have to go through this kind of training. Each one of you has to go some place where your English doesn't work. You will have to use every other part of your body to communicate with the other person. You will feel lonely on such a boat and if you say, "Oh, I'm sick and tired and have to go home," there will be no way to go back. Then your experience here in Gloucester will be just like heaven. Do you still want to go on with this training course? One day this season I heard a sister shouting out to me when the *New Hope* went by, "Father, I want to be in Ocean Church!" She sounded almost like a crazy person. That's how we should feel.

We are preparing to have refrigerated warehouses in the major coastal cities. We would open them all tonight if we could find someone to manage these plants. However, you are not ready yet. I am wondering if you will be much different in three years time. I am depending on you American brothers and sisters. If you don't do it, then the European, Asian or Hispanic members will be mobilized to do it. I will mobilize the Asian and Hispanic members. If you Americans don't want it, then the minorities in America can earn the fishing industry. If you don't want it and don't like it, there is no choice but to offer this opportunity to minority members.

In Japan there is already so much preparation in fishing-related fields, but I want you to be the central people in this providence. That is why I have hope in the international Blessing. One way or another we shall do it. If Ocean Church can't do it, then Asian members in America will have to do it. I am giving you the best education now. You can learn something for your entire life. For ten years I have been working so hard to train you. If you gain success it will go far more quickly than if the Asian members have to do it.

The ocean has everything to do with the future. Don't you know that? You have to become interested in the ocean or otherwise you will just disappear into history. In the future, the qualification for leadership will be to know about the ocean. The basic knowledge will be how to handle a boat. To know about the ocean and to be able to go upon it will become the two basic qualifications for leadership in the future.

You don't know so much about me. I'm giving every ounce of my sweat to maintain the prestige of America in the world. How many days could you continue, working at such a pace? Are you thinking about sleeping each day you go out? Are you playing every day, just looking around and thinking about the pretty boats? Don't just be light and say, "Oh I love the sea!" It's actually very difficult to really love the sea.

I want to send the brothers to Surinam and train you there, then bring you back and make you into captains of a large boat. I have been thinking about that for three years, but I look at you and you are already tired with just the *One Hope* boats. In Alaska, the thirty knot winds are nothing. That's normal--a calm day. On the rough days, you don't even see other boats between the waves, maybe just the highest light. Think about that. Think about the couple who would live in that situation. How wonderful it would be. They could be loving each other in that kind of weather. That's really exciting, isn't it? The way you live all depends upon what you think. It depends on how you look at it. If your spirit is willing and joyfully giving for the cause, you can do anything.

If I had not come to America with that kind of spirit, our movement could never have spent the millions of dollars that it has already invested in so many programs. We are even spending and investing more now. And yet, at the same time I am accused of hiding tax money from the government. It is exactly opposite to reality, but they can't see that yet. It doesn't make sense. We spent more than four million dollars for the last science conference and almost two million dollars for the World Youth for God conference and world tour. Tax evasion? It's really a great mistake that America judged me that way. However, I only answered the judge with a smile. I have no grudge against America. That is the kind of man leading you. No matter what kind of persecution comes towards me, I will just stand where I am. Nothing will move me from the will of God. This is happening in the free world. What do you think the Communist world would like to do? They are really against me. I am the most fearful person to them. Why? Because they cannot defeat this ideology. Instead, our ideology can easily defeat them, so they will come against me at every opportunity. You will see it. We have to work in every field to bring it salvation.

Religion is the center or the core of our life, but we cannot be separate from all these other areas such as education, business or politics. That is why America cannot understand me. They cannot see in such a large way. I have had to focus on the court case rather than many other more important projects. However, it is not just my own battle; it is to educate you, to educate America. I have to fight.

It is an indemnity course, but by following it, I will become even more famous. The same principle applies to you. Here in Gloucester you receive persecution, but if you keep working hard, the public will begin to see you as you really are. Are you a dirty boat Moonie, or are you absolutely clean and orderly? I should inspect each boat and make sure. I have a great idea and a great concept for your life. How many of you want to go to South America and receive training? The best training is to go to another country and receive your training from that low, lonely place. After receiving your training, you should then come back and work very hard for America. When you fish in South America it takes several months to fill the quota which means you are out fishing for at least one month before you even get to where the fish can be caught. Here you complain about what kind of breakfast or dinner you have, but out there you can't complain about the food. Out there you might get a letter from your lovely wife, but the captain won't let you have it until the end of the fishing period. Even if you are upset about that, nothing will be done to change it. On those boats, there are about thirty crew members. Think about their life. When you come back from fishing, there are thirty families waiting for the crew member. Everything depends on the work that they did, how much they caught. It depends on their result; they have no choice but to work harder than other boats. I see that as really good training for you and that is why I am thinking of sending you down there.

I am going to do this anyway, so why don't you just catch the spirit quickly? Don't just wait for it. I am thinking about sending one or two persons immediately to Surinam after this summer, or Berlin. The German fishermen also go out into the cold, harsh seas for three or four months duty. After that, if you are still willing to serve the ocean providence, you are truly ready to be an Ocean Church member. After you come back from that experience, if you still want to serve the ocean, I will choose you. Then, you can someday be trusted with a large fishing boat and a fishing career as a captain. I have great hope for the ocean. I have great hope for all of you. I would like to send you out and have you come back ready to serve America and become a great leader.

Your Foundation is with the Fishermen

I know history very clearly. In the near future, those who are fishermen will really deeply appreciate what we have done for them. When Karl Marx started communism he supported the laborers, but he himself never once experienced that kind of work. He didn't do his own front-line work. I am very different from that. I am truly a good friend of the fisherman because I myself have pushed and worked hard in this area. I truly understand their effort and their heart. That is the great difference.

You can't complain to me because I am always doing first whatever I ask of you. When you go back to your regions, learn how to catch the fish of that area. If you are in an area where there is striped bass, you must really research them. I want to help you, but you also have to study and do your own research.

You have to build your own foundation also. While the husband is out catching fish, the women cannot stay at home all the time. The wife has to develop a fish related activity. The husband and wife should both be active and interested in the ocean world. I am making prototype foundations: one in the East, one in the South and one in the West. On that base, we can expand. After building the foundation, we can even begin to make all our own equipment, boats, gear, clothing, everything. I am always studying and researching. I am always thinking of ways to make the fisherman's life better. We can use the fish that people usually throw away and invent a way to pre-cut it as chum. Then, the fishermen can come and ask us for the #3 chum which catches blue fish, and the #4 chum which catches tuna, and so on. Our future is unlimited. You have to use your imagination and create your own foundation. Once you do that, you only have to spend a few hours each day with your own personal business. Then, you can go out and meet the other leaders in the community. You can find other churches and help their programs. They are looking for something to do with their young people. You can train them on your boats. That is what they are for.

How many boats would you like to have in each center? How many big trawlers would you like to administrate in the future? Your desire may be very large, but if you are going to accomplish these things you have to start now. That is why we made these *One Hope* boats. You need education and training. How many boats can you be responsible for?

With the *One Hope* you have to learn and experience how to manage a boat. That will help you understand how to manage a larger boat in the future. How many small boats can you control? You have to go all over the sea coast and explore every opportunity. In Florida, you have many friends already, so you won't have too many problems. Anywhere you go, you can find friends. Most fishermen don't have such friendship and help, but you know how to serve people and make friends wherever you go. How can you even worry about the future? You will always have some place to go and someone to help you.

You have to study how you can make a fishermen's association.

You can help the fishermen in your area. Sometimes a captain may need some help. The fishermen don't have any association or organization. They are looking for that. They are looking at us with great big open eyes. They are waiting to see if we have the ability to do that. They need that kind of help. Every environment needs preparation. We can begin an American organization, but then cover the whole world, sharing with fishermen everywhere.

That is why I am wondering how many boats you can be responsible for. Can you take care of 100 boats? Not now. Someday you should be able to guide and manage a fleet of large boats. That is why you have to train on the smaller boats for the future. You are on a small boat now; this is where everything starts for you. You can control the smaller boat now and find out how to catch the smaller fish, such as striped bass, but this is training for you. Some of you will move on to take care of much larger boats and to catch large amounts of fish.

Training on the One Hope Boats

After you graduate from the *One Hope* boat, you can go on to the next size boat. You can become responsible for a forty foot or fifty foot boat. You can even live on that size of boat as well. You can make the ocean your way of life, every area of your life. You have to be interested and capable in every aspect of fishing. Do you know anything about tackle? Do you know how to handle and take care of fish? Do you know how to repair engines and make boat modifications? If you don't know these things, how will you survive upon and live from the ocean?

The *One Hope* boats have to go everywhere so that people will see them and come to respect what we are doing. It's a dream, and I am holding onto that dream in my mind. That means that it is in an invisible form, but it will become visible. We will see it in the future. We will see it soon. A man who believes can do anything. A man who acts can achieve anything. "Believing man and Doing man." That is how I am and that is how I envision you to become. Actually, it isn't a dream. It is what I know.

Even the *One Hope* boat is not the final standard. I am now researching how to make it better. One problem is that the balance is too sensitive. This has to be corrected. We have to research and correct that problem. I want to make this boat useful for every kind of training. I am also looking at how it cuts through the wave. If the boat could go faster, the boat could cut three waves at once. Now, it can cut two and if you go slowly it has to cut each wave, one by one. I have already tested this out. If the boat goes 3,500 rpm it is more stable and cuts the wave cleanly.

Can you suggest anything that would improve the *One Hope* boat? Let's really study this boat and make the best modifications. It is already designed very well and whenever we have taken it to boat shows in this country, we receive very good comments. We make the *One Hope* boats twenty-eight feet for a specific purpose. We can store them easily because we can trailer them anywhere in the country. We can mobilize from one city to another city this way as well. It's more difficult with larger boats. The twenty-eight foot boat is stable in winds up to twenty-five knots. Winds higher than that are not the best for fishing anyway, so the twenty-eight foot boat is an excellent boat to train for all kinds of fishing.

What is unique about this boat is that it will never sink. There is no limit to our use of such a boat. This is great for Home Church. An entire family can use this boat; they can go almost anywhere. This as a very convenient and wonderful boat for any family. That is why I designed the boat this way. When we begin to mass produce other boats, you can sell them for your own personal business. Through Master Marine company you can order the boats for those in your local area who want to buy one for themselves.

Don't take this effort lightly. It's very difficult to come to an old establishment like this industry and set up a new tradition. We have to study it very carefully. Money is not the problem. The key point is, do we have the ability? One good example for us is the *Washington Times*. Our members did not have the same abilities as the people we employed, but they were able to administer and manage the direction of the paper. That's the key point for us. You should become that kind of person, who can administrate and take care of many people. You have to be able to guide people in all areas of life.

The same principle applies to things as well. Make a basic formula for all the boats and follow that standard in taking care of them. Engine and boat repair are expensive to do; you have to do your best to prevent the need for repair. You must make periodic inspections of your engines and boats. Each region, West Coast, East Coast and Gulf Coast has to make a system to maintain the boats. How many of you can repair an engine? An IW should be appointed for each coastal region. Each region has to have at least three spare engines so that if an engine breaks down, you can use that engine while you are fixing the broken one. You should be able to fix an engine in one night, even if you have to stay up the entire night.

If you need help, get the person in charge of the boats and spend the whole night with him. The IW can direct those responsible for the boats to stay and work with him, even if it takes all night. You should have that kind of experience. The IW has to teach all the others what to do. If those engines break down in the same way again, they have to go back and teach everyone again how to operate an engine and repair it. We have to learn these lessons very well.

The engine is most important. Without a good engine you cannot use the boat for anything. So, the regional service men have to go immediately wherever the boat has broken down. Who has confidence to repair an engine in this room? You have to learn both, gasoline and diesel. You can't say, "I can fix gasoline, but not diesel." You have to fix both. Also, those who fix engines have to know the electrical system. You have to be able to repair anything wrong with that system as well. The *One Hope* boat is so small, there is hardly anything to learn about.

However, if you go through this course and get experience and skill, you can open a maintenance and repair business for larger boats. You can repair trawling boats and big ships. You can train yourself to repair anything. Engines have common points or parts that break down.

In each center, start with one boat. If that boat breaks down, then fix it. If you have two boats and one is older and it breaks down, don't just get on the new boat and go out. You have to fix the older boat and use that boat. That's the tradition. If you have an older boat and it breaks down, you have to come up with the money to fix that boat. This will teach you the tradition of responsibility.

Catalogue everything: boat number, parts number, engine number. Then, you can order by number the parts you need for repairs. We should have that kind of inventory system and relationship with the factory. If we have spare engines in New York, and California needs a specific part, they can order from New York and it can be sent over night. Then, we can repair our boats within two days of breaking down. We should develop that kind of system. After one year, we can see which parts break down more frequently and we can stock those parts. The same goes for the electrical system. Everything has to be listed by number, every part that goes onto and is used by the *One Hope* boat. This includes doors, anchors, fire equipment, everything. Then we can keep track of what we lose more often or what breaks down more often. The number system has to be unified and used by every center in the nation.

The responsibility here is great. Our future is great, but we have to be serious with what we do now. Someday you will be able to repair even the largest of boats. You will have to be able to repair Navy ships. That day is coming. I am thinking about going around in the *New Hope* to directly supervise the fishing activities of each center, but that might not be possible. However, we have *Sea Hope I, II*, and *III*. One of these boats should be sent as a flagship to each of these regions. Then, with the *One Hope* boat and the *Sea Hope* boat, you can spend the night out together fishing. You can teach from these boats all the activities of the *One Hope* boats in your region. Each center has to have at least a *One Hope* always ready to go, so that whenever I call, you will be immediately ready to go out. That is the standard for each center, to have one boat completely ready to go at any time. I would like to send my representative to you. The moment he arrives, you must take him out. Someone like Dr. Durst or Colonel Pak may come; you have to be absolutely ready. No excuses. So, please, study the fishing grounds in your area and know the right places to go.

The Purpose of One Hope Training

Why should we have this standard? I want to explain this to you. You should be able to take out anyone at anytime. You should be able to take out a world class person and impress them with your standard. We could prepare a fishing tour from Alaska down the West coast, through the Gulf area and up the East coast. That would be a six month fishing tour. After such an experience of catching fish in each of these coastal areas, they would become crazy!

Then, we could create fishing tours all over the world. Fishing in Africa, Europe, South America. We have to prepare for that right now, beginning right now. In this way, we are connected to people all over the world and can connect people to the ocean all over the world. They would never forget their experiences. There are many fishing and hunting groups all over the world, but their purpose needs to change. They need to be ignited to do something for the sake of helping the world. Therefore, you have to study your area. Ask yourselves, "How can I make my seaport more and more beautiful?" You have to prepare your area. Study how to catch flounder, striped bass and tuna. Then, we can advertise in Japan. They can plan their trips to America by the kind of fish they want to catch. You have to experience by yourself how to catch the fish in your area. Do you understand me? If you want to take charge of this area you have to go to Europe, Africa, South America and Japan on a regular basis. Are you that kind of person?

When you are catching tuna, do you remember anything sad or happy? You forget everything don't you? Your mother or wife may have recently died, but you can forget that sorrow in that moment. The excitement is so great that you are lifted up out of any sad or depressed mood. That's true! Modern man is looking for a way to get rid of his tension without leaving his business behind for a long time. They are looking for a way to get rid of a great deal of tension in a short amount of time. Something that is great and exciting can do that. Fishing in America can do that.

I want to stop here at this point because you forget everything so easily, but we have to continue. I have been teaching you how to catch tuna, how to catch striped bass. I feel that I am the champion of the tuna now, but I have not graduated from the striped bass. The striped bass is very smart, even smarter than the tuna. The striped bass is very hard to catch. When you first start to fish for a species, you don't know anything about its habits, such as where to go to catch it. You have to study what the other fishermen are doing, then you have to inherit that and improve it. You have to go fishing with them, find out their spots. Then, study the area and mark the spot on your own map.

Follow the professional fishermen. Be like their own sons. No one will inherit from them, so you must do that. One by one you can talk to them and tell them what you are doing. Ask them if they want to help you. Many of them will say "yes." You must move them deep inside, one by one. Then, start an association in your area. Make friends and bring them together. Take them out in your boat; it runs so fast that they cannot help but become excited.

Bring them together for a banquet, tell them all your plans and share with them. Cook all kinds of seafood for them. They will respond to you and want to help you. Make them your friends. Bring back some fish that you catch and give it to them. Share your life with them and they will share with you. By doing this, you can inherit from them and they will want to help you obtain your goals. You have your own experience, plus you have the fishermen's experience of that area. You can then make a textbook for fishing by combining all your experience and knowledge from these different areas. We can make a textbook and update it all the time. This kind of effort helps everyone.

Take your fisherman friends with you to another area to fish. Ask them, "Won't you go out with me? I already bought a ticket for you and I, so let's go." And he will answer, "Yes!" Take your friends to Alaska. They will be so excited. How about if I ask you, "Don't you want to go to Europe to fish?" What kind of answer do you have? "Sure!" So, you can teach them and raise them up. When you really need them you can call them up on the phone and say, "Come here quickly!" They will surely come to help you. We have to start from here, but this is where we want to go. We have to constantly keep the future in front of us. Otherwise, nothing happens.

Have hope, great hope. We are doing so many things and I have to guide so many projects. I remember when I started the Science Conference. Many people could not grasp it. Many members opposed it. When I started the seminary many members didn't want to support the idea either. Then the *News World* came and many members didn't like that idea, but the *News World* gave birth to the *Washington Times* and everyone can see how great a newspaper it is.

Am I crazy? I don't think so. You think so, don't you? Sometimes? I understand. Anyway, let's understand this much; if I don't go to the spiritual world too soon, this venture will be successful. There is no doubt about that. What will you do if I go to the spiritual world tomorrow? Will you give up? You are very strong, very firm and even heaven hears your "No!" However, even if you give up what I am saying to you today, there will be young people in the future who will risk their own life to achieve this idea. Once I have touched this industry, then it shall never perish. Now it is declining and in serious trouble, but we will pick it up and resurrect it. Therefore, you have to make up your mind. Make it up very strongly to go this way. Do you want to do this? "Yes." Okay, then. Thank you very much.

Question and Answer Session

If you have any questions for me, now is a good time.

Member: "Will you start Ocean Church in Africa?"

If we accomplish Ocean Church in America, it is no problem anywhere else in the world. However, first things first. We have to make the foundation here. Surely, we must go everywhere in the world, after all almost every country has a coastline.

Member: "Have you any ideas about aquaculture?"

Fish farming is the real way for the future. We should intensely study about that. Someday, we have to start a fish farm for almost every kind of fish. We have to do that through the academic side, so we have to start a university and that program will begin there.

Member: "Will we have other types of Ocean Challenge programs?"

Yes, we can go to places like Key West, Florida. We can do king-fishing there. Wherever we go, we have to prepare.

Member: "What is the relationship between Ocean Church and Home Church?"

Ocean Church is the place where we raise the spirit of people, but the mission is the same. We have to reach out to people and raise them up. This actually takes a long time. You can stay all your life in either mission.

Member: "How are we connected to the members in Japan?"

The foundation is laid in Japan and it moves from there to America. From America, we have to think about the whole world, Africa and South America especially. Members should see themselves connected in this way. Since fish is an excellent source of protein, we are working to develop ways of sending fish and fish products all over the world. Japan is ahead of America in this sense. However, the best fishing grounds are here in America. Our hope is to connect these two countries so that many other nations will benefit.

Member: "After this season of tuna fishing, what do you want the members of Ocean Church to focus upon?"

You should study how to catch the striped bass. You should study all about the striped bass, especially how to increase its population. You should study all kinds of fish and fishing techniques, but first study about the striped bass. Your reality is that you have to support yourselves somehow in the local area. If you graduate the "tuna course" and then the "striped bass course" using the small boat, you can begin to operate larger boats and go after other kinds of fish.

Tuna is the king of fish and the striped bass is the prince of fish. When you see a large striped bass come up, you really fall in love with that fish. It's completely beautiful. The striped bass is the gentleman of the sea. Other fish, such as the bluefish, go behind their prey, but the striped bass comes head on to meet its intended catch. Even after hooking one up, they fight without extreme violence, just steady and determined to get loose.

I asked one brother to bring home a striped bass, but after an entire day he only caught one. If you can find out how to catch these fish, it is no problem to discover how to catch many other kinds of fish, such as the bluefish which is the "ocean wolf." Bluefish are so aggressive. When they pass through a school of fish, they tear into everything and nothing is left. The taste of that fish is not so great either. If they tasted really good, they could be forgiven, but they are one of the cheapest fish to buy.

Flounder is the "ocean cake." It's smooth and delicate. There are all kinds of fish and you have to learn about them.

Member: "Why are there so many dogfish and what are they good for?"

There are also lots of dogfish in Japan and in England. They are all over the world. I want to make fish powder out of dogfish, for protein bread. Then, that bread could be sent to third world countries. They could eat cheaply, but also get some protein. I think about that all the time. We have to make a factory which can produce this kind of bread. Man can eat any kind of fish. The only problem is how to process it. If you know how to do that, it's no problem. You can make fish powder thousands of ways. You can eat it everyday. People can think of what they want to eat and say things like, "Oh, today we have fish pancakes!" I would like to hear words like that all over the world. I am deeply concerned about that.

Member: "What are the future plans for Master Marine?"

Essentially, they will build many boats, big boats and more small boats.

Member: "Everything we do is for restoration. I am wondering what that means for each one of us personally. For example, what did Jacob restore with Uncle Laban?"

Jacob's course in the land of Haran was to receive training. He trained for twenty-one years and he worked under all kinds of circumstances. Everyone is in this process; they are each on their course of restoration. For example, some people are on their way to Washington D.C. and they get a flat tire. They have to fix it. Next, their engine breaks down and they have to fix that, but they don't get discouraged. They are on the way and their final destination is in front of them. That's important. It is the same for you. Don't be disappointed by the things that get in your path. You have to know the essential point in the course of restoration. Some of you sisters are really good at singing and dancing, but how are you going to make a living? You have to remember that you live to love others. Don't expect to be loved. With that principle you can always go on. If you are accused by your husband for something, how will you take it? Will you cry out or just be grown-up and go on quietly?

When I look at some of the couples, I am really amazed. I wonder to myself, "How did I make such an ideal matching?" The more I look, the more amazed at myself I become. For example, this brother here is like those bluefish I was describing, so he needs a soft, beautiful girl such as his wife who is sitting next to him. I didn't know these details when I matched you, but as time goes on, I am truly amazed at how well you fit together. There is another brother here, Steve Taylor, who also has just the right kind of wife. His wife is what I usually call an "eye-laughing" or "laughing-eyes" girl. This kind of sister has a complicated heart and mind and sometimes it is easy for others to misunderstand her. When you look at her husband, he looks angry day and night. He can pick up the good nature of his wife, and together, with good give and take, they will pick up the good qualities between each other.

I am sympathetic towards them. I know this brother truly loves his wife. She may think, "Oh, my husband needs to be different, he should have a better shape or a better mind." She may think this way, but it isn't true. For this sister, her spouse has the kind of character that best suits her. It is a perfect match. You will have especially good children. Wait and see when your children come.

When I look at you, I can see right away your inside and outside. When I look at the nation I can also see its character and future. When I came to America in the early 1970's I proclaimed that America was heading for destruction. I was anxious to proclaim this in every city and state. When people heard this they questioned why I was so intent to proclaim that kind of thing for America. They didn't know that if people heard that and united with me, America could be saved at a much earlier time. Look at the gay men and women in America. This is sad and miserable. Those people have a special kind of cancer in the blood system. What can be done for them?

Even in simple electricity the flow of energy can only occur in polar relationships, between positive and negative. Plus and plus, minus and minus is completely out of line. From that, all kinds of problems arise, even resentment and sickness. This is a state of confusion and chaos, men looking at men and falling in love, kissing and making love. Biologically, men and women are meant to get together. Man is made to give and woman is made to receive. Men smell different from women. That difference actually attracts one to the other. God is really a great scientist. Even that small detail was taken care of. Even the nose between men and women has a purpose. When you understand this, you can understand the essential course of training that we go through and you can understand the essential course of restoration that we have to accomplish. You can understand the final goal.

Member: "Is the two year fundraising course and the eighteen month ocean church course for everybody?"

Yes, everybody. Including me. I myself have gone this course. We have to experience many different things. That's what is important.

Education System for Ocean Church Members

You have to train and study. The first process is to train Ocean Church members about fishing. The second is to help Ocean Church expand and gain a foundation. From there, you can move to other kinds of fishing. This way you will find out how to prepare for all kinds of fishing. You can compile the information: this kind of fish is "a-type" and this kind is "b-type", and you can write down what kind of line to use, what kind of tackle and what kind of bait. This kind of information is very important.

We have to gain our own members in Ocean Church and we have to find a way to raise them up. Use the video system. Each guest comes to see the entire video program, which is several cassettes long. However, people are happy to learn in this way. In Japan, we have gained more than 100 dedicated members from this form of education. People can come and study for themselves.

We can design many programs, such as education programs about current affairs and other things. The guests can come and gain not only knowledge in Divine Principle, but also about society and the world. If you set up your centers and you are busy, you don't have to teach them everything yourself. Use the portable size video player. Just hook it up to the television and you can provide all kinds of education for your guests.

You can create this kind of situation. Everything can connect together. You just have to use what you have and whatever is around you. People are looking to learn and improve themselves. Now there is so much confusion and people are really suffering. We showed these Divine Principle lecture tapes to many professors and they were really impressed. They said, "This kind of education is very good." We don't have many teachers, so these tapes can fill the gap. We should make 2-day, 7-day, 21-day and 40-day lecture courses where the guest can come each day and learn from the tape.

While listening to the tapes, they don't have to stop for questions. In this way, they get the whole idea of each lecture first. This will help them understand more clearly what we are teaching. Sometimes people stop the lecturer all the time with so many questions, but this prevents them from seeing the whole idea. It's better to ask questions after the lecture is given in its entirety.

We have to find the way to teach Divine Principle. How can we teach the entire world? How can we teach the highest quality person? We have to get the highest quality teacher and then make an excellent video series on the Divine Principle. Now we are starting to do this. If we were welcomed by the environment, it would be easier, but this is not our situation, so we have to give all our effort to teach the people. You didn't know about the spiritual world before, but now you must clearly experience it. People don't know that their life is forever; they only live half of a human life. They don't understand the purpose of their physical life at all.

The Parents' Course

Let us think more seriously now. My life has not been so easy. I don't have even one day for myself. I know the spiritual world, so there is no escape for me, no hope to get away from my task. I know how you feel sometimes, but I can never turn around and go back. There is absolutely no way other than this for me to go. I know the reality of both worlds, so I must continue with my work. Do you understand? You too must understand the spiritual world. Now, you are starting from the miserable place in your course of life, you are preparing for the future. You cannot see that, but I know what your future will be like. Now you cannot see it, but eventually, everyone has to go this way. There is no other way.

This is critical. During your short lifetime you can do it. Thousands of years of problems in the spiritual world can be solved by you. You have to do it. No one else will. That is why I must be hard on you. I like you, but I must be hard. I must tell America the truth about itself. Otherwise the nation has no hope, no future. The same holds for you. You decide now. Each day you decide your own fate and the fate of your nation. God blessed America, but you are responsible for that blessing. Otherwise, God will find another nation. It is very serious for you. America doesn't want to hear about its problems, but it has to listen. The problems of this nation are very serious.

Who will solve the problems in America? If America doesn't solve the problems of drugs, free sex, the breakdown of the family and the decline of Christianity, it will perish. Intelligent people in the Communist camp look at these problems and work to make them worse. They won't have to shed any of their own blood to ruin this nation. Therefore, they support drugs and free sex and push towards the breakdown of the family and the decline of religious life in America. This is true. In this way, communism will just walk in and take over someday.

Can you understand my heart? Really? I am so serious. I began all alone. There was no one to lead me, no one to guide me along the way. It was a miserable, lonely course. How could I have had any hope. How could I have continued? The only way I could continue was because I had found the way to solve mankind's division and this unlocked the way for mankind to receive God's blessing. Cain and Abel have to come together and stand and work together. Then, the position of the parents can stand and God can work his power on earth through that.

Upon that foundation, the parents can come. All the levels have to be achieved: family level, tribal level, national level and finally, the worldwide level. That is the way of the providence. It has always been this way. Today, that providence is working the same way, but centering on Asia. If we can bring the nations together, the world can start anew. If an individual Cain and Abel become one, the family can stand. If a Cain family and an Abel family become one, the tribe can stand. If a Cain nation and an Abel nation become one, the world can stand. Do you understand? That is the way of the Principle.

I now stand in Abel's position. I started alone, so I had to create the foundation on the individual level and work up to the worldwide level. I couldn't think of my own family. Abel cannot think of his own family. He has to go to Cain and Cain's family, and to the entire world of Cain. Then after that, he can go to his own family. This has been my situation all throughout my life.

Think about my heart. There is so much pain. The worst persecution comes from those closest to the heart. My own family wanted me to be concerned for them, but I could never once think of them first. This caused incredible pain for them. This has been my course. Sometimes, I even have to hear the cries of my own children, but I can't take the time with them that they need. My time is for others instead.

The parents are in such a severe situation. Cain and Abel have to come together. That is the only way to save your parents. Do you understand? When you fight one another in the church, do you think about that? So much depends on you. You will understand later on, but not now. Sometimes you are like a robber or a thief. You are taking things without earning them. You cannot steal the parents' love like that. You have to come together first and then God can send the parents love to you. You have to bring others together centered on God's providence. Then you can taste the parents' love.

Cain and Abel have to become one. With this, the True Parents can be revealed. Parents cannot become parents by themselves. They must have the children's position fulfilled. We have to solve the division between Cain and Abel, from the individual level to the tribal level to the national level, all the way to the worldwide level.

Solving the Serious Problems of the World

The world is crazy now. Everyone is working for themselves, or at the very most for their own nation. Who is really thinking about and working for the entire world? No one. That is Satan's character. Selfish. The Oriental world is more occupied with the spiritual world, with philosophy and meditation and spiritual practice. That is its basic history. The Western world is more or less occupied with the physical world, with science and technology. That means one is more internal and the other is more external. What does that indicate to us? Cain and Abel. They share a relationship. Without them, True Parents cannot stand. In the court case they asked me, "who did you meet in the spiritual world?" I told them the truth. Our purpose is to proclaim the messiah isn't it? When they asked me this question, I said, "Jesus, Moses, every kind of saint." They replied, "Oh, amazing." They didn't believe it. Neither did the newspapers. I explained that I met Moses because he was the founder of Judaism, and Jesus because he is responsible for all Christians, and Buddha because he was the beginning point of Buddhism. Some Muslim people came to ask if I met Muhammad. I said, "Yes." They asked, "Was he Muslim?" I said, "Yes, of course, indeed he was Muslim."

Jewish people also wanted to know about my meetings with Moses. They didn't believe me, but they asked anyway, just in case. They were curious to find out what Moses might have said. They were curious about what he might have said to me. Others were upset that I had met with Jesus, but what is wrong with that? There is nothing wrong with that. Few people can meet with Jesus because he is so high in the spiritual world, but there is nothing wrong with meeting Jesus.

We have to defend the free world because here these things can be said openly. We can at least discuss these things and investigate whether they are true or not. In the Communist world, this is not at all even possible. We have to bring these two worlds together. Not just East and West, but also the spiritual and physical worlds. Then we can proclaim the messiah and people will understand without too many problems.

During the time before World War II, there were many groups in Korea receiving messages directly from the spiritual world. They had ideas similar to mine. They could understand parts of the message. They had a certain amount of preparation, but they didn't understand me completely and this foundation was lost. After World War II, there was the Korean War and during this time I had to go and re-create the foundation. After that war, many people were searching and could hear the message.

Now we are centering on America, but they don't have the same kind of spiritual background. They have liberal theology, liberal thinking. They are not concerned with the spiritual world. However, what is true is true. The spiritual world exists and everyone lives there from the worst sinner to the highest saint. Anyone can find out for himself. American people don't understand who they are and they are confused about the purpose of their life. If 50% of the families in America end in divorce, how can they understand the concept of True Parents? Are you going to take care of that? Do you know how to solve that? It's very serious.

Who can save American youth? Who can straighten out their situation? There are all kinds of situations. Do you believe that you can solve everything? Can you say, "Father, we will do everything"? Can you American men and women say that? I like you, but what is happening to your nation? Do your congressmen care? Do your senators really care about how young people will remain pure and reach God? Do they truly understand how to solve the problems if they recognize them? No, but Reverend Moon understands these problems and he is working day and night to solve them, to clean up the youth of America. What has been your experience with me? Are you better or worse now?

It looks like you are worse. I make you work all day and night, in any kind of weather. In spite of that, you feel better. Is that right? Why? Because you are fulfilling your purpose in life. The ideal world will come from you. That's true. In this world, all you can find is persecution. No matter how hard it is, you have to go on. I came here more than ten years ago. During that time many powerful people came to persecute me. All the newspapers and news media and government officials were against me. They started then to prevent my work in America.

However, from this time on, people will begin to see our work and they will welcome us all over the world. Many people in South America already want to meet me. Third World nations will understand me much more quickly, but my greatest concern is the Free World. It has a mission to the Communist World. If you take care of the other nations in the world they will come to help you when you need it. Your mission is at least to take care of South America. America has to understand that.

Japan's mission is to take care of America. Western people have to follow the Oriental way. That will be the way for them. Western civilization is an empire built on technical ability in the physical world, but the Oriental way has traditionally been more concerned with the spiritual way. You have to inherit that. How about you sisters? Why do you want to marry an Oriental man? And why do the brothers also want an Oriental wife? That is because the two worlds now want to meet. They can meet through you. That's true. The future world needs both. Then we can create the original family, starting with Cain and Abel. The world can start a new family. How about you? When you first came here did your parents become angry? Many of you are nodding your heads saying, "Yes." Why? Even my family couldn't understand the path I was taking. Your parents said, "Don't go, don't go," but you went anyway.

Everyone says, "the Unification Church is an evil place." Why don't you believe them and leave? You came here to solve your problems. Instead, you were inspired to solve the problems of the world first. First help the world, then help yourself. Now, everything is in perspective for you isn't it?

You need to experience the spiritual world. Three nations represent three positions. Adam, Eve and the archangel. To save the world we have to bring three nations together. Actually, we need four nations because we solve the problem of the archangel through the restoration of Cain and Abel. Therefore, we need Adam, Eve, Cain and Abel nations. If these four nations unite, the world can unite. When this happens, the spiritual and physical worlds can come together as one.

Why We Have an
Ocean Church

September 5th, 1982 -- East Garden

THOSE WHO do not wish to continue in the Ocean Church mission, please raise your hands. I would like to speak about the ocean providence today. Until June 1981, Master Marine built 150 boats, and when they finish building 300 of these, the factory can move to Alabama. Once it moves to Alabama, it will make small and major fishing vessels in the fiberglass division. In the future, boats up to 100 and 120 feet will be built, the basic plan being to create a boat that can take Alaskan waters. This boat would have the fundamental design for other boats that could fish in Southern or Eastern waters.

At the same time, we originally planned to create thirty Ocean Church centers along the coast line of the United States. Then, thirty major boats, each something like a "mother ship," could have been sent to each center. In one year's time you should have gained enough experience to captain those boats. On October 1, 1980, I gathered all the members in Gloucester and gave the details of the vision of Ocean Church. Were you there? The original plan was for you to go to a major port and begin training young people. Each *One Hope* boat was to be used to interest young people in the vision of fishing and the ocean. If they were responsible, we could have even turned over the boat to them, a minimum of five young people per boat.

The initial stage or foundation was for each center to utilize and be responsible for ten boats. With five youths per boat, you should be training fifty young people by now and they could have been working with Ocean Church members. Our plan was not just for fishing, but to create a network of people with a vision for the ocean.

The problem has been our understanding of Ocean Church. Why do we add the word "church" after "ocean"? Ocean Church is a church movement because it is founded upon and guided by a belief. That belief is a philosophy, meaning that our main concern is internal or spiritual. That is the essence of Ocean Church. The future is for those who develop their spirit; they are the ones who can truly take care of creation, of the world.

Basic Structure of the American Movement

I designed the basic route for the core of our movement who come through the Seminary at Barrytown. After graduation, they should first go to CARP and train on the campus. Then, automatically they should come to Ocean Church. That is the plan for educating the leadership of our movement: from UTS to CARP to Ocean Church. After that kind of well-rounded training, the seminarian should go on to state leadership. Every state must have that kind of leader.

Anyone who wants to qualify in the future for state leadership must first qualify for leadership in CARP and Ocean Church. The movement is growing beyond the level of the present state leadership. So far, no matter how clear and creative the directions were, they have not been digested and accepted. The message dwindled with each step, from the leadership to the members, until it no longer made sense when it got to the members. However, the leader who moves from CARP to Ocean Church and then to state leadership can understand and respond to my direction. They will be like a special task force, ready to respond and go whenever they hear new directions.

In the future, the Unification Church hierarchy, or means of leadership and direction, will be on the state level. It will not be a strict federal system, but more a state system. Each state will become a strong unit able to take care of its own situation and create its own direction. For example, there is a federal government in America, but each state has its own government as well. This is a source of strength for America. I would like to emulate that system in our movement. We will group together the states into regions of five states, which together would form one group. Therefore, we would have ten regions and each region would have its own director helping each state leader. All that would be needed then, would be a good connection between headquarters and the regions. The mission of headquarters should be small. There isn't so much needed by the central point, except to gather information from the local centers and be able to understand the whole picture. Then, headquarters can give general directions centered upon the work of each region. Each region would have an IW who would go to each state and see exactly what is going on, what is good, what needs changing, etc. They would report directly and only to headquarters. The IW should be connected with me and know about our tradition and way of life, as well as church administration. The mission of the IW is to go to each state so that the members are educated directly. In this way they can give guidance and counseling to all the members.

This is how a unified system can unfold across the country, even though each state takes the major burden of responsibility for itself. What shall our education center upon? Tradition. And what is that tradition? That tradition will include CARP tradition, Ocean Church tradition and state leadership tradition. We will educate members to become well-rounded and capable to take care of others in any situation.

Why am I interested in that kind of organization? There are three categories into which people fit in this country: those who live inland; those who live on the coast; and those who are young, the next generation. The young generation includes high school and college students. Thus we need to have both a campus (CARP) and a high school (HARP) movement.

It's not possible to deal with those who are old-minded, who are so set in their way of life that they don't want to move and change. We have to pioneer a new world with young people who look to the future and are excited by adventure. Young people are the most creative and productive group in the world. However, there is division there. There are those who are serious and those who are turning to free sex, drugs and all kinds of self indulgence.

We are dedicated to creating young people who are morally clear. We have to clean them up and challenge them and channel their resources. That is CARP's mission. From 1978 on, there was almost no focus on state level church activities. CARP members were pushed so hard to create a strong CARP movement. CARP members have many enemies who are strong and willing to face them. In almost every college in America there have been strong Communist and leftist groups actively at work for many years. I knew there would be angry confrontations. On many campuses the leftist and more violent organizations almost took over. It has been and continues to be a real problem. The members of CARP have to confront that and show a winning spirit over the ideology and tactics of communist-related groups on the college campus. In 1978, CARP was initiated in America, however, real activities on campus didn't begin until a year later. Before we set up our national network, we have to create a solid tradition of victory. The goal for CARP by the end of 1982 is to pioneer 300 campuses. I want to save your country. How about you? If we save America, the entire world can be saved. America is the microcosm and the world still looks to America and follows its example.

Since 1978, we have confronted many Communist groups on the campus and many of them have retreated. I am absolutely sure they can be won over. The first step is the university campus, for it is in the universities, where future leaders are being prepared, that one can begin to approach any nation. From America, the CARP movement will grow all around the world. I would really like to see CARP expand, especially in Germany. The greatest sight would be to see young people in CARP come together and break down the Berlin wall and re-unite the country in true peace. I would truly like to see this accomplished through what I call the "women's force." Women are the spearhead; when women move forward, the opposition cannot stand. That is vision. Can you understand?

Relationship Between Ocean Church and CARP

Since CARP and Ocean Church are growing up side by side, they should work together. They should have a spirit of cooperation. CARP members can ask their college student friends to come with them to their boat and this will create a great deal of interest in the more adventurous students. Then, Ocean Church members can take the students out and teach them about our vision for the future. College students will be very excited by this kind of program and plan.

The inland movement should be linked to the coastal movement. That is CARP and Ocean Church. Most college students are inland, but through Ocean Church, they can be introduced to a whole new horizon. We have the system and the program, the plan and the vision. So, why not? We can go to the college campus and form a club. We can let them be responsible for a boat in the same way that I've already outlined. We can just say, "You can have them!" All they have to do is get ten people and form a club. Many students would work day in and day out to use such a boat.

Up to now detailed directions have been given, but they were not fulfilled. Ocean Church members, have you done any of these things? You should be seasoned fishermen by now so that when the university students come, you will be able to intoxicate them with a sense of the ocean and everything within it. You should be able to take them on the journey of their life and teach them how to fish.

When a big boat of ours comes to each port, you can take them out on the *One Hope* and show them the boat. You can tell them that if they want to, and if they work hard, they can surely have a boat like that in the future. Many young people would go crazy to have that kind of goal. You can give them something to dream about, something to live for.

You can let them fish on the weekends on the big boat. During the week, teach them by taking them out in the *One Hope*. They can use their weekend work towards their college expenses. They can study for their MA degree and PhD degree with their earnings. What a great opportunity for them. They can graduate with intellectual and sea-going skills; with intellectual, mechanical and spiritual skills.

That's the vision and the goal. What has happened? The years have been virtually wasted. Why don't you work towards these goals? I have to tell you again and repeat everything. It's disheartening. The major leaders in our church should become an advisory group and feel responsible, either for the failure or success of Ocean Church.

What do you CARP members think? Are you excited to exist side by side with Ocean Church or are you reluctant? Young people are still very much wanting to get into life. Think about it. Locate the boats at different schools. Come up with the ocean-going youth. If you can't find such youth, then CARP members should take up one boat and show the way. Ten CARP members should have two boats. They can attract young people to come out and use the boats. It can become a program of great pride in that school. CARP can even give scholarships based on someone's performance in the program. These boats meet with the spirit of young people. They are sharp, modern and powerful. I wanted a boat that would move like a knife in the water and cut right through the waves. I designed the boats for the sake of young people, to excite their hearts and minds. This is the love that I have for young people.

I expected Ocean Church to take off, but it hasn't quite done that. You are clunking along. We are in an emergency all over the world, so I cannot waste one minute. When we first started to build these boats, we knew nothing about it, but we created an absolute miracle. Master Marine started from scratch. Members came from all over the world to work on those boats. Why? I wanted Ocean Church to go to the entire world. Therefore, once a member is successful here, he can go to the rest of the world. Ocean Church members are responsible to win the support of local governments. From the mayor and police chief to the governor. They will look at your work and proclaim you. Will your parents be negative about that? Not at all. The problem is that Ocean Church never took off. There was an eight year plan prepared for Ocean Church. I had hoped you would complete the program in that amount of time and be able to move on to the international level.

I had expected Ocean Church to be so successful that everyone would envy Ocean Church. Ocean Church members are well educated and many of you came from the seminary. Your experiences in Ocean Church should make you into great leaders for this country. You should deal with college professors, teach them our principles and show them our vision. Give them lectures. You can do that; it's not a strange thing for you to do.

I made up my mind. I know that you can become such people. Even the PhD graduates must come to Ocean Church; they have to go this course. By training in this way, we will surely develop the kind of leadership that can truly teach this nation and show it the way into the future. I sincerely want to see you become those men and women. Look at the path I have walked. I have trained myself as a fisherman. Why? Not for myself, but to save the nation. I have determined to find the way over and beyond communism. I have been fighting all my life against communism. America must not be lost to this ideology. That is why for more than thirty years I have given every inch of my life for this cause.

I have already studied and pioneered your course. CARP members, do you know your mission? Communism is seeping into America through the college campuses. You have to expose that and confront it. Ocean Church members, drugs are coming into this country through the ocean. You have to protect the true freedom of this nation. You have to protect its original dignity.

This is a monumental task. When Americans wake up to their situation, they will look around and ask, "where is the person who can lead us out of this?" Someone has to come and revitalize Christianity so that it can truly stir the conscience of the people. God has directed me to do that. You are seminary graduates: Go out and work all day long on the ocean and then come home and teach at night. This is exactly what I have done for you. Now, are you awakened? You don't like Ocean Church? You don't like CARP? This is how we will save the nation. Do you think the government will praise me and come after me for help? They will do exactly the opposite. Knowing that, you have to be tough.

Around the world, brothers and sisters are sweating blood. They are literally sending blood money to this nation, to save this nation. You are riding the boat and the wind is blowing hard; you should yell at the wind, "I am going to go forward to justify the blood money of my brothers and sisters!" This is their hope in you. Seminary graduates in CARP, raise your hands. Are you ready to go to Ocean Church? Your accomplishments in CARP will come with you to Ocean Church. I appreciate your willingness to follow this course.

Taking Responsibility for America

Even so, I am so deeply disappointed. At Provincetown this year, the members were reluctant to go out. I had to do all the pulling and pushing to get people out. You are young; you should be exclaiming to me, "Father, forget about the high winds, let's go out!" When you know you are going out, you have to work hours ahead of time, get everything ready. When I come, the engines are out of order, the bait isn't bought and the hooks aren't the right size. How can you hope to move the world with such a sluggish approach to things?

What are you worried about? Your life is taken care of. God has already given you your destiny. You should just be serious about fishing. Someday your wife and children will depend upon your work for their life. Don't you know that? Most of you just look for excuses not to do things. Do you understand exactly how I feel? Do you think that I want you to bring money to me so that I can steal it and take it back to Korea? It's exactly the opposite. I am bringing money from overseas to help you get this project started. The government can't even see that much. They are so blind they want to kick me out of the country. However, I am determined to help you, to help this nation.

I would like to have some comfort somewhere, but there is no relief. The government is persecuting me and that is difficult. However, if you don't fulfill the simple responsibility given you, that's even worse persecution. Go to your campuses and ocean cities. Do it and it will be accomplished. Just give everything that you have and go out.

Where were you before I came? Many of you were just like human trash. Were you thinking about America or saving humanity? Were you thinking about spirit world and eternal life? Were you thinking about the quality of your own life? Did you have any real concern even for yourselves. Did you ever think about the will of God? Far from it.

What have you to fear? You are free. You are American citizens. You have the right to work twenty-four hours a day for the sake of your country. Can they put you in jail for that? They chase after me day and night, but they will not come after you. You are born here, but you cannot feel what I am feeling for this nation. You cannot feel the emergency this nation is in. This is what pains me more than anything else. You have no idea. We have to have a heart-to-heart understanding. I want a firm foundation before I depart from America. Are you tired? That word doesn't exist for us. I should have been tired years and years ago. I am over sixty years of age. I am almost at the age of retirement. And yet, I am going at twice the rate you are.

When I first met Mr. Masters, I noticed his hair was completely white and thought he was an old man. I treated him kindly and didn't push him too much. Then I found out he was only fifty-six and I thought, "Oh, I should have really pushed him much more, he is only a young man!" Why is this man here from Britain? Does he have a separate destiny from you? No. The world is only one world. America is not just by itself. No nation is just by itself. We share whatever happens. However, America will choose her own destiny. I am always thinking about other nations that can fulfill this role if America fails. Sodom and Gomorrah received judgement from God. They were given many chances to decide their own destiny. Finally, Lot and his wife had to leave. God told them to not look back, but the woman did and turned into a pillar of salt.

If I leave this country, I will not look back, not even once. Do you want to see the day that I pack up and leave this nation? What stops me from leaving this violent nation? You do. Looking at you living this way of life and giving your absolute heart keeps me here. Many countries are even begging me to come. In South America and Africa, many countries are asking for me to come. Shall I go? Someday I will go, but do you want me to go in a way that abandons America?

If you want to succeed in this nation, you have to pay indemnity.

That is my way of life. I will never change one iota of it. When God told Abraham to go, he had to leave. Abraham couldn't say, "Well, what am I going to do about expenses?" He had to take off right then and there. I am a serious man. If I have to leave America in that way, I will not return, not even if the State department realizes something and asks for me to come back. I will have to cut off and that would be absolute.

Now do you understand the importance of CARP and Ocean Church? Master Marine members, do you know how important those boats are? Master Marine members, what kind of heart do you have about your work? Ocean Church, I had expected you to realize some of the great potential of your mission already. All right then, today is the day you receive new direction. You have to remember this day deep within your heart. Your mission is so vital that the survival of America hangs on you. You have to feel this to the bone. There is no other way for this nation.

If you participate in this crusade and lift this country up to serve God and mankind, will you be forgotten? Will your grave be left unattended? Do you think this country will think of you someday? I can answer that one clearly. You will become old and tired and want to hide, but the public will search you out and make you serve even further. Can you think about just getting married and taking care of only your own family? I have treated you like royalty. You were men and women without any concern for the world, just at the bottom of life, but I picked you up and glorified you. You have been given an education. I have been lifting up your heart and spirit so that you could lead this nation. What more can I do for you? What more can you expect from me?

The survival of this nation, the hope of the free world is on your shoulders. Just go on for ten or twenty years. That is all I am asking of you. Then you will see. This nation will be desperate and needing you. You will be able to bring this nation up. Can you feel tired thinking of that? You will be in your prime when you are forty or fifty years old; that is the prime of life when you still have energy, but also experience and wisdom. Don't just be a drop-out. You will see. In ten or twenty years time, you will harvest the fruits of all your efforts.

I am now fishing for striped bass. This fish is very difficult to catch and that is why I have pursued it. The whole area talked about me all summer long. While I was fishing, no one could even find any striped bass, but I caught them everyday. You have to be like that. People have to respect you for what you can do. I never said a word, but my actions caused everyone to talk all summer long. Be like that. Just have a single-minded goal and work day in and day out for that goal. What kind of man am I? Then what kind of person should you be? I want to train you to be great men and women. Absolutely.

In Provincetown and Gloucester, I did most of the work, but when everyone was talking, they didn't say, "Reverend Moon did this and that." No, instead they talked about the Moonies taking all the tuna and striped bass. I want it to be like that, because all my efforts are for you. I want to push you up and up. Look at this little brother here. He just works on the *New Hope* engine and cuts smelly fish all day. His hands are dirty all the time and his clothes are smelly. No one even sees him, but if they did they wouldn't want to be near him. Ten years from now he can be the mayor of Los Angeles. Why not? Why not? If he takes responsibility and works desperately, he will grow and become a person to whom others give great respect. Just work, don't talk, don't look for comfort. People will then notice you and they will ask you to take care of things beyond your imagination.

Look at Bo Hi Pak. When we first decided to start the media providence he didn't even know what a newspaper was. But now there is the *Washington Times* and it will produce far more than its own publication. Who did that? Bo Hi Pak? No, not at all. He just worked, uniting with me and following Heavenly Father completely. Then a miracle could happen. When you make up your mind, you can become somebody. I am that kind of person. I can start any kind of company. What if I came looking for you and wanted you to be the president for that company? I want you to be capable people who can take on any task. That is why I push and train you so hard. This is a true father's love.

Testing Ground for Future Leadership

Ocean Church and CARP are a testing ground. I am looking for future leaders here. When you prove yourselves, you will then have to take care of international things. No one else is doing this with the youth of the world. In Russia and Red China there are already newspapers which have criticized me, so I know that I am making an impact. I know that they are even afraid of me if that is their reaction. Do I look fearful to you? Then why do the Communists fear me? To you, I am like a father, but to them I am a fearless and relentless fighter.

I want to design a martial arts program which is so tough that when members go through it, they will beg to come to Ocean Church. Then, when they leave martial arts and arrive on the boats, I will request that the same program be taught on the boats! They will be so shocked and want to jump into the ocean, but there will be a welcoming guest there: the shark. The shark can take care of you very well. No problem. Then, what would you do? Would you jump in, or would you survive and really learn martial arts once and for all? That's the kind of training I want you to have in life.

Cuba is right around the corner. Ocean Church may have a confrontation with them. You may be harassed by them. You have to be prepared for that. In Japan, when we made a declaration against communism we also prepared thirty gun shops around the country. We gave them a direct message. "If you come out to fight we will defend ourselves." These guns are just air rifles, but they can at least stop someone if need be. We had to do at least that, otherwise the Communists would resort to violence.

Anyone can buy these rifles and have them in their homes. The Japanese government was really worried that open fighting would come about, but our goal is not to come out in violence. Our goal is to overcome the ideology of communism. However, people have to have self-defense if they are ever attacked. This makes the Communists think very hard. They didn't dare to come out in violence, not even one time. Finally, the police in Japan said, "Reverend Moon is a wise man. He made a great strategy to stop the Communists from street violence."

In the meantime, we have been making an ideological offensive against communism in every CARP campus. Communist theory has no comparison with Unification teaching. They tried to win on the Japanese college campuses by debating, but they lost to the point of humiliation. Our truth was so compelling and so clearly beyond theirs. Also, our Japanese members worked so much harder than they did. Finally, they could only resort to their own bottom line. They came at us with violence. They wanted to take to the streets and fight and intimidate us. Often they charged and attacked our CARP members. We stood up to that. We never wanted to attack first, but absolutely we defended against their attack. The Japanese CARP members studied the best Korean martial arts and they were ready to die. Many of them were attacked, but they defended themselves.

Don't you think that American CARP needs that? Wherever you go, communism is the same. If you aren't prepared they will attack you and hurt you. Don't wait until then to say, "Oh, we should have been ready." Then it's too late. Without a deep resolve, you cannot fight for the sake of God's will. This is what I am teaching the members. Look at us: only one theological school is teaching martial arts and that is our own theological school at Barrytown.

You cannot go on unless you realize that this is a life and death matter. The American government is pushing me down. Fine, let them try. The time will come when the senators and governors will convey their deepest apologies to me. I am going on in spite of everything they do to me. No matter what hits me, I go on and even grow larger and larger. This is true of Unification Church. No matter what, it will never be crushed. Do you have that inner resolve? If so, Unification Church will go on forever.

The Era of Video Education

This summer, the Blessing for 2,100 couples occurred. I want every couple to be a success, a champion for God. Should you follow me or ignore me? If you don't go this way, who will suffer? I am not going to be the one to suffer in the ultimate sense. However, you will suffer greatly if you don't fulfill. I know that so well and that is why I am so serious to instruct you about the Blessing. Anyone who doesn't take me seriously will end up following those who do. I am not a "maybe" person. There is no such thing with me. as "maybe so." I am the truth. You have to clearly know that.

In Madison Square Garden, there were more than 2,000 couples, more than 4,000 people walking upon the platform and dedicating themselves. These people were not brainwashed; they were intelligent and serious people. What can America think about me? They have to consider me more seriously; they have to consider us more seriously. Actually that battle is over. People can see so clearly that our ideal is truly great. Our marriages have a serious responsibility to uphold this ideal. When people watched the Madison Square Garden event they were deeply moved; they felt something great had happened. We can put that on tape and show it without sound. People can watch in silence. I think that will be more effective. Just by watching our marriage, people can understand what we are all about. You don't need to explain what is going on, if they are sensitive people. You Blessed couples should have a tape of this wedding in your Home Church home. You can show this tape to everyone in your area. They will watch and look at you very differently after that. You can become very popular and in demand. People will even want to pay you to see the video.

American people will view that tape and become so intoxicated that they will feel as if they are living in a dream. When they finish watching, they will wake up from that beautiful dream and they will become positive towards you. They will think, "What wonderful people these young Moonies are. They are the hope of the world." You should keep a video of your wedding at least for your own sake and for your children's sake.

Apart from theology, this is a great gift to America. Everyone who finds out that you are a Moonie will want to see the tape of your wedding. They will be so curious. Then, they will see you, your spouse and your family and when they see how you began they will have tears in their eyes. Their own families will be in such a state. You know, almost one half of American families are breaking apart. They will see your family and want to stay with you.

The Moonie couple will be the showcase of the model family. In front of every Moonie home should be a big flagpole with a flag twice the size of a normal American flag saying, "Moonie couple lives here." The pro-Moonie relatives will have a flagpole too saying, "Moonie relatives live here." Then, when people come to visit you, you can first show them your wedding tape. After they are completely intoxicated, they will just sit there. Then you can show them a six-hour tape with all the contents of Divine Principle.

People are so curious in Japan about what the Moonies are doing that they now pay to come to our video centers. Most of them are young people and intelligent college students. They know that the future is vital, so they want to study a new idea and see if it is connected to the future. We made over 1,200 tapes and these can be watched at any time. Every month, over 100 people are signing membership. I want this to increase ten-fold, so the Japanese members are making 12,000 tapes and showing them all day and night.

When this project first began, Mr. Furuta who was then president of Happy World said to me, "It's impossible and will cost millions of dollars." Then I said, "Do it!" Somehow they found a way to do it, and after trying it for one year, Mr. Furuta came back to me and said, "You were absolutely right and now we are gaining 100 members each month."

Ocean Church you have to realize how to do this. All you have to do is set the tradition. Once there is a foundation, anyone can inherit the way to success. CARP members, you should create video centers with an entire curriculum. Great teachers and artists will come to us and we will help them express their ideas on tape. We can get the highest quality people and create an entire curriculum from them; we can educate young people in America in every field...business and philosophy, music and religion; any field.

Japan has shown the way. We will do this in America and then take it to Germany, England and all over the world. People can educate themselves in any area of their interest. The top scholars can teach any interested person directly. Even poor people can get a degree from a university. After taking a video course, they can go to the university and take an exam and earn their degree that way.

In order to do that, we have to create cable and broadcast television. Through satellite courses we can educate anyone in the world. Initially it may be hard to attract attention to this kind of education, but eventually people will line up to come. We can serve the entire world in this way. Thousands of people can earn their degrees this way, satellite degrees.

The Standard of a Champion

I am a very different kind of man. My mind is very different isn't it? Do you want to spare me or use me all up while I am here with you? I am getting older. You don't want to spare me? All right then, we need a spare tire for when I am all used up. You have to become Reverend Moon's spare tire. That's only fair isn't it? I want you to become a "spare" of me.

You really are different people now aren't you? You Americans look and see differently than other Americans, because your vision is for the whole world. Because of your connection of heart all over the world, people will want to come and work with you. You watch and you will see it happen. Maybe now you don't realize how you are connected, but because of me, you are linked, hooked together all over the world.

I didn't set out to be a famous person. I would rather be hidden behind the scenes, but year by year I have attracted the attention of the world. When I go fishing in Provincetown, people are looking everywhere for Reverend Moon and asking, "Where is he?" Usually, I'm right there and they don't know that it's me. That's different from you isn't it? You Americans like to show up and be seen. You really love to be in front of the television camera. It is quite the opposite for me. I enjoy it when people don't even recognize me.

What if I offered an exclusive interview? Would they jump on that or ignore me? You are right. People are just dying to find out about me. There are people asking Colonel Pak all the time for some way to interview me. People are just dying to interview Reverend Moon. One person was just begging Colonel Pak to get an interview with me. She works for an internationally famous magazine. When I said, "No," and Colonel Pak relayed that to her, she just replied, "Well, I understand." So far, Colonel Pak has refused many magazine editors already. They never get angry, they understand. They sense that I am not that kind of person. What is the speediest form of transportation in the world today? You say "jet, rocket, Apollo and Concorde." That's fine, but then, you Unification members should be 100 times as fast. How can you do that? With spiritual, mental speed. They can go to the moon one time. In that amount of time, you can go back and forth ten times. If they learn one thing, you learn 100 things. If they lecture one hour, you lecture ten hours. If they work or run for one hour, then you work and run for ten hours.

You look at the seasoned fisherman and say, "He is catching more fish than I am." Well then, determine to go beyond him in three years time. Look at him and say, "You work during the day; I'll work day and night." Say to yourself, "I'll go beyond the record that anyone set; I'll set the new record." Work more hours and do more things than the other fishermen. In that way, build up for three years and then you will overtake anyone. Eventually, everyone will come and look at you.

In the same way, I came to America and said, "I will love America more than any other American ever has. I will love America more than George Washington." Then I had to think seriously, "How can I be superior to such a man?" My answer was that I can teach young Americans why they should love America. I can teach them the spiritual significance of their lives. I can teach them the will of God. I can teach them the mission of this nation.

I can do this in a systematic and organized way. I shall restore the youth of this nation. I determined I would do this. Not even George Washington thought of these things. No matter who has set the record in the past, I have determined to break that record in serving America. When I came here I traveled by car on the highway and went to each state. I went through all fifty states without a break, dedicating holy grounds. After that, I returned to many of those states and spoke to the public. Throughout the speaking tour, I traveled without stopping and pushed myself to exhaustion many times. All the speaking campaigns were like that.

Ocean Church is not a random whim. I have a vision for America and Ocean Church plays an integral and important part in that. My mind is very deep. Everything that I do has a purpose which covers thousands of years. When Allan Hokanson gets in the *New Hope* and drives, he has a purpose, but when I take the *New Hope* out my purpose is much wider and greater.

No matter who set the record in the past, I am determined to break it. On that foundation I have begun and made the American movement. Do you believe that I truly love America more than anyone else in its history? If I go to the spiritual world, will I receive guidance from George Washington, or will George Washington come to me and receive guidance from me? If that is the case, the President today is in the same situation.

The Lonely Position of True Parents

Do you think that I live inside the house looking at trees and birds all day long? Do you think that's my way of life? I want you to know that those people who lived rich and carelessly are in a completely different position in the spiritual world. They are deeply ashamed. When you review my life, you will see a life of deep suffering. My standard has been incredible, going beyond poverty and pain. I have suffered every humiliation possible, but my mind was never changed from loving God.

I have never taken comfort, even in East Garden. Instead I have used this place like all the others, as a place to shed tears. Constantly. You have never known this; however, throughout my life I have wept and wept for God, and God knows. God knows precisely how Reverend Moon has lived. Therefore, even when I die, God will preserve a shrine for me. God will never forget what I have done all my life for him.

You've been destined to meet me. When you met me you felt something. That is an invisible tie. It is because God knows about me. Still, I am teaching new things every day. The leaders have known me for twenty or thirty years. Even so, every day I have new ideas, new material for them. I am still a mystery for them. You think they know me and are accustomed to meeting me everyday, but this isn't so. They are almost fearful to meet me because they don't know what I will do next. They still don't know exactly what I think. You like me, but even if you feel close, you don't feel completely familiar with me. You also feel some dignity, some awesome power within me. I live in this house as a lonely man. No one truly knows me. Not even Mother or the children.

So, if I instruct you, don't take me lightly. The Japanese members know not to take me lightly, but the Americans haven't found that out yet. The Japanese follow without question and this is a great strength. This is fidelity. Many people have criticized what I did in Korea and Japan. They criticized me for taking so much from Korea and Japan and using it all for the sake of America. They didn't understand why I did that. After all these years, the vision has begun to take shape and form. Now, people are seriously looking at my work and they are truly awed. Christian scholars and theologians just shake their heads in disbelief. Our vision is so great.

Don't you really want to know about me and be close to me? Then you have to walk a very rare and unusual way of life. You have to follow my instructions and walk a narrow way of life. You have a destiny. Now, many very famous scholars are asking the leaders, even the members, if they can see Reverend Moon. How about you? Do you have that same desire? Do you want to meet with me often? Have you ever thought, "I am not worthy to receive direction from him. I shouldn't be in that position. People more prepared than I should be here. How honored I am." Have you ever thought about that?

Have you thought deeply in the middle of the night, looking at the moon, or in the early morning when the sun is just rising? Have you ever looked out over the ocean? Have you thought about your position, your destiny? Have you ever thought, "I am so special to be connected directly to True Parents. I can receive instruction and direction from them." Have you ever thought that the entire universe is envying you?

How much honor have you felt working for me? What about the disciples who worked for Jesus? At the time of Jesus, the people could not receive it, so Jesus could not teach the Principle. The disciples were uneducated men. They didn't know anything; they just felt something from Jesus and they tried to follow. They didn't even know how to help Jesus make any kind of foundation. He died truly alone. Completely alone.

Peter was his chief disciple. He was an unlearned fisherman, an almost primitive person, but today everyone honors him as a saint. You are the seminary graduates. Are you going to be less than Peter? If Jesus had left even one place in the Bible, just one word, two words actually, "True Parents," I would not have suffered as much.

If Jesus had taught in the Bible somewhere, even a little bit, about the fall of man, how the fall happened and how sin crept in, I would not have had to suffer as much. Now, 2,000 years later, it's an entirely new message. Today, I am teaching the way of life. People are reading my message and it will be the same message for those who come 2,000 years later from now. It will not only make sense for them, but it will truly be their "blood and sweat," their way of life. That's the standard I am teaching today.

Have you ever thought of that? You often say, "Oh, Father, you are always saying and teaching strange things." Naturally that is so, because I am speaking to an audience that will be here 2,000 years later. I am thinking, "even if I am in the middle of the mission and I work so hard that I drop dead, I will not regret it." How about you? Are you thinking like that? Do you have that determination?

Do you understand now? In particular, do you seminary graduates understand? You have a special privilege and responsibility. I want you to set and keep the record for the movement. You have to work more than average people. The time will come when I will go, and afterward, each one of you should record your own "Acts of the Apostles." You are deeply indebted in the sight of God. For three years I paid extra attention to the seminary. Almost every day I was there. I attended to almost every detail. Every extra moment I could find the time, I went to the seminary. That three year period of time is over and I have consummated my mission to the seminary.

I am never irresponsible toward you, but you are irresponsible for Ocean Church, irresponsible for CARP. As leaders, if you think nothing about the mission, you are unacceptable to God. If you just do everything that you want to do and then think about the mission, that's not acceptable to me; it's not acceptable to God. For twenty-four hours a day, I think of nothing but the mission.

You don't need any further message. You have the message. Every ounce of energy that comes out of your body and soul, invest that into your mission whether it be Ocean Church, CARP or Master Marine. Don't you think it's important? I am not tired. Every time my legs start to hurt, I scold my own body saying, "You leg, how can you complain? How can you not follow me? I will disown you! You have to help me do God's will." I push myself forward like this, sometimes I even hit my own legs.

I push to go out every day on the ocean. When the engine breaks down, I am disappointed, but feel that for some reason God wants me to stay on shore for that day. Then I search for that reason. That is the only way for me, but for you, sometimes without any reason, you just want to stay on the shore and take a rest and nap. My conscience will not allow that for myself.

The Extraordinary Course of True Parents

Do you want to follow me? Do you want to become a companion of the True Parents? Yes or No? "Yes." So when you go up to the spiritual world, everything will be shown. Nothing will be hidden. Therefore, what do you think? Do you want to be ashamed for eternity or proud? Then do something. Do something that no one else will duplicate. Do something unique. Do something that others cannot imitate. What kind of leader am I when I push seminary students to achieve the highest level of academic studies and then, after graduation, send them out on a boat in the ocean?

It seems crazy. Why do I do this? I want you to know those fishermen, dock workers and crewmen. Among those men are some strong patriots. I love America and I love the world. I want you to become like that: strong men who love their country and love the world. Then you will become teachers and you will restore the people in that field.

I don't want all of you to become fishermen for your entire life, but you have to reach into that realm of life and become teachers so that you can bring salvation to that area. You must become people who have a truly loving heart for these people. You must be one in heart, brothers and sisters centered on God, with the fishermen and workers in the coastal cities. What's wrong with that?

Sometimes I go out on a boat and there is no bathroom. After several hours I have to pass water and there is no place to go. I simply have to do that, even if others are on the boat. That's embarrassing in one way. I know that, but I myself have to walk ahead of you. I have to go first the way you have to go, to be a public person. By doing so, I am teaching the example and laying down the path. Don't worry and don't complain. Even if you are in a situation someday where you become naked and have to pass your stool in public, don't do it with shame. You have a great destiny and you will fulfill something. You have to do everything with dignity.

The saints in the spiritual world will then look down on you and they will acknowledge you as a serious and holy person. So when you pass your stool in a small boat on the sea, all your ancestors in the spirit world will look down and envy your position. They will say, "I wish I could go down there and experience that." Your descendents will also want to follow you and would buy their turn to go out on a small boat and somehow share that experience. In fact, you might have many people coming to your boat before the end of your life to do this thing and you might make a lot of money by charging a small fee to take them out. You are laughing, but in a way, this is no joke.

I can eat with my own fingers, without using a fork or spoon. I can eat out of my lap, using one hand to hold food and the other to eat with. It doesn't make a difference to me. If I have to do something like that to bring salvation to others, I wouldn't hesitate to eat out of my lap a million times. No matter what you think, my way of thinking is entirely different from yours. Do you want to think in a similar way to me? Do you want to make your thoughts parallel to my thoughts? When I landed in America in 1972, no one had heard of me, but I was determined that within three years I would turn this nation upside down, and then right side up. Millions of people have landed on this nation, but my first footstep was different. I planted my foot thinking, "No one else has ever come to this nation with my thinking and my mission. However, I'm going to do it and bring this nation to God."

If you had this same heart when you first went to the Ocean Church mission, Ocean Church would not be like it is today. If you listened to the weather report, you would know that it's rugged up in Gloucester, but calm down here in New York. Okay then, where do you want to go fishing? You have to develop your mind to at least think, "The East Coast is my area. I'm going to go up and down it and work every part of it." However you have to get there, find a way to get there. Fly by plane, fundraise for the money or just walk. Whatever you have to do, just get there. Then learn about that area, learn about the coast. Find out everything about the fish and how they are caught. Once you do that much, practice and improve every technique you learn. I do things so differently from you, because I think differently, see differently and hear differently. That's why my results are so different from yours. People say, "I cannot do it." I can never understand how people can say that. There is no such thing. If your life hung upon the one thing that you were doing, whatever it is, how would you do that? You would do it with desperation, if your life was in the balance. You would just apply yourself and give every ounce of yourself.

Do you follow what I am saying? My thinking is like this and far more. It is not ordinary thinking. When I arrived in New York, I took all the leaders to the top of the Empire State Building. I had just come to New York and didn't even know what was going on there. Yet, I told those leaders, "we will buy some of the major buildings in New York, maybe even this one." Within three or four years, we did indeed buy some large buildings. I even thought about buying the Empire State Building when the negotiations were going on, but it was too late for us at that time. However, another time will come. I know absolutely that "where there is a will, there is a way." I think through every problem, day and night, until I find the solution. I never let it go. My thinking is very different from yours.

What about you? What is changing within you? Did you just grow a beard and become different like that? Or did something change inside of you? If you really chang inside, the result will show up. Where is it? What have you been doing? Well, your beards look very wonderful, outstanding. To me you look like Paul Bunyan. Did you put as much care into your boat? I would like to inspect and see which you love more, your beard or your mission. I dress in ordinary, simple clothes. I am ready to go to sea right now. I know that I was born for a unique destiny. I am going to live it out. What people say about me or do to me doesn't matter. I listen in one ear and let it go out the other. I am only thinking about fulfilling my destiny and completing my mission. That's all. That's how I think. Ocean Church is rare. There is no other organization like it in the world. Who created it? It is not that simple. Can you explain Ocean Church to others? Can you explain why it exists and its philosophy? I want to have a wives' program in Ocean Church. One day, I will announce that the wives will be the pilots for the boats. On that day, the husbands will have to train their wives. If they don't do that, their boat will be taken away from them. Anyway, these boats are not your boats. You are taking care of them, just as you would a church center. Unification Church has something of every variety. If you want something, send in to Unification Church for it. People around the world are beginning to see us like that. We should have a catalogue and if someone wants fisherwomen we will make them if we don't have them. You are Americans. I am Korean. You think, "Well, because Father is Korean he thinks like that." However, you should be even better than me here in America. This is your country. You are born here, your culture is here, your way of life is here. You should do more. You should break every record that I set here in America.

Shall we do it? "Yes." Well, are you just "yes" people or "deed" people? I cannot know just by talking this one day that everyone will do well. I cannot assume that. I want to have a closer look at you. The leaders of Ocean Church have been too good to you. They have been too kind and soft towards you. You need the "iron fist" method. This will bring you greater success, quicker success. You saw the movie, "An Officer and a Gentleman." That was really the "iron fist" method. I was sorry when I saw that, because I could have done so much more for that soldier than his sergeant did in that movie. That movie showed a great training method, but the morality was wrong. We have to go beyond that movie. Our training has to be more than the Marines, but our morality has to be as high as the saints.

So then, let us change from today and accomplish the mission completely. Thank you and may God bless you.

The Ocean Church
Foundation

June 10th, 1983 -- Gloucester

TODAY, I want to speak to you directly, but it is difficult because I speak one language, you speak many different languages from each other, and all of you speak a different language from me. When you learn Korean, you can pronounce anything. You hear how the Korean members can speak English very well. What upsets me is that the translation process only leaves you with half of the meaning. Many things get mixed up this way. In the future I only want to speak in Korean and not have to translate into English or Japanese. For this purpose, please learn Korean so that you can hear me directly whenever I speak.

Work Hard for a Solid Foundation

Are you working harder than before? You shouted out "Yes" so loudly it must be true. However, think about this. Some members of Unification Church (you are also members; you put all your effort into the Ocean Church project), are working in some of the communist countries and they are risking their lives. No matter how hard you are working, compared to them, your life is still an exciting and happy life. It is something to reflect upon.

Our movement has so many other projects going on simultaneously, all over the world. Yet, I am taking precious time every day to be with you and give you guidance. I am working even harder than you are, so your position is one of sympathy towards me. To give you just one example: Do you know how much the Washington Times is costing? We have already invested several

154

million dollars. At the same time, the providence in South America has already begun. However, I cannot think about only the things our movement is doing right now. I must also think about the future.

One thing I know is that the era of catching fish on the open sea will end soon. So, the era of fish farming will begin. Sooner or later, mankind will be looking for how to gain access to the ocean. The land will run out of room and resources for man. If you really make the effort to be successful, you will be supported on your way. Already, in Gloucester and in many other fishing ports, so much support has been given. Yet, I see that Ocean Church doesn't have the foundation to be trusted. Although we should have already begun to invest in and build tackle stores, there is no foundation for that to happen. These stores were to have been just the beginning point. I am concerned about you for this reason.

I want to go fishing with you all the time, but there is not enough time to do that. I am concerned about everything going on in this nation and in the world. Now I am worried about IOWC, so there just isn't enough time. I expect you to make even more effort than you have ever done before. Have you done the things I've already instructed you about? Does the Coast Guard of your city like you? Do they have a concept that Moonies are doing bad things or good things? There is a universal law. The easy way will never win. The hard-working way will never fail. What is the easy way? That is the losing side. Alternatively, you have the hard-working way. No matter how difficult the task, he who pursues this way will be successful. That's the truth.

So, what do you think? Some of you older and more experienced members, do you need a bigger boat? How big? Yes, you need to go beyond the training level of the Good Go. If you take the project and make it a success, then you can ask for and receive support. It's not a problem. However, you have to make up your mind that you will do it. Then, it is really no problem. It's no problem to build a 120 foot boat; we are already making the foundation for it to happen. We have to think about making that kind of large boat with fiberglass. Do you want that kind of boat? Okay then, make your own personal foundation first.

Those who are over thirty-five, raise your hands. Only a few of you raised your hands. You are all so young! You can still go to the army at your age. When you are as young as you are, you have to go through many experiences that will be part of your life. Do you mind? Sometimes you are working long hours, getting up early, going to bed very late. Well, you have to learn how to support yourself and your family. This is your training time. You never know what I am preparing for, what I might be doing next. I have already met many important people in my life. So many people are against me. They pray, "please God, help me in my effort against Reverend Moon." They have very strange concepts of me and because their prayer isn't based on really knowing me, God cannot answer them. God cannot answer prayers that are not based on truth.How about you? Are you a brave man or not? I faced all my enemies. How about you? Look at this brother. You are too small. How can you overcome those tough fishermen who might try to stop you from working on the ocean? If you are too small, it will be difficult for you. You will have to work twice as hard as the big men, you will have to have twice the spirit in order to succeed.

Can you do what I have instructed you to do this time? Do you feel your mission is to become a good person in front of the mayors of your towns? Unless you can establish good relationships with them you will never succeed. This is my absolute instruction to you. Those who are the chief of police and the mayor are already successful people in their city. You have to make a good foundation with them by earning their support. You have to go through them and with their assistance, make something successful happen. You have to come to the point of being able to call up the mayor at his office anytime. Unless you build that kind of relationship, you cannot become a public person for that city. I too have gone this course. I have tried to deal with Nixon, Ford, Carter and Reagan. I spoke out strongly about Carter and clearly told him what was wrong with America. Wrong is wrong, bad is bad. You have to tell them clearly. I have tried to meet with every important person in society. Even if they didn't respond, I tried to meet with them. Some of them would never see me. Inside they feel some kind of fear, but I'm not out to get them. However, they sense that I will tell them the truth. Then, how about you? Why don't you see the small-time mayor in your town? He isn't as big as the President.

Really, it's nothing. Just walk in. You have to make some kind of relationship. Go in there and make some tea. Have an afternoon visit. Make the atmosphere delightful. You can do that. It's more difficult for me. I don't know the customs that well. In that sense, I am very much a stranger here in America, but you are familiar. You just go in there and make friends.

I started the science conference years ago. At first it didn't seem like much. It took lots of thought, money and manpower to make that project go. In the beginning we had almost nothing. If you have a strong conviction and know within yourself that what you are doing is a righteous thing, nothing will stop you. You will meet difficult problems and you will overcome them, and you will just keep right on going. That's the way of life. No matter where I go, no matter what kind of clothing I wear, no matter how humble I look, I feel comfortable. Many times I have gone to the grocery store wearing my fishing clothes and people have come up to me asking, "Do you know when Reverend Moon is coming back here to fish?" That is a wonderful experience for me. No one even really knows what I look like. I prefer not to be known and seen like that. I can be natural then.

Sometimes I go to the department store and I am not even wearing shoes, just some house slippers. The sales girls who are working don't even notice I am there. I go to the department stores in particular when the sales are on. I want to buy the expensive shoes for less than twenty dollars. I am wearing shoes that are made out of snakeskin which are supposed to be more than 100 dollars. I will let you guess how much I paid for them. People don't think of me wearing sales items. I have a big, old Lincoln car, but I don't mind going straight to McDonald's with it. It's a long car. No other cars in the parking lot are like that. Such cars are usually in the high class Chinese restaurants, but for me, this kind of meal is normal. I enjoy treating the members to high class places, but I don't like to eat at those places myself. McDonald's is the usual place for me. If I explained precisely and clearly where we are going to be in just ten years you wouldn't work so hard, so I'm not going to tell you. What is precious is that I am teaching you how to do it yourself. I don't want you to miss out in getting due credit for the result. So then, will you work hard and make your own success? How many times have you prayed to God with fear in your heart? I pray like that all the time. I am serious to the point of my life. What do you feel when you go out to sea in a boat? What do you think about, what do you pray about? These are precious moments for your life.

We have to know the difference between farming on the land and going out to sea. Especially on the sea, you have to depend on God and the spiritual world to guide you. Farmers also depend on such things because they have to sense when is the right time to plant and harvest. They have to know a great deal about the weather, but on the ocean you have to be even more spiritual and religious. You are completely dependent upon nature.

I love to have that kind of experience with nature and God. That is why I go to sea. Even Mother sometimes doesn't understand why I go so much to the ocean. Sometimes I am so tired. However, I understand the heart of God. Without help from spiritual world, you cannot do anything on the ocean. I know this point very well.

Do you think that God is helping you? What do you think? Is God helping me? If there is a difference, why is it so? If you understand why there is a difference, you are on the way. The ocean even misses me and I too miss the ocean. The spiritual world assists me and God comes very close to me. There is a deep bond of love that is there. I make an appointment to go out on the sea and I am anxious to get there because Heavenly Father is waiting there with intense longing for me.

I push you so hard and it seems to be cold-hearted and severe. Maybe you feel God should stop helping me because I am so harsh with you. It looks harsh to you. When you look at things as they come to you, from the front side, it looks like persecution and hardship. However, as you look back you can see that actually God was caring for you, giving you direction and guidance for your life. An ordinary person cannot receive the kind of blessing that God and

I want to give to you. Do you understand this point? Love is a discipline. It is not an easy thing to do. You cannot just love some people and not others. You have to develop three things: a high spiritual antenna, a keen sense and mind for analyzing, and many experiences in life. Those three elements are necessary. You have to think of these things clearly right now. You are young and should fulfill what you are doing with your whole heart.

Specific Instructions for Ocean Church

When you go back, are you going to work even harder? I sometimes feel your words are cheap. Today, you say you will do it, but when you come back again next time, you might say, "Oh, we're sorry because we didn't really fulfill it." So, do your best. Please do your absolute best. You have studied my previous instructions, but I want to give you more specific instructions today. Please write them down:

A: SELF TRAINING AND MANAGEMENT

1: Train yourself
Before you train others, train yourself first. If you think you are already well-trained and disciplined, you have already made a big mistake.

2: Practice
Practice what you learn immediately. Fishing must be learned through experience.

3: Management of boats
Take care of your boat with a sincere heart and prayer. You have to make sure that you clean the boat and manage the boat. Learning comes through practice and training yourself. This is all under self-discipline. This summer you are going to stay and sleep on the boat. That is also part of the training. The boat is the place for your training. You have to learn how to

love your boat, how to really cherish it. Then it will provide for you everlasting memories for which you will always have a special fondness.

4: The boat is your objective purpose.

The boat is your life. You have to take care of it with just as much love as you would give your wife. Each day, before going out, you have to make a checklist of what is needed. You have to check each thing in order. By doing this, you must make sure that everything is in good, perfect working order. You cannot have the boat break down. You have to maintain a constant check list and go over it every day. Make sure you have the proper oil and gas, everything. If you do not properly maintain your boat, you may die. It is absolutely that serious. You will be out on the water and something may break down. This should never happen. Do you understand clearly?

B: RAISING UP MEMBERS

1: Witness to others (and create yourself)

When you are witnessing to others you are also creating yourself. As you educate others, you are also educating yourself. Therefore, in order for you to reach your own perfection, you must raise others up along the way. If you bring 100 people and educate all of them, you become the person who can manage 100 people. You will grow and create yourself by that same amount. Membership is the foundation. From there you can raise funds for your programs and develop your programs. Without membership, you cannot do much of anything.

2: Teach the future plan clearly

Make this your motto, "Let us prosper together, you and I." You have to clearly teach the vision for the future and share it with your members.

3: Move towards the great promise of the fishing industry
I have already explained the tremendous potential and future of the fishing industry in America. You have to develop it at all costs.

4: Create the local support group
Create the five member group for each boat and form a committee organization that will guide the ocean related interests of your coastal city.

C: OBTAIN THE SUPPORT OF THE LOCAL LEADERS

1:Create the sponsorship to restore your city
Find at least one good civic leader who will sponsor your committee and support it. Unless you create that kind of sponsorship you cannot give away the boats and let them be used for the public purpose. The restoration of such people, your mayor and local leaders, is very important for the restoration of your coastal cities.

2: Re-develop the coastal city itself

3: Educate those who follow

4: Bring Unification to your city
Prevent divisions in your city. Unite those who care about the future of your city. Especially prevent the use of your city as a port for illegal smuggling.

5: Education and Fishing business
One supports the other. Ocean Church members, you have to eat don't you? Your programs cannot be successful without economic support of some kind. You have to create that support.

D: OCEAN RELATED CONCERNS

1: Import and Export

Study the relationships involved in import and export. You don't know much about this area, but it is very important.

2: Process factory

Study about process factories and the fish processing industry.

3: Other related industries

Learn about ocean related industries and equipment, such as netmaking, tackle and fishing gear in general.

4: Research Institute

Ocean Church should develop a research institute. You have to use the boats, take them out and accomplish something with them. That is your foundation. Unless you follow this direction, you cannot fulfill my idea for your future. You really have to study the different ways of fishing, such as longlining. Check into the kinds of baskets you have to use. Study the lines and hooks. You have to check and study and learn everything. Then improve the system.

Although I made the course for UTS graduates to go first to CARP, Ocean Church and then state leadership, those graduates who have special desire and ability can settle down in Ocean Church. This is how serious I am for the success of Ocean Church. I want the kind of member who is deeply interested in the ocean.

These are my specific instructions. I am serious about all these things and want you also to be serious with me. Use the boats for which you have been given responsibility. Go to sea. This is the only way you will make your foundation. I have given you my direct instructions, but you have to think about, find out and create ways to catch fish. You have to learn about longlining, gillnetting, and all different kinds of fishing. You have to practice and find out.

If you are in Ocean Church, that must be your focus. If you come to Ocean Church, that is your primary concern and mission. Don't go the complicated way in life. If you have more than one mission, you have to put them in order of priority. Move quickly between two or more projects. Make sure, though, that you accomplish your major goal. I want to establish a clear tradition for the graduates of the PhD program. When they finish their studies, they should come and experience Ocean Church.

They can go to the local cities and meet the Mayor and civic leaders with the members. I am concerned that Ocean Church not only be a fishing project, but a religious movement as well. The PhD graduates have studied theology and can explain our ideas in a clear and precise manner. However, in order to become a true PhD in the spiritual sense, you have to go through many, many experiences. So, think of yourself as going through my own special school. This is my intensive course for the spiritual PhD.

I have a special PhD program for you. For everyone. You have to pass that program before you are qualified to be a church leader. You may have a PhD, but that is just external knowledge. You have to also learn internal knowledge. You at least have to pass through the ocean-going experience. This course doesn't just apply to you, but to anyone who wants to teach, lecture, or guide others in the spiritual life. There are many graduate students in other church departments and they have important roles, but if necessary, I would take them out of their positions and put them in a boat. We should witness to the professors in those areas and let them take on the responsibility.

I am sending many PhD students to work in New ERA while they are still studying, but the first one to graduate from the doctorate course is our example today. It's important to understand the core point. He should go to the local cities and witness with the members to the leaders of that city. Now, it should be clear that I want to make Tyler into a great person. He isn't such a tough kind of man, so he needs to go to the ocean. From now on he has to learn everything that the members already know.

However, he is worried because he also has to teach at UTS and he has responsibilities with New ERA. Why should he worry? Don't worry! It's simple. You know you have to go fishing this summer, so just go out. Don't be so complicated. Only ride on the boat, only catch the fish. That's all! Ocean Church is not so difficult. I myself have many responsibilities, so I understand how this brother feels, and I know how you feel when you receive so many detailed instructions. However, please use your time on the ocean. It is necessary. Otherwise, why would I do it myself? I am making a point to all these departments, such as New ERA and ICUS. I am making a point to the PhD graduates. The point is to focus on the present task and work really hard.

I have many different and difficult situations to deal with right now. So, I'm worried about all these problems. I know your situation very well. The question is, how quickly can each of you be developed into real leaders. That's a real problem. Ocean Church, you have to encourage and advertise about the summer program. Then, many people will want to come for the summer program. The summer program is a core training program. If the Ocean Church members, if your own manpower cannot do it, then I will organize the sisters, woman power. At this same time, I am preparing and thinking about a boat run by computerized electronics. It isn't any problem. Physical power is not important. Dedication is important. You can make up for power in many ways. So, if you cannot accomplish, I will find other members who will.

Some of the most famous fishermen in the world are Koreans. The Japanese are very good too, but they don't take many chances. Koreans love adventure. What ordinary people would never try, Koreans gladly do. Thus, the Korean fisherman has earned respect throughout the world today. Many fishermen are trained in Korea. They come from all over the world to be trained by Korean fishermen. Do you think you can do it? I am serious when I ask you this. I am not only asking about this summer. I am asking about your whole life. Can you do this with your whole heart? Can you do it? Will you do it? Your answer encourages me. Let us go forward. Let us pray.

Who Will Inherit the Ocean?

July 3rd, 1983 --- Gloucester

HOW MANY of you have never seen me before? Please raise your hands. Thank you. I came by boat today and it was rolling quite heavily. There was a dense fog, so my eyes are not yet in focus. The trip took one and a half hours from Provincetown. As I came from there I couldn't help but think, "how critical it is to know the direction." In that fog, all we had was the compass. So, by the direction of one wheel we traveled through the fog. How appropriate it is that life is exactly like that.

Mankind has been searching for its direction in many different ways all throughout the earth from generation to generation--the entire history of mankind. By now, man has tried everything and failed everything, and has pretty much given up. Nothing has satisfied his search, but now, we can narrow things down and be more clear ourselves. Before we have direction, we have to have our destination, our purpose. We first have to have our purpose before we are concerned about the direction.

Before we conclude how we live our life, we first have to conclude for what reason we live our life. This has been the question which all mankind has asked since the beginning. Since religious people at least accept God, they can say that their life should somehow serve God's purpose. However, look at those people who don't even believe in God. No one has been able to really teach them about their life.

165

The Purpose of Life

This question has been raised millions of times and even great scholars have not been able to answer it. Here you are, just ordinary people, and even more than that, you are just ordinary Moonies. Do you know the answer? Do you know for what purpose you live? You might say to me, "Well Father, we live to fulfill the purpose of creation," because you have some understanding of the Principle. What really is that purpose? In our church, when we think about God's providence we immediately think about establishing the four-position foundation. The perfection of the purpose of God is the perfection of the four-position foundation. And what is that term? What does that mean?

First, man and woman become perfect and then God can realize his ideal. What is that ideal? When two--one man and one woman--are united in perfect love, that is God. Do you understand? When man and woman are united together in perfect love, there it is, that's, God. What does the love of man and woman center upon? The man? Or like it is in America, upon the woman? No, you don't think so? Then, who is that love centered upon? You are shouting out, "God," and yes, that's right. The love of man and woman, the love between them, is centered upon God.

Well, somehow man and woman are united, but where does love come from? Does it first come from man or from woman? Neither. Then, to whom does that love belong? You are right again to say, "God." So, to come into contact with that love, you cannot do with it whatever you will. You have to cherish it and respect it, because it is not yours to begin with. It comes from somewhere other than yourself. Then, how does love come to you? Does it come directly to you, just to you? Does it come directly from God? How does love come to you? The man may have lots of love, but it comes from God through his spouse. It's really easy to understand. Here is a man. He is equipped with everything, but by himself there is no satisfaction. In order to have love, he must have someone. That is the nature of love. When you think about love, realize that it comes from your spouse, not from you. It is the same for man and for woman. There first has to come give and take action, then unity and then love emerges. If you have love, it is always because of someone else. You should think about that.

With love, there is always some force to push it and some force to pull it. Here is a man and a woman, meeting each other in first love. The man completely gives to the woman and the woman gives completely to the man. They sacrifice themselves for each other. Then, where is God? In the center. God is the force which brings that man and woman together and moves them to give to one another.

In the center, God fills up everything. There is no need for discussion about who is greater, man or woman, or if they are equal or not equal. Both man and woman reach to God in the center, but look, they reach from opposite directions. In any motion, you must have a center and an axis. That is God. The axis of man and woman, of the universe, is God. Every man, every woman must be centered on God. Every family, tribe, clan and culture must be centered on God. Every nation, world and even the universe and cosmos must be centered upon God.

Then, if God is the center, what must that center be focused upon. What is the center? Power? Money? What will hold together everyone, even those of the past to those of the future? Well, how does life begin? How does it start in the first place? From the very origin, how did we come into being? From love. Where do individuals come from? You come from your parents. Do you come from their life or from their love? Life or love? Then, what are you? You are the participants in the love of your parents. That is why you can never separate from your parents. The relationship of natural law is that parents are willing to die for the sake of their children. We see that all the time in the animal world. The mother or the father fight to the death to protect their offspring.

What about man, the highest being on earth? In that aspect, man must yet acquire the respect of all creation. Children cannot exist without first having parents. Their life comes from their parents. If their parents are united in perfect love, there would never be a separation of those two people. The father's love and the mother's love together become the replica of God's love. This is the explanation of being. If parents and children understand this, they can never separate from each other. They live together and die together. Anything which is separate from God's love does not truly exist. As simple as it is, no one has known this absolutely for sure until now.

The husband would love his wife as he would love God. The wife would love her husband as she would love God. Then, they would love their children and their children would love them, all in the love of God. This is the four-position foundation, the perfection of the love of God. That is the purpose of our life. Once man and woman come together in this love, they cannot separate. And once they have children in such love, the children cannot be separated from them. When we know this and see what we see today, it is truly a serious and grave matter. It is a painful tragedy. One-half of American families are suffering separation. All children want to live with their parents' love forever, but they are denied this one simple and basic thing. There is no greater crime than this. How can a husband and wife separate? They are breaking God's love. The children are lost. The only name for this tragedy is Satan. What is Satan? He came and broke apart God's love. Nothing else. We have to establish the standard absolutely opposite from that. When you come to have love between you and your spouse, you must raise up that love and keep it. Why is love so precious that it has to be regarded so highly? For one thing, love, and love alone, can motivate life. Nothing motivates more than love. When love awakens you, your eyes and ears and all your senses are focused. You are not looking at two or three different things at once, but only at love and love alone. You don't need a translation for that. You know. Mind and body become one when love awakens you. The power of love can unite your spirit and physical body. Without love, your mind and body can never reach full unity. Without love the spiritual world and physical world would not be able to come together. That explains why God created man. God must have man before even He is excited to love. If God didn't have a purpose in creating man, He would be just a mischievous being with no value. He had to have a goal and a purpose for all that He created.

What is your direction as a man? Your direction is to meet woman. Well, why don't you look around. There are lots of wonderful men and lots of wonderful women. Why don't the men just find another great man and go live with him? Why don't the women find some other great woman and live with her? You are frowning about that. Why? Since you have this explanation, you understand the formula of the universe. Anything which defies that formula defies life and eventually perishes.

Love comes from God and life comes from Him too. Love and life are the same. The quality of love is the quality of life. When we go with the natural law we become part of the universe and contribute to it. Then, we grow larger and larger. However, those who live against that law become smaller and smaller until they no longer even exist.

What is the purpose then? It is to build the foundation of love, the four-position foundation. Here, all points meet; God, men, women and children. What more could you want? Here, there are no separate bank accounts, no separate ownership. The father belongs to the mother and the mother belongs to the father and together they belong to God. And the children belong to the parents and to God. It's so simple and so reasonable.

Why do you wash your face in the morning? You should look at your face and ask that question. Your face answers, "I want to be intoxicated in true love." Your eyes and ears want to feel the intoxication of love. Once love is in action, you don't mind anything. The man doesn't mind the woman smelling strange and the woman doesn't mind the man smelling even like old dead fish. This is the most important thing in life. The man who jeers at women or looks sideways at other women besides his wife is the one Satan likes to be inside of. On the other hand, the man who can only look at his wife and see the whole universe in her is the one God wants to dwell within. What is the virtue of man? What is the virtue of woman? The true love that they offer to each other. What is a perfect man or a perfect woman? One who brings his mind and body into perfect union.

The Ocean and the Future

What is the value of a person? Look at me. What is my value? I am a religious leader. Many people get angry about me and say, "Why doesn't this man just stay in the church? Why does he come out fishing and why does he do so many other things?" I sometimes think about that. I could put on a robe and stay in the church all day long. That would be very easy. I wouldn't have to worry about all the things I have initiated. There are so many projects now and more to come. If Christianity had fulfilled all its goals and ideals, I would not have that much to do, but that is not the case. Instead, without even thinking deeply about my work, Christians have come out strongly against me. Who has ever supported me?

Even though members in the Unification Church have supported me, I had to first initiate and explain everything. Even my own family needs time to understand me. Why is it so difficult for the world to accept me? It is because many religious leaders would have to change their own ideas to accept me and they don't want to do that. Some people admire me and want to help me, but they are also afraid of me because of my penetrating mind and spirit.

Communism has a system of thought behind it, an ideology that guides it, but democracy does not really have such a unifying thought. However, Reverend Moon's thought surpasses the ideology of communism and this is very clear to them. They are not afraid of physical power such as the United States military power. The race is already over in that area and they are the winner. However, unification philosophy is a bigger problem to them. They are far more afraid of that.

I have pioneered a new path in every area, beginning with thought or philosophy. I have also demonstrated how to begin economic projects, business and technical projects such as the factories in Korea and Germany. Then, why did I start Ocean Church? Why have I given it such importance? You can see, I am working day in and day out on the ocean. Why am I doing that? You have heard me speak about this before.

The ocean is an orphan. It has no master, no real owner who loves and takes care of it. The fishing industry is also going under. The industry can't move an inch, it's so tight. In a few years it will be difficult for man to live off the land alone. The population is now almost four billion. It will increase by ten-fold. What will happen? The land itself will be crowded. There will be less space to farm and more people to feed. The population problem is one of two very serious questions. The other is pollution. To me, the problem is how to see these questions in a new light. The worst aspect of pollution is in the air, exhaust fumes from cars, factories and such things. In the future, there will be a limit upon anything that produces exhaust, even cooking. Any kind of extra smoke or gas exhaust will not be tolerated.

That means that we will try to eat foods without so much cooking, which means we will eat more raw foods, raw vegetables, raw fish. Anyway, it's good for their health, so people will turn to it. For a while, mankind may try to escape to space and live up there, but the difficulties and expenses will be too much and he will come right back to earth. Then, man will have to turn to the ocean. It is only a matter of time. The future of the ocean is inevitable. Is fish good for the diet? Ten or twenty years ago, Americans never even dreamed about eating anything raw, much less fish. Now they are going to Japanese restaurants and trying out the sushi and sashimi.

If fish is going to be the main source of the human diet, what kind of fish would be the best to supply it? We have to produce a large fish and utilize all its qualities. What kind of fish should we use? Whales? Tunas? And what else? Shark! Actually, whales are not good to use for feeding lots of people. They are too large. They only give birth to one calf per cow and it takes a long time for them to gestate.

Let's look at the tuna and the shark. They contain the tastiest kind of meat. That's true! You may not have tasted it, but I have tasted many kinds of shark in different ways. Shark is good for dry meat. It doesn't have so much fat. On the other hand, tuna has lots of oil content in the meat. So, these two kinds of fish are the best for providing a wide variety of fish taste to humans.

In Japan, they are now studying how to farm tuna. This is a very serious enterprise for them and it means a great deal for the future that we envision. Here are some things to consider. One female tuna lays about 1.5 to 3 million eggs at each spawning. Now, in the natural setting only a very few of these eggs even survive to become baby fish. Most of the eggs are eaten by predators. And then, to survive the first few years is almost as difficult, so very few tuna live to maturity.

It takes about two years for them to grow to where they can escape most dangers. A fully grown tuna can travel with speeds from seventy-five to one hundred knots. That is their "get-away" speed. However, when they are just cruising they go from twenty to thrity-five knots. That's some cruise. If you study the anatomy of the tuna you will see that they are created for speed. The shark is also capable of speed, but not at all like the tuna. All the fins fold in and the tuna takes on the shape of a torpedo. Tuna not only swim fast, but also travel great distances--all over the world.

Think about the mature tuna. It often weighs 700 or 800 pounds. If you catch just one tuna and then use the dressed meat, around 80%, which is approximately 550 to 750 pounds, you have that much meat to feed people with. Most people eat two or three pounds of meat each day, but they should eat only one or two pounds. If they were to eat like that, you could feed 500 or 600 people each day with one tuna. If you catch 100 tuna, you feed that many more people.

You can use every part of the fish for something. Shark skin can be used for jackets and shoes. The skin is very durable and rugged. The teeth can be made into jewelry. Why not? One day, Daikan came up with the bright idea to dry and smoke the shark meat. Later on he gave up, but that was the right idea. All parts of the fish can be used. You can crush up the left-over parts and make it into fish powder. With that you can make bread and feed people. That will not only fill them up, but provide protein as well. Think about what this would mean in Africa. There is no such thing as waste when it comes to fish.

Well then, if we are to catch hundreds or even thousands of tuna, where can we farm them? You cannot put them into a fenced-in place. The whole ocean can be populated with tuna. Then, the fishermen will have to develop the means to harvest them. Tuna sushi and sashimi are beginning to be popular. Who discovered this way of making fish for eating? I once thought to myself that if the white people had first discovered tuna sushi, there would be no way for the world to have tuna in the future. They would have taken all of them by now.

We can plant all kinds of food on the ocean floor. We have to study about that, but the possibilities only stop with us. The ocean is that vast--our minds are too small for it yet. The future is coming and there is so much there. Ironically, young people in America are leaving the fishing way of life. Look at Gloucester. It used to be the hub of the fishing world, but now it is run-down. It is not because the fish ran away. Young people ran away. That's what is happening.

Many fishermen go out and fish long days and weeks. They come back and haven't made so much money. When that happens, the wife and husband often fight. Then, he goes out and comes back and one day the wife has run away. So, the young people and the wives are running from the fishing way of life. That means eventually the fisherman himself will run away.

When a serious man loses his wife, he no longer thinks about marrying again. The same thing happens when the reason to continue fishing is gone. The serious fisherman just gives up on fishing altogether. Today, you can see so much corruption going on in the once prosperous fishing harbors. The Mafia is prevailing, there are buyers who fix the prices against the fishermen and cheat them at the dock, and drug smuggling is a problem in every harbor.

Uplifting the American Fishing Industry

By and large, America's trading tradition is based on the Merchant Marines. America and Mexico should have an inseparable tie to the ocean, and to each other. This is not something new. We should have known about this. Your ancestors were dead serious, much more than you now realize. They suffered religious persecution and so they came here, risking their lives. They had no guarantee that they would make it here alive, much less survive here.

The evidence is everywhere. The biggest economic centers are not in the center of America where Chicago is, but right on the coast. For example, New York with the Hudson River and Bay, San Francisco and Los Angeles. It's evident that the ocean is vital to the economy of the nation.

If the jet had not been introduced, our dependence upon the ocean would be even greater. Can we afford not to care about the ocean? Look at the boat building industry. They all moved down to Alabama or in that general region in order to find cheaper labor, but almost all companies have closed down. Now, our movement is starting companies there. Why? Because the re-development of the ocean is soon coming and we have to be ready for that. Not only in America, but in other nations as well. We are developing boats for fishing in Brazil and boats for long-lining tuna. Now, everyone else is giving up on the fishing industry, but someday soon, people will see that the only person who has a pattern for success is Reverend Moon. That is why we have to make a foundation now. Then, people will someday wake up and see that we are way ahead. In the world today, when an industry goes down, that is when people leave it and give up. However, that is not our way. That is when we really buckle down and invest. There are four great fishing grounds in the world. Three of them are right here near the United States. People can fish anywhere in the world, but the American fisherman can easily go to the best places. Japan and Germany, even the Soviet Union desperately want to catch fish for their own markets, but America makes it very difficult for other fishermen to come in. However, the market for fish in America is much smaller than in other countries. It doesn't make sense.

The best way would be to combine fishing-ground rights and market strategies between three nations: Japan, Germany and America. If these three countries could make a responsible agreement towards the fisheries today, the rest of the world could center on that. At any rate, these other countries are coming in to fish, and this makes the position of the American government so difficult. They don't want people coming in, but there are so few American fishing boats. Since Americans aren't utilizing these great fishing grounds, the other countries that really invest a lot in fishing come into these waters anyway. America is in a dilemma to defend it's fishing waters. Who can step in and help this situation? Reverend Moon can. He will organize young people and send them out to develop the American fishing industry. This is my vision.

Eventually, the Moonies will be a strong and positive force in the industry, not to destroy it, but to bring it up to international standards. So, even though the American government doesn't want Moonies fishing and becoming successful, they will encourage us because of this situation. Now, Gloucester wants Reverend Moon to leave, but at the same time, they want to keep the same price standard for their tuna.

In Korea, they make the best fishing equipment and gear. Japanese fishermen are now saying that the best fishermen are the Koreans because they are so tough and courageous. The Koreans have guts when they fish. They'll go for a huge catch and strain the net, even if it costs them a million dollars for the net. When they lose, it's tough, but when they gain, they really gain. The Japanese don't do that. They compute and calculate very carefully. Sometimes they miss the chance.

Coming from that background in Korea, I noticed the fishing gear companies in America and couldn't help but think of how to make them better. There are many boats in the New York area, but so few equipment stores in New York City. We could distribute fishing gear so easily in America. Eventually we could build a highrise in New York centering on the fishing equipment business. In every area the fishing industry needs improvement. The ocean industry is open to us. If we make our foundation now, nobody could even think about catching up to us in the future. As time goes on, people will say, "No one can even compete with the Moonies." For example, look at the tuna fishing situation as it is now. People used to wake up around 6:00 or 7:00 a.m. and go out. However, we have been waking up at 3:00 or even 2:00 a.m. People look at our hard work and they have to say, "The ocean business is for Moonies, no way we can beat that." When I first came here, more than eight years ago, the tuna price was five or ten cents per pound. Now, the price recently jumped to two dollars per pound. We bought a great deal of tuna and helped to raise the price. Then, all the other buyers had to follow. That's exactly what happened. From the businessman's viewpoint, Reverend Moon is bad, but they never concerned themselves about the fishermen. From the fishermen's viewpoint, it is another story.

The price of tuna should go up to $5.00 per pound and even more. This is important for the entire industry. If tuna prices go up, then other fish prices have to go up. Fishermen in other areas have a better chance to make money. Today, fishermen catch tons of fish, but they only get thirty or forty cents per pound. Let's look at ourselves. We are buying tuna at a great cost and even though we are catching tuna, we are not making money. Why should we do such a program? Think about it this way. A tuna weighing around 1,000 pounds, (and with tuna at $5.00 per pound) is a $5,000 tuna. Don't you think this would attract many young Americans to come here and fish? Since you have already gained the experience, you can teach them. Think of how the coastal towns in America will benefit from our work.

I have a clear idea, but most Americans have not understood me. I cannot make you do anything just by telling you. So, I have sacrificed myself; I have worked day and night to show you how to do it. The need is there. People understand that, but they won't do what is necessary. I had to come along and show you. Then, you too have to show them.

I know what motivates people. You can't just say, "Father, I can't do that." I have already shown you how it is to be done. People try to keep up with me, but even those in their twenties and thirties can't do it. They ask me, "Father, how can you do that?" I am always thinking, "I am doing this for those who are yet to come. This tradition will stand for thousands of years and millions of people can live by it." Therefore, I don't mind the pace that I have to keep.

I have dreamed of training women captains in America. When those women go to sea for a month and the husbands don't run away, what will happen? That husband will be longing and longing for his wife to return. That husband won't run away after three days, but instead wait for his wife and rejoice to meet her. When I came to

America, I realized that the Divine Principle would be best taught by showing the people exactly what it is. Then, if there was one person who inherited this tradition, everyone would understand my teaching. The woman would be happy with such a husband and that man would be happy to have such a wife. That's how much power the Principle has. When the man is happy, the woman is also dancing. Is that bad? It's BAD! No? You are shouting "GOOD!" at me. Since you are speaking the truth, you win. Do you like that? Well, what if I don't like that? You are really shouting at me now. So, you know. You know the truth. You think I am a 100% genuinely smart man. And how about you? If you weren't smart, you wouldn't have followed me, but here you are. In this declining industry, everyone is bailing out. However, our movement is spending millions of dollars every year. We are spending and investing in America, researching boats and the fishing industry, teaching and educating young people, and developing fisheries.

True Love for the Ocean

The real Moonie is the one who loves the ocean. Why? Because the head of the Unification movement loves the ocean. Reverend Moon loves the ocean. So, if you are a Moonie, you have to come to that point as well. What about you women? Are you a real Moonie or a make-believe one? How about you men?

The child inherits from the Parent. How about you? Have you inherited from me? You didn't know that I have been fishing way ahead of you, days, months and years ahead of you. If you worked harder than me, my conscience would bother me. I am hard on you, pushing you, but still you feel love from me. That's because I am already working way beyond you.

Those who really think that I love you, even when I push you so hard, raise your hands. Why did you raise your hands? Are you crazy? When I see someone like you, I am relieved. All put together, do you feel fortunate to be here? When you first came here, you probably secretly made a painful face. Americans are very diplomatic. They don't show how they really feel. You probably smiled really big, but inside you wondered about doing this.

Of all the fish to go after, why did we choose the tuna? Because I found that once you catch a tuna, you never forget it. You can catch many other kinds of fish and forget about it, but never the tuna. So, this is the best way to catch young people. You are Americans. You are here to stay. Many guests may come, but eventually they have to go away. They may come from many different countries. However, you Americans have to inherit your own future. For the rest of your life this is your responsibility. This is a really great responsibility.

Once you hook and catch a tuna, you can never forget it for the rest of your life. Every occasion that reminds you of that moment connects you to all the events that surrounded it. Once you connect to the ocean, you never forget it. We go out and everyone looks at us and shouts, "Moonie, Moonie." But once we catch tuna and no one else gets a strike, they have to look at us and think again. As we come by with a tuna on the line, we have to yell, "Get out of the way!" At that moment, they have to do that.

After that, they are silent. When a small *One Hope* boat has a tuna and is going towards a big yacht, you just shout out, "Get out of here!" Then, they have to get off their anchor. At that moment we can feel very proud. We are earning our way; we are earning their respect.

Suppose you lose a tuna after a hook-up. When you go back home and someone else is there with a tuna, you don't even want to look at it. That kind of experience is very precious. Then, your dreams are consumed by the thought of getting a tuna. You can't think without thinking about a tuna. "Tomorrow, tomorrow," your mind is always thinking about catching a tuna the next day. You have to learn how to live and pray and sweat for tomorrow. You have to pray even for the tuna.

Tuna also have spirit. If you really love the ocean and love the tuna, you can attract them to you. It works this way. When you cut fish for chum, don't just cut them. Think about them and talk to them, "Since you are a small fish, I will cut you up and send you down for the large fish. I am fishing for the sake of mankind and would go down there myself, but you are doing this for me and I am grateful to you."

When you pray like that and think like that, it makes the difference. Everyday, every action becomes special. You should say, "I am sorry to catch the tuna, but I am doing it for mankind." You are doing what others do, but your heart must be different about it. When you see me catch a tuna, harpoon it and bring it to the land, you may wonder, "Why does a religious leader do that to the tuna?" I do it as an offering. This will help the providence, this will save lives from further suffering. We can't joke around and sleep on those boats. Our work is even more serious than the other fishermen's.

Only twice have I ever laid down to rest on the *New Hope*. I had to at one time because I had a severe headache, but even then I prayed and apologized with great sincerity. Allan Hokanson was so tired one time that he was dozing off at the wheel. So, I allowed him to take a rest at that time because to steer the boat is a serious matter. I took responsibility for that and then, Allan could rest. Our work is so serious, you have to know that.

The Special One Hope Boat

To catch a tuna, I had to develop a way to communicate with them. Sometimes, there is a small craft warning and still I go out to fish. Why? Because I don't want the members to look at difficult weather and be afraid to go out. You have to be concerned about safety, but you also have to know how serious our work is. We cannot go out just because the weather is calm. The goal is very difficult to reach and very far away. We have to go through so much training to get there. The boat is one way to train. The *One Hope* boat is very tough. It won't sink. I wanted it that way. Twenty people can ride in it and flood the vessel, but still the front part will stay up. With your life jacket on you can just hang on and the boat will support you. This already happened with several people in a *One Hope* boat, so we know for sure the boat is very safe and strong. We made it that way. When we run into somebody or something, the boat doesn't break. I designed the boat, but behind me is a deeper inspiration for it. This is a multi-purpose boat. You can easily trailer the boat. It can be a speed boat, a sight-seeing boat, a tuna boat, a fishing boat, a teaching boat, any kind of boat. It can go to many kinds of programs and any kind of place. There is no limit or specific way to use these boats.

The *New Hope* is not such a good boat for catching tuna. It is too big and makes the job somewhat complicated, but the *One Hope* boat is a perfect size for the job. You just get away from the lines and the tuna gets tired from pulling the boat. Before I designed this boat I researched everywhere: Japan, Alaska and Germany.

We built this boat with specific things in mind. One thing is that the *One Hope* has to be able to cut through the waves. Then, it has to have speed. It cannot roll when it's going fast. Some boats have this problem and I wanted to prevent such mistakes from happening. For these and other reasons I researched for two years just on the design of the *One Hope*.

Now, I watch the boat and I am very happy. When you turn as you are going fast, it holds very well. Some boats would throw the man out, but the *One Hope* has real balance. There are a thousand tiny details that make this boat very different from other boats. However, when I first brought up the idea, Americans said, "Father, you need an expert to design such a boat."

The first one was built by members who didn't even know one thing about building boats. Such a thing can never be done by other people, but now as we build more and more boats, the members are looking and seeing that a bold new tradition is being set in making fiberglass boats of this size. We use the highest quality parts and this makes the boat a very expensive machine. You have to think seriously. Not only is it expensive, but it is also built by the sacrifice and hard work of the members. You have to realize that I designed and built that boat out of my own sweat and tears. You cannot just get on the boat and take off. This is the wrong attitude. In the years to come these boats will become very famous. You don't see it now, but this is true. You have to have a serious attitude about your boat and you have to have great pride in your boat. In the future, the record of your boat will be studied. People will ask, "How many fish did this *One Hope* catch?" One of these boats will catch the most and be very,

very famous. Which one will that be? You have to do things with the thought of the future.

The Kind of Leader the World Needs

We are not playing. This is very, very serious. No one knows me. You don't know how serious I am. I made a condition in the beginning. More than twenty days I fished for tuna. I had to catch a tuna. There was a reason. Every day, every day, I went out. You don't know how serious that time was. When we finally caught the tuna, you don't know the feeling inside when we said, "Mansei!"

Now the Moonie members go out and catch a tuna. You just laugh and smile. You don't know the meaning of it. I am looking for the member who is strong and really researches how to catch the tuna. I have thought deeply about modern civilization. What kind of leader will fix the foundation upon which civilization stands? I have that kind of purpose in teaching you how to catch tuna. You have to be clear and pure. I have to make you pure. You are just looking around at the other boats, but you don't understand why you are out there. You have to dedicate your heart, otherwise, there is no meaning.

You have to endure hardships. It's a serious matter. I have been thinking seriously all my life. Tuna are not easy to catch. If you were to catch them so easily, it would not have such a meaning. I want to find members who can understand the meaning of catching tuna. I want those people to give lectures. I don't have time to always explain everything. If you inherit my heart this season and have a victorious season, you will want to come back next year. Between seasons, you have to go to other places and speak to the fishermen there about catching tuna. When you go to the ocean you have to think about many serious things. You have to think about making a living.

If you catch ten tuna you have made an entire income for one year. You can support your family with one season's work. To catch ten tuna is really no problem. To catch thirty tuna can be done if you develop the skills. That kind of ability is precious. How great it is for you. How great this is for Ocean Church. You must know what is behind you when you work. Don't just work with an external attitude. You have a boat and everyday you go out to the ocean. Every time you catch a fish, think very deeply about what you are doing. You are doing this for the future of mankind. You have the *One Hope* boat. After the tuna, I want to develop fishing for three or four other species of fish. Then, you can fish the entire year. If it's too cold here, you can go further south. I have taught you the foundation for catching tuna. Now we have to study secondary species of fishing. From five years ago, I have been thinking about the kind of fish we have to research and catch. Tuna, striped bass, flounder, fluke, salmon, trout, snapper and a few others. You have to think how to support your family and take care of your children. You can take the boats and fish in any area of the coast. Fish every season of the year. If you work as hard on the ocean as you do on land, you will make twice the amount of money. You will see this happen if you practice it. You have to find out and examine it for yourself. I am deeply convinced about this way of life. It is for your future.

The fiberglass boat is going to be the future of fishing boats in America. You wait and see. It will become the standard for boats in the future, even up to eighty foot boats. If such a boat has a break or a puncture, we can fix it more easily than if it were steel. I am thinking about the future of the fishing industry in Alaska. I am determined to develop the boat that fishes best up there.

I am so serious about this providence. If the Western members don't inherit it, I will push the Japanese to take it. If they refuse to pick it up, I will offer it to the Koreans. If they miss the opportunity, I will give it to the blessed children. If they fail, then my own children will establish it. Why? Because mankind has to inherit this tradition. It is for the future of all mankind.

Inherit the Future Through the Ocean

I don't blame you if you don't understand everything today. In ten years you will understand what I am talking about. So, please just do your very best and inherit what I am doing upon the ocean. It's important for you, it's essential for mankind's future. For example, look at Tyler Hendricks. He was the first PhD graduate. As soon as he graduated, he was asked to come to Ocean Church. He couldn't believe it. I had been working for seven or eight years before I could become the top fisherman, but Tyler came along and had to inherit it in one season. No matter how tough it was, he had to do that. It's really impossible, but anyway, he had to find out what it is like.

I have been fishing now for ten years. However, I cannot do that anymore. The purpose for it is in you. You have to research what I have done here and go on from this point. The first thing that you must do is gather all the information around you. Find out about the fish, how it runs. Then, find out about the currents in the waters and the shape of the ocean floor where you are fishing. If you do that for tuna fishing, you then know how to do that for any other kind of fishing. Also, don't just take my word, or anyone's word. Find out for yourself. Never believe what others say, but first find out for yourself how the fish run and what the water is really like. You have to train your mind to think and question and research like that. That is what you must inherit from me.

Those who stay in the Gloucester area should research the catching of tuna. If you catch tuna in the morning, you have the rest of the day to do other things. Research the catching of other fish. Go out and try to catch the striped bass, the flounder and other kinds of fish. Yesterday, I caught almost 200 pounds of flounder. If you watch me you will discover what I am teaching you. I am already thinking far ahead and researching how to sell fish that are still alive. That fish can be sold for the best price directly to the restaurants. Many restaurants will keep an aquarium for the customer to choose the fish he wants for his meal that night. The best seafood restaurants will develop this system. This is not new in Japan, but will be a really new thing in America.

There will be a day in the future when the best restaurants will advertise "live fish." Even the President of the United States will express his liking for such fish. Also, we have to research about live bait. We have to develop live bait stores. This will be an enormous business in itself. However, keeping fish alive is a very difficult thing to do. That is why we began with lobster. Lobster is the most difficult to keep alive. If we find the best ways to do that, developing ways to keep fish alive will not be a problem. I am thinking of how to revive the American market. That is the market which really needs new development. We can start by keeping the fish in seawater and sending it to Japan. That will generate the funds and give us practice in the market itself. Then, we can develop the market here in America. The better seafood restaurants will quickly see the good points in having live fish tanks. We can make the market expand quickly.

You may think, "Oh Father, that is not for me," but how do you know that this won't be a success? I always think of things that everyone else never thinks of doing. Look at the *Washington Times*. No one else even thought it could be done in three years, but in less than one year, we brought it to a brilliant level of success. Everyone is admitting that.

I won't let Ocean Church members even come to the office in the future. Don't sit behind a desk! Just put my ideas into action and you will find the success I am talking about. The only hope that Unification Church has for the future lies in Ocean Church. Don't you see how serious your position is? What is the limit of the future of those who go to the ocean? I can say with complete confidence, "there is no limit." Now, Russia, Japan, South America and North America are competing, but there is no limit. We can really inherit the future through the ocean. We are people for the future. Our thinking is always for the future. So, the future is for us. In America, the retirement age is sixty-five, but I started at the age of sixty. Can you follow me? Why can't you follow me if you are so much younger than I am? You have no excuse. If you come to a difficult point, think of me when I started Ocean Church from nothing. Think of me when I went out fishing with no knowledge and then created the way to catch tuna. You have to go even beyond that.

This has to be done. For the future, someone has to do it. You are my hope. If you don't know that, you cannot understand even who you are. The one who is close to me is the one who will determine to be successful on the ocean. After telling you this, should I stay here or go on to something else? Ocean Church members, you shouldn't worry where I might be. As long as you have the same mind and desire that I have, then Ocean Church will succeed. And if you lose all hope, remember that my mind is always with you. I will never, ever forget Ocean Church.

Why We Go Tuna Fishing

August 31st, 1983 -- Gloucester

WELL, WITHOUT a doubt, everyone now knows that the Moonies have entered the fishing industry. One thing which has happened as a result of our fishing is that the fishermen can see exactly what kind of people we are. We go out in every kind of weather, rain or shine. We even have women fishing, doing just as well as the men, sometimes better than the men. The fishermen of Gloucester can't help but see that.

Surely, they have been talking about it, so the news traveled, even to the city officials, the mayor included. They know what kind of transition has taken place in the last ten years since I first came here in 1974. At that time, the typical daily working hours of the tuna fishermen went something like this: around ten o'clock in the morning they'd get out on the sea, and then come back around two o'clock in the afternoon, with or without the tuna.

At that time, there was no price for the tuna. If they caught a tuna, they'd come back to the docks, take a picture standing next to it, and then leave the fish behind. It was only five cents per pound, so it wasn't even worth the effort to try and sell it. Sometimes, the fish would just lie there on the dock until it rotted.

The fishermen also remember how the price of tuna went up every year. Just by ten to fifteen to twenty-five cents a year, or less. The price never increased by any great amount from year to year. However, this year, the price came up to close to $5.00 per pound. This trend will continue and they know it; it's almost a fact. They also realize that our movement has had an impact on this trend.

If we can catch 200 tuna at the price of $5.00 per pound, we will break even, or even do better than that. We won't have to suffer this loss that we now take every year. Please understand that there is a vision guiding our effort; we will not end up every year like this. In the next few years, we will go beyond the loss column. Don't have faith in the results before you. Have faith in the process. We are going towards a goal. Have faith in that.

Establishing the Tradition

We can suffer our losses year after year until we finally come to the gaining point, but other people cannot do that. If they lose out one or two years, they simply quit. One thing we never do is quit. That is truly our secret. Once this process reaches a certain point, we will begin to gain rather than suffer loss. When that day comes, and that day will surely come, people will establish the undisputed conclusion that as far as tuna goes, Reverend Moon is the "king of all kings."

We also know that we are the ones who value the tradition. Our tradition is always this: first to create the solid foundation. No church, no business, no family or person can be successful without a solid foundation. We know that. Even now, they begin to see it, but not as clearly as we would hope. However, in a few years, they will see very clearly what I am doing and they will know I am building up a tradition so that the fishing industry will not go up and down every year, but go solidly upward, year after year. Clearly they will begin to see that this effort is not solely for our own profit.

America has only one last frontier. That is the fishing industry. There is enormous potential in the fishing industry. Everyone knows that. 70% of the major fishing grounds in the entire world are in America. The other 30% is shared by Norway, Japan and all the other sea-going countries. You can imagine what 70% of the entire world's catch could be. It's staggering to the imagination how much that could be, if you think in terms of pounds and sizes of catch. That ocean, of which 70% belongs to America, is more than twice the size of the land we now live on. The ocean occupies two-thirds of the globe and land occupies only one-third of the earth's surface. The potential catch from the ocean produces far more protein than we could ever bring from the land. Fish, if you catch them wisely, are consistently there from year to year. If you take something out of the earth, such as oil, when you are done with it, there is nothing left. On the other hand, if you have the consciousness of harvesting fish, that industry can go on without ever stopping.

Does the average American really care about this? Not so much. They don't think about this and they don't think about what it means for the future. No American at all would ever dream that the next generation after Reverend Moon will be fishermen, but you will be, and so will be the next generation after that, and after that. Generation after generation we will become better and better fishermen. Why would we want to do that? For the sake of mankind, that is why.

Americans are not thinking like that. They are thinking, "Well, I will live this hard life, but I don't want to encourage my children to sacrifice like this." Some even stop their children from going to the ocean. Why? Because it is a hard way of living and the income is not that great. On the contrary, I am thinking of how to raise up these very same fishermen. After all, we are going into the same thing for which they have already lived all their life. We will embrace them and take care of them. As fast as we grow, we will bring them along with us.

This fishing industry is an important and vital industry, and it will become even more so in the future. Even though our church members may find something they have to attend to somewhere else, we have to make sure that American fishermen inherit the tradition and spirit of making a solid foundation from us. And they must carry on this vision, even if we are absent from it for a time.

People who are now fishing cannot find satisfaction in their work, unless they can get at least 50% more from their income through fishing than any job they might take on land. This includes working on shore or on a dock with boats. Why? On the land, you can plan what you are going to do, even though it rains or the weather is difficult. But on the ocean, you cannot plan like that. There are some days, even if you are ready to work, you cannot go out. The weather simply prevents you. Therefore, they cannot always depend on their income to be steady. That is, you have to gain at least 50% more of an income than if you worked the same amount of time on the land, in order to have an equal amount of income in the long run. They have to take in the factor of losing days due to hard weather.

However, the fact is that, in these times, fishermen put in the same amount of effort which others put in on the land, but often receive up to 50% less. Sometimes more, but usually less. The result is that most American fishermen eventually choose to work on the land the first chance they get something on land that is a little bit better than fishing. So, whoever will make this fishing industry viable has to manage some key areas.

The first is, how to sustain the working hours. We have to get up earlier than normal and to stay out as long as possible before returning. Others are working only one day, but we have to work two days to make up for our inexperience. The second is, technique. Since we have to compensate for the long hours that we put in, we have to find the better method, the faster method to bring in the fish. We have to research and study and experiment. We have to establish a new pattern of fishing. We have to study seriously several points about fishing. We have to study about the bait, the lines, how to use the lines and how to use the boat in different waters. All these things have to be studied and carried out. We have to think deeply about these things, and plan each area very thoroughly.

Tuna Fishing Techniques

Those who have joined the tuna fleet for the first time raise your hands. This is your first season. You almost outnumber the experienced members. Do you expect to catch tuna? Automatically, just like that? I don't believe in that. If I left you to do things your own way, if I didn't care and just let you go out and catch tuna however you imagine it to be done, it wouldn't work. If I left everything up to you without giving you instructions and covering every detail with you, you would have never caught one fish. I know that; you know that. Every experienced fishermen knows the same thing.

Let's think about that. The first thing that is most important in catching tuna is the boat. The *New Hope* is an example of this. It is simply too big to catch tuna and I lost several tuna because of this factor. Once the tuna bites your bait, no one knows which way it will go. It will go one way and then turn around and go the other. The *New Hope* is simply too big to change direction and go with the tuna. It's not fast enough.

There are two propellers in the back of the *New Hope*. When the tuna comes back and goes underneath the boat, it often catches against the propeller and cuts the line. The tuna is trying to escape and it's absolutely frantic. The *New Hope* is trying to move around and follow it, but because it is a bigger boat, it takes a long time to maneuver it. The lines get tangled, and when we are following the tuna, the propeller is also moving. So, the line just needs to touch it and the tuna is cut off, lost.

I thought about it for many years and I kept asking myself, "how can we improve this boat so that it's 100% able to catch tuna?" It was a very important question, because the result of those thoughts became the design for the *One Hope*. You can see that. You have already experienced the abilities of the *One Hope*. It can turn very quickly while following tuna. The boat is actually almost the same size as a tuna. You can move and fight the tuna, even going easily between many other boats. You simply cannot do these things with the *New Hope*. As you have already experienced, it is easier to manage when you tangle up the lines between your own boat and other boats.

We used to have to cut the lines all the time, but in doing that, catching a tuna became so expensive. If you cut all your lines, it is almost $1,000. I wanted to prevent that loss, not only for ourselves, but for other fishermen. They can't afford to lose their equipment either. My major concern was how to avoid having to cut the lines after the tuna strikes. You could not work on the *New Hope* because of this problem. If you were on one side of the bow and the tuna went under to the other side, it was very difficult to get the lines around, especially if they were tangled. It became too expensive just to catch each tuna.

Before you plan or design a boat, you have to take all these things into consideration. The kind of fish you want to catch and the kind of boat you design must go hand in hand. We first worried about the problem of the lines. We had to design the boat with that problem in mind. My first thought was how to prevent or evade tangling, and then how to separate quickly after tangling. What you must do, is make sure that when the tuna strikes, the line can be isolated from the other lines that are still in the water. Then, you don't have to worry as much about bringing in the lines. One person can get those other lines in while the first person works on the bow with the tuna line. Why is it so important? Most people, before we started fishing, used only one or two lines because they couldn't solve this tangling problem. I wanted to fish with five, six, seven, even up to eleven lines, because the chances of catching a fish are much greater. Now, I am confident to fish with that many lines because we have solved this problem.

To space the line according to the depth and current are the expert techniques. We developed these things. Furthermore, the line we are now using is a perfect set-up. The line will not snap, the hook will not straighten. All of these things, we developed. You may have wondered about the line. You may have wondered why it is constructed the way it is. The reason is so that you can untie it very quickly. If you can untie it, you can prevent having to cut it, and so lose your line.

The line, if you take reasonable care of it, will last ten or twenty years. You have to understand there is a technique to all these things. You have to develop the technique. I realize that this is your first year of tuna fishing. You didn't understand everything when you got on the boat, why things were set-up the way they were, but you fished that way and learned how. Now you have gained the experience of seven years. This means that after one season, you are in your seventh year of fishing, so to speak.

I have now explained to you how I considered the size of the boat and the tuna line technique. Thirdly, I considered the problem of the anchor line. If you put yourself in the position of the tuna underneath the water, you can see a great deal of things. There are all sorts of lines hanging down. There are many, many anchor lines. If the tuna hooks up, he will head in the direction of the anchor line. He will try to wrap around the anchor line and get loose from the hook.

The worst problem is your own anchor line because the tuna has such a little distance to go in order to get to it. Once the tuna strikes, you cannot let go of the line, no matter what. Often the tuna runs out and then turns back in, heading straight for the anchor line. If he can get to that line while it is still attached to the boat, he will cut the line holding him. We understood this by our experience. When this happens, you have to give some slack to the tuna, but you run a great risk of losing him from your line. If, however, you are already cast off from your anchor, the tuna just wraps the anchor line around its line. You have to get to the buoy and unwrap the line, but it will not cut the tuna line because there is not the same tension as when it is still attached to the boat.

Getting off the anchor line is one of the most important maneuvers that you will make fighting the fish. Once you drop the anchor line, you will have a much better chance, fighting the fish one to one, just yourself and the fish. You always have to keep the tuna line tight. Once there is slack, you can lose the fish so easily. The tuna may go up to the surface. Once the tuna bites, you keep pulling and the fish goes against the pull. But it does not always happen that way. Sometimes the tuna runs back directly against your pull, then it gives a jerk and tries to get the hook out of its mouth.

Whenever you make any maneuver with the tuna, you have to think about keeping the hook in its mouth. The *New Hope* lost six fish this summer and three of the cases were just like this. We lost it because the tuna was able to escape the pressure of the line and get off the hook. Once you can clear your boat from the buoy line, you have a 90% chance of bringing the fish in. Even though you are on the boat, you have to visualize the tuna underneath and analyze how it is behaving. I am trying to teach you everything about the techniques as well as how to think about catching the tuna. It is just like you are in school again. While you are learning, you don't understand it right at that moment, but afterwards you say to yourself, "Ah, that is what the teacher meant." By now, by the end of the summer, you should be able to understand what I am trying to teach you.

The last point to consider is harpooning. As you know, you harpoon the fish in order to insure that you can bring it to the boat. After you successfully harpoon the fish, your task is to bring the fish close to the boat in the minimum amount of time. In this one last moment, since the tuna is getting tired and you have been constantly pulling, it comes up to the surface of the water, close to the boat. And then, he gets a glimpse of what is going on. He sees the people, the boat, everything. It is completely strange to him. When this happens, the tuna often makes one last powerful move and heads again for the deep ocean. You should expect this. Don't pull, but give the tuna the line that he needs. Don't let it get slack though. This is the one last chance for the tuna to survive. Then, pull it back up to the boat. Often the tuna will go straight down deep again. This may happen once or twice, even three times or more. The Japanese members didn't understand this. Once they got a tuna harpooned and next to the boat, they thought it was a disgrace to let it go down again, but they should have done so. You have to handle the fish and expect what it is thinking to do next. If you don't do this, then you will lose fish the more often. If you let the fish get away, it could mean thousands of dollars lost. Worse yet, it probably means the life of the fish as well.

Tuna Fishing is Training

For some people, one tuna is more than one month's entire pay. You have to think more seriously about this. If you had $5,000 cash in your pocket and you let it drop down into the water, how deeply would you regret it? You should think about this. It is even more serious with the tuna, because you not only lose money, but the tuna probably loses its life.We are more serious than anyone else. Such seriousness is absolutely important. If we lack a serious and respectful attitude the tuna will be able to get away. Catching tuna requires the highest techniques used in all of fishing. Of course, you may not have known all these things, because you started out with little knowledge of any kind of fishing, but now that I have explained these things, you have to think about them. These techniques will be with you wherever you go, either in the fishing or ocean industry or some other kind of work. This is because you are learning to apply an attitude of the mind.

Whatever you do in the future, whatever problem you might have, you can solve it because you can connect it to the lessons you learned here. You can apply this to any other kind of fishing in the entire industry. Do you understand? It's a little bit abstract, but it means that you are learning a type of thinking which can be applied in any other area of fishing activity. Actually, it can be applied to any kind of activity.

As you may have already experienced, this kind of fishing demands very quick and instantaneous decisions. It doesn't leave you even a few minutes to think about it. Sometimes you have to make a decision in that very second; a man's life may depend on you. Certainly, success or failure depends on your decision in that very moment. A wrong move and something very dangerous can happen. We always have to think in a serious and not a frivolous way. This brings us to reflect about the danger of our lives as we look to the future. At any time, something, some emergency can occur. You have to think about your life in this way. It really is serious from moment to moment.

Also, you have learned a great lesson about unity. When all the people on the boat are united and all the boats are working in harmony, no one gets hurt and the tuna does not escape from the hook-up. The tuna strikes, the tuna is pulling and you are pulling too. At that time, you are thinking about ten things or more. When you are pulling, you have to think quickly ahead, "next is this and next is that."

Everything is going on in your mind at once. You have to know exactly what you are going to do next. For example, Jin Sung got a hook-up. He began to pull and that was all that was on his mind.

The tuna came up to the surface, but no one else knew what to do, they were just standing around and all the lines were everywhere. If you were in his position you would have to decide what to do.

Keep everything in consideration and concentrate on what you do. Always know why you are doing whatever you do and always think about the next thing that you must do. These things all have to go on at the same time. I thought for a long time and very seriously about these techniques and I want you to learn them. It is important. Never waste a moment or you might lose the opportunity. That's what I want to teach you.

Investing in Youth and the Future

Why are we fishing for tuna? There are so many other kinds of fish, flounder, salmon and so forth, that are good to catch. Someday we will catch all of these fish. However, I am thinking first of how to catch the imagination of young people. Once a young person catches at least three tuna, he is hooked for the rest of his life. Every summer comes and this same person wants to come again. They are thinking, "It's so hot and humid on the land, but out on the ocean it is so calm, so beautiful and sometimes adventurous." The young person cannot but help be drawn to that.

Moonies are basically the same as anyone else in the world. Maybe getting a little bit better, but basically the same. Anyway, we need incentive in life from time to time. Don't you think so? With tuna, we have so far been losing money, but I am never worried about that. I will never let go of the line, never let go of my belief in this. I know it is the best species to establish this tradition. Nothing changes a man quickly, not overnight or in one year. I know that it takes at least ten years for an individual, an average American young person, to take his mind and really apply it. This is especially true about the ocean. To really love it takes one, two or three years to begin. After a long time you become involved to the point where you can say, "yes, this is my future."

Once you understand how to catch tuna, the excitement cannot be contained. When someone who knows this starts to talk about catching tuna, he cannot talk calmly, but has to get excited. He has to recreate the very moment when the tuna struck the line and go through every detail of the fight. You are laughing because you already know about this point. This is such a positive influence upon people who have never caught tuna. Sometimes you are pulling so hard on the line when suddenly the tuna gets to the anchor line and cuts off. You fall back on the boat and crash against it. These are truly experiences that make life fulfilling. Even though we lose so much money, we are not worried.

We are not fishing for one or two years. We are looking into the future, even far beyond ten years when this starts to spread and is shared by more and more people. Then, the whole tide of American youth will begin to turn towards the ocean. I am sure of that. In order to insure that, we have to spend at least ten years laying the foundation. If we do that, they can easily come to our movement and benefit from their experiences with us. Even in our own movement we have to learn. I first began to fish, and after six, seven years of fishing myself, I initiated Ocean Church. In the beginning the leaders of Ocean Church were hardly able to understand anything, but now there is a point where some of the leaders understand and they have some maturity. Don't you feel that? So now is the time when we can begin to invest more money and practical effort.

I am always ahead of you. When you weren't even thinking of what to do for the future, I was out there learning how to fish for tuna. Now you are fishing for tuna and I am already in Alaska. Alaska is something else. There, you can literally work through the night, because there is no night. And all that time, you are catching fish. In Alaska, you can catch halibut. They weigh up to 150 pounds and more. However, they are as big as the tuna because the halibut is flat. The tuna takes the line and just pulls straight ahead, but halibut pull by jerks. If you really like fishing, once you get to Alaska, you will say, "forget about Provincetown, forget about Gloucester."

There's so much there. For example, when you see the school of cod fish, you can see all the colors of the ocean. They move like a huge island of solid fish. If you had a big enough net, how many millions of pounds that would be! You have to find the way to catch them and send them all over the world. From there you could make a new tradition for the American fishing industry. Do you understand a little more clearly why we go tuna fishing? It is the best fish to start with. Once you thoroughly learn the tuna techniques, you can go on to any other kind of fishing with confidence. If you can fish with confidence, you can revive the entire fishing industry and in so doing, revive America. This is my hope for you.

Let Us
Begin Again

February 8th, 1984 -- World Mission Center

I HAD EXPECTED a great deal from Ocean Church, but those expectations have been somewhat betrayed. Today, let's start again and make a new beginning. You have no idea how important the foundation of Ocean Church is for this country. You have no idea how wonderful Ocean Church could be for America. You are part of an important providence, an ocean providence. I am always thinking about the kind of foundation that should be made here in America. More than anything else, I spend most of my time thinking about this. I have thought about where we should start. There is so much waste in this nation that I first thought we should collect together the scrap metal in America, the old rusted out parts, and recycle them. We should salvage these things and put them to good use. Also, there is an incredible amount of paper that is used and thrown away. We could recycle that as well. There is a tremendous need in this nation for someone to do that. However, at this time, it would be very difficult for us to set up a program like that.

What kind of life do you want to have? In the world today, many people are looking for an easy way to make their living. They want to make their fortune overnight; going out everyday and working hard in the environment is too much for them. When I thought about this, I looked for a place that would not only provide good training for your character, but also a good way of life. The way of life upon the ocean then, is a good way of life for us.

I studied the ocean-related cities and recognized that the best way to help America is to help these cities. So much comes through these cities and then filters into the country. If we develop these cities and clean them up, we will set the direction for this nation for the next century. The Coast Guard is very important in this regard. They are trying to safeguard the country against the infiltration of drugs, but the Mafia is bringing in cocaine and other drugs by the thousands of pounds. If we are to enter into the ocean way of life, we have to cooperate and help the Coast Guard with its work. In that way we can help this nation clean up its drug problem and at the same time we can even help the American fishing industry. There is a danger that these cities might come under Mafia control. In Korea, long before I came to America, I explored the possibilities of the ocean. In America, I have been laying the foundation for the ocean providence since 1974. How long have you been on the ocean? Some of you began since 1980 and others since 1981. In 1980, you were given instructions to go out to many of the ocean cities and revive them through evangelical meetings. You should have invited the key officials in those cities such as the mayor and the Coast Guard leaders.

I designed the *One Hope* boat. It is a strong and yet fast boat, and I know that young people will be easily attracted to it. It was designed with young people in mind. I wanted them to use the boat and do things together with you. In the ocean cities, the young people have no hope. They don't have anything to do and just hang around in the streets. They are open to being contaminated by the drug traffic. They have no equipment to go out fishing and even if they caught fish, they wouldn't know what to do with them. They have no way to gain pride in themselves or self-respect.

Where are those boats? They are still sitting in storage. There should be at least ten boats in each ocean city. If you can get five people per boat to learn with it and take care of it, you can go on to use a large ocean-going boat. Out of fifty people, you can train a full captain and crew. If you had gone to your cities and followed this plan exactly as it was outlined, you would have a solid foundation by now. You would already have experienced incredible victory by now.

Before you can accomplish anything however, you first have to think of how to achieve the spiritual foundation.

I emphasized the spiritual foundation first. You have to unite with the city leadership, then embrace the young people. This formula would have been successful. No matter what, no matter how difficult, I want you to win the friendship and trust of the local leadership. The ministers and civic leaders are so important. Even now, you must go and follow this course. You have to go through this principled path.

Without the young people in the local area you will not succeed. You cannot just ask for help from other members. You have to earn the support from young people with your own effort of heart. You have to go through a struggle. You are going there to stand for justice. At first people will form a "hate Moonie" fleet, but you need all of that persecution and rejection. It is a cleansing process for you and it is also the way you win support. The Coast Guard and mayor will come to support you because you are standing up for the right thing. Use your boat to help the drug patrol. It is a very expensive boat and the Coast Guard will be surprised that such a nice boat could be used to help their work. Once you let people use the boats and share with them your ideals you will win their respect. Persecution will just bring you to the attention of good people who care about their city.

I believed that three years was good enough to lay the complete foundation. After three years, I hoped you could begin to use even bigger boats. I wanted the people in your local city to take turns in learning how to run the trawling boat. Then, what would happen? You could have even obtained support for your program from the government. You could have built an entire fleet for that city and coastal area. Theoretically, you could have trained fifty captains. You could have helped that coastal area build an entire new fishing fleet.

The mayor and Coast Guard would have recommended you and the government would have helped you based on their appraisal of you. Your purpose must be to help the fishing industry here in America. Their purpose cannot be fulfilled without you. Creating this relationship is critical. By having the support of the Coast Guard and local leaders, there is no doubt that the ocean providence will succeed and become a powerful work in America. However, not even one of you lived up to my expectation. Not even one of you made friends with the mayor or made a relationship with the Coast Guard. Not even one.

Those who started in 1980 raise up your hands. Did you do this much? Did anyone of you accomplish at least with one mayor or with one Coast Guard official? No? Then, we have wasted all our time. This is a shame for all of us. Therefore, we are beginning again and we will recreate the foundation. You must first learn Divine Principle. Unless you can teach Divine Principle there is no way for you to gain the spiritual foundation. There is no way for you to gain success unless you can teach your ideals.

You have to become attractive to your city. You have to be able to add something. When the Moonies come to a city, they always watch you, afraid of what you might do. If you go and build up the local area, they will see that the benefit goes to the local population. Then, they will not oppose you. You have to organize your battle, because you will have to prove every point to them. They will not believe you automatically. You have to be disciplined and organized. You have to be teamwork people. There is no doubt about it. If you are going to train others, you must also train yourselves. This is the course of Ocean Church.

Sometimes ocean-going people are sloppy. We have to be absolutely meticulous about every detail. You cannot successfully win over the ocean without disciplining your mind. You must have an absolutely scientific and organized approach to your work on the ocean.

You have to take constant care of the boat. It must always be in the best condition and it must be spotless. Otherwise, you will be put in a dangerous position. This mission is very difficult. However, if you achieve in it, there will be no comparison with other leaders in America. That is why I chose the ocean as the basis for our work in America. And that is also why I picked seminary graduates to lay the foundation.

However, you have to follow my instructions exactly. Your spiritual state of mind will determine everything. You must always pray, especially when you are out on the ocean. Then, you will be guided from danger. Use your mind and develop your faith. Ocean Church members are very rough sometimes. They say things like, "Why do we need Jesus?" That's a strange way to think. If Jesus isn't needed, then we don't need Moses or Abraham or Adam. If we don't need the first Adam, then we don't need the second Adam. And then, we don't need the third Adam either. So, finally you think, "We don't need Father." That becomes your conclusion. What we are doing now, Jesus also wanted to do. We are working to liberate Jesus in the spiritual world. Jesus is working in the spiritual world to liberate mankind, and that is also our task. If we cannot liberate Jesus and the spiritual world, then we cannot bring the Kingdom of Heaven on earth.

You have to have the correct mental state. If your mind is not spiritually tuned, the fish, who are also part of creation and have sensitivity, will never come close to you. Unless you have your spiritual foundation and can fellowship with the city leaders, you can never win any kind of victory for Ocean Church. You have to go to every level and win people to your side. In your city you might meet all kinds of very rough men. Some of them would throw away their own parents, but you have to win them over. You have to convince them that you really care for them. Some of them will come to that realization. Then, you will find people in the city who will want to come with you. If your mind is tuned spiritually, they will come to support you because you have the right attitude. They will be attracted to you. As you gain the reputation of being decent and honest and dedicated men, the city leaders will let the young people come to you and they will watch your work with them. Then, they will bear testimony to you. You have to go through this course. You can ask some really rough person to come out with you and bring his own son. You can treat his son with such concern that he will be moved. Every city has parents who are agonizing over the problems of their youth. Ocean Church members will help these difficult young people. You can become their counselor by listening to them and training them on your boat. Then, the parents, the mayor and city leaders will come to your side. The people who oppose you and are negative are the ones you have to turn around so that they welcome you.

You have to grab these negative people and win them. If you can do that, you will succeed very quickly. Do you understand what I am saying? Work with the young people mixed up in drugs. No one else can help them. You can help them.

I believe that Ocean Church will succeed more than the IOWC and state centers. Why? Because the work you do with your boats will quickly gain recognition by the city. Someday you may even become the mayor of your city. The people will elect you based on your contribution to cleaning up their city. Some of you might even become congressmen or senators.

You are taking care of a boat. Go out and catch fish. Use the boat for evangelical programs and train the youth of the city. The boat can supply you with all you need. How many years have we wasted already? Well, even now we are going to do it. Don't get other members to work in your local centers. No. You, the leaders of Ocean Church must go to your city and win support from the local youth. Pioneer the city with only a few members. We should have built 300 boats for this purpose, but you were not ready to receive them. You even didn't want ten boats in your centers; you said, "Oh Father, we only need one boat. Don't send us any more boats." I was deeply disappointed.

Where did this disillusionment come from? You should have more hope than any other church project. You lost your hope because you didn't follow instructions. Tuna fishing is not Ocean Church. Not in the real sense. It is a good way to train, but it is only the beginning. You have to earn the respect of local fishermen in your cities. Then, you can begin your Ocean Church. When you can train young people to be responsible for even a big ocean trawler, you have truly begun your work. Do you see how you can gain success for the future of Ocean Church and for America? Then, you have to start. You have to start again right now.

While you are developing in Ocean Church, you should learn from the Japanese. They have to cooperate with you and help you. You have to support them as well. You have to go out to the ocean. That is your role and mission. If you Americans fail then I may ask the Japanese or Koreans or even the blessed children to accomplish the mission. I am absolutely determined to succeed. Repent for the past and make a new hopeful beginning. Now is the time. Shall we do it? Then, let us make a solemn promise today. Let us determine to succeed, following this course.

You may not know where I am, but I might arrive suddenly to go out to the ocean with you. You have to be ready for that any time. Keep your boats ready for that moment. It will come. As soon as I arrive in your city, you have to leave the coast in ten minutes. Be ready to leave your dock in that amount of time. Always have your boat ready for that. When I come, I will call you and say, "Ready?" Then, you have to answer, "Father, let's go."

If Ocean Church stops the drugs from coming in by the drug-running boats, then the Coast Guard will really come to support us. The Moonies will be recognized as the ones truly trying to help America face this serious problem. Drugs are crippling the youth of this nation. By cleaning up the drug problem, the youth of this nation will have a future. I see the ocean as the way for a new foundation to be laid in America. I am disappointed because the Ocean Church providence has not kept the pace. You are way behind schedule.

So, please study hard and review my instructions from today. From here we will march forward. There is no doubt anymore as to what we must do. Will you do it? [Yes!] Yes? Absolutely Yes? [Yes!] Then, do not lose your determination. Thank you very much.

Why We Have
Ocean Training

July 2nd, 1984 -- Morning Garden

LET'S LOOK at the Good Go boat. Water can come in as much as it wants. You can bore a hole in the bottom of the hull and make a test. Even if people are inside the boat, they can still stay there because of the foam construction within the hull. It's been built for safety. At the same time, it's a very fast boat. If a storm is coming, you can outrun the storm. Of course, it's not the most economical boat because it takes a lot of gas to run it, but for a training program, it's well worth it. We want a boat that is safe and fast, rather than slow and economical. For training purposes, the Good Go is best.

The Value of Training

In any training course, the harder the training is, the more you learn. The training itself is what makes the program worth it. Ultimately, we want to go into the fishing industry. That's the future. How can we help America and the world solve its problems if we don't have any money? In the fishing industry the work is incredibly hard, but the return is good. In order to accomplish any task however, one first has to accomplish the training period.

Some members are now in the process of creating Japanese restaurants. You may think that a restaurant business is just a small thing, but it has many implications. First, it is a business where many customers come in and out. You can reach out to these people. You can talk to them and make good relationships. You can serve them and display the real spirit of service. We are religious people, and we also have to work in this world. For this reason, the restaurant is an excellent type of business for us to be involved in.

Now, the Japanese restaurant is in fashion. Everyone wants to try out this new kind of food. When your customers come, it will probably be their first experience. You can serve them with your full heart so that they fall in love with the food, with your restaurant and come back again and again. We are beginning with Japanese restaurants, but we need not confine ourselves to them. We come from many backgrounds, Italian, French, Indian and all kinds of cultures. Our members will have no problem making their own special restaurant because they come from all over the world.

There are not too many businesses where you can invest all your money and then, in just three years see the return. With restaurants, a certain amount of money is invested and within three years one can see the investment come back. We can make even more restaurants, and after the success of these restaurants we will have made such a track record that we can borrow money from the bank and they know it will be safe. It will be no problem to pay back all the money. We will lay that kind of foundation. Most importantly, we will teach people how to eat fish. The future diet will be fish. Once we make our investment and make success from that, we can branch out and further success is guaranteed.

In your restaurants you can serve many people every day. You can make a difference in your community in this way. Think about it. The spirit of America can be uplifted in this very meaningful and yet practical way. The American people can be making friendships with us. They can get to know us in a real way. How can we save this country? In a real way, how can we do that? We are making a foundation to really save this country through everything that we do. We can reach people through practical service. We may be selling machines, boats, cars, fish or sushi. What's important is that we truly serve people and make a good relationship. We are simply making our foundation and though it is modest, it will someday extend all over the country and have a very good effect.

It's your country. Don't you want to see a good future for it? You have to be able to offer your time, your money, your effort. People misunderstand us now, but in time they will see the real motivation behind our work.

In the fishing industry, we have to make a whole new foundation. We will go out and catch the fish. We will buy it and sell it to our restaurants. We will be the distributor and the retailer. Why is the fishing industry so low at this point? It is because fish is too expensive to take home every night, so most people don't think of buying it, except for special occasions. However, is fish expensive when it comes from the boat? No! The fisherman gets the least of anyone for all his work. From the boat the price is so cheap, but who gets the money? The middle man--he buys the fish cheap and sells it at too high a price. That isn't fair. It isn't fair to the fishermen and it isn't fair to the consumer.

We have to think about the profit for the public. We will have to supply a good meat for a cheap price. Someday, people will welcome the Moonies because of this consideration. When we began to train for tuna fishing there was nothing but ridiculous opposition. That was because everyone was so afraid that they just panicked. However, when they fished with us, side by side, they saw how we behaved and they knew that we were sincere. Then the price went up for the fishermen. Our movement had an influence upon that price hike. We lost everything in that investment, but the fishermen were really happy. They could sell their fish to us for a higher price. This year they were even expecting and hoping for something of the same. They were concerned about my having to go to Danbury. They were wondering about the price and they were worried that we would give up on helping them. You can reply something like this when they ask you if I am coming at all this summer: "You put him in jail. Everyone for so many years wanted to get rid of Reverend Moon, but now you see that if he isn't around, the American people suffer." Make them think about that point.

We must train now. That is the only thing we have in mind for this summer. I have been looking at your faces and I have studied them. Your fortune brought you here. You may not be extremely happy to be here; you may be thinking about the hard work ahead of you, but there was no choice in a sense for you. You did not arrive here by accident. You felt something calling you and pulling you here. However, you must focus and put your heart into what you are doing. If your heart is not here, then something may happen.

I am especially concerned about accidents. Don't make bad relationships with one another. On the boat this is serious. We have to be careful and train ourselves. On our own boats, with one another, bad things should never happen. It is even more serious if you work on a boat where no one has any religious background. On a regular commercial boat, if you make enemies, it would be very easy just to "lose" you over the side of the boat. An "accident" could happen and no one could prove it was otherwise. Do you understand? Things like this happen, so we have to learn here how to make good relationships.

The ocean is a very difficult place. Always follow all the safety procedures on your boat. It's important to know how to swim. If you don't, you must always wear the life jacket. You will see many different things on the ocean. Sometimes a huge whale will come by your boat and mess up your lines. You are students and you will have to learn all kinds of things this summer. You will learn about fishing, but you will also learn about life as well. Think about the future, about the past, about the people around you. Think about your life of faith and why you joined.

Don't be anxious. Take your time. Don't try to be a PhD while you are still in elementary school. Those who are PhD's may look at you "greenhorns" and think, "Oh, when are they going to have experience with things like me." We must understand that there are many unexplored areas in the ocean. We are going to discover things in the ocean that others never even dreamed about. Such things will come to pass. I am serious about developing a submarine which will explore deep underneath the water.

I am also extremely serious about building a marine college here in Gloucester. We bought the land to build that college, but the community became scared and cried out, "Oh, Reverend Moon is going to take over and exercise some kind of tyranny." Well, now they know that this just isn't true and they are beginning to accept us. Someday we will make the marine college come true. Imagine, America is such a developed country, a nation that honors God and is a first rate nation in the world. However, this beautiful house was closed to us for four years. They didn't allow one person to come in.

They said, "The Catholic Church was okay, but the Unification Church--no!" Is there any other nation in the world that has freedom of religion like the United States? We had to fight back and claim our rights. We had to threaten to sue them in order to use the Gloucester property. They thought about it and realized in the long run that they were going to lose. Our motivation was not to fight, but we had to challenge such an unrighteous act.

Now we are to begin our training and this is a new era for the ocean. A new age is beginning. This is a truly historical happening in which you are now participating. Why? Because someday in the future, all the people in this area will know clearly about Unification Church. And many of them will join. Don't you believe that? There will be millions and millions of people who will join from all around the world.

They will come here to this very port of Gloucester, to this very house in Gloucester where you were able to hear from me personally about the meaning of this training program. You, the class of 1984, just seventy-six members will be considered the "Pilgrim Fathers" of this new age. Now, you have responsibility for a Good Go boat all your own during this summer. In the future, people will have to be selected. Maybe only one out of one hundred thousand can be selected and only seventy or eighty people can come here and be allocated a Good Go boat. Today, you can train to be a captain for a boat without much competition. Those of you who came here and are already complaining about the long hours and hard work, raise up your hands and tell me, "I want to miss this chance to pioneer and be the forefather of Ocean Church." You are free to leave. If you have no vision of what it will be like ten years from now or twenty years from now, you can go. You must realize that this is a historical moment we are in.

Each year that I came fishing here, every single fishing day, I went to the boat, whether there was a storm or good weather. No matter how late we had gone to bed the night before and how early we had to rise, I went to the boat. But now, it is not as safe for me to go about freely. This is a reality that I have to contend with. I am making a firm stand against atheism, against communism and many of them would like to strike me down. It is difficult for me to be with you every day as I have done in the past ten years.

I expect you to be autonomous. You must become independent and pioneer your own way, especially this year. Otherwise, how will you become a self-supporting person? How will you support others on your way? Each and every one of you have to understand the meaning of this training period and live up to its standard during the next two months. If you experience how difficult it is to go out on a boat every day, think about my experience on the *New Hope* for the past ten years. Never once during any of those ten seasons, did I lay down and sleep on the boat. I put my entire will power and whole heart into this training. Every moment while I was on the boat, during the long tedious wait for the tuna, I was always praying to commit myself even more for the sake of God and mankind. That is what I want you to inherit here.

The Tuna-Fishing Training Course

As you know, the tuna also has some spiritual aspect, being part of creation. Sometimes when your spirit is dull, the tuna may even be more spiritually sensitive than you. The tuna which you are after weighs more than 500 pounds. To get to that size, it is eighteen to twenty years of age. Think about it. To get to that age, what kind of dangers has that tuna already escaped, time and time again? Over and over, the tuna was on the verge of getting caught, but it somehow escaped. By the time a tuna is 500 pounds, it is a very smart fish.

The tuna know that the lines hanging down are there to catch him. For a tuna to bite the bait is not a normal thing. It is an accident. Just like human beings who have an accident after drinking alcohol, the tuna gets drunk on eating the chum and then, in one mistake, it reaches out and bites the bait. The secret which makes the difference here is for you to concentrate and with all your heart, mind and effort, draw the tuna towards you.

If you really concentrate and become spiritually attuned, you will wake up one day and while you wash your face and prepare to go to your boat, you will sense at what hour that day you will catch a tuna. Sometimes you are waiting and waiting. Your mind starts to wander and then, you have a sharp awakening in your mind. At that moment, you realize, "Oh, in five minutes a tuna is going to strike the line." As soon as you feel that, the tuna strikes. Every one of you, if you apply yourself, will experience this at one time or another.

There is some kind of law or principle at work here. If you invest all your heart, you will catch a tuna. You have to be able to know and envision what is going on underneath you, when the small fish are coming in and when the tuna are moving with the currents and tides. You must be able to see it without even seeing it. This takes concentration.

I am thinking about dedicating the money made by the *New Hope* to some charity in Gloucester. If that is the case, then wouldn't you expect the tuna to bite even more? The spiritual world would encourage the tuna to bite the *New Hope's* lines. This year there is a quota and I am hoping that two-thirds of the quota is caught by Moonie boats. In order to do that, you really have to love your bait. Bait is the direct cause of catching the tuna. You have to connect with God's love and then put that into the bait. You are the connecting point.

A clean boat reflects a clean spirit. An orderly boat also reflects an orderly spirit. This means that all your jigs, rods, reels, lines, hooks, everything is in the right place. I can tell immediately if your boat has received a lot of heart or very little heart. And if you are praying deeply, the spiritual world will help you, inspire you and bring tuna close to your boat. Through these experiences you will discover that God is alive. If something bad is going to happen to you, you will be sensitive to that. This year, we have to be concerned about safety. The best way to avoid accidents is to be serious and put our whole heart into what we are doing. You must take care of yourself spiritually. Always keep yourself orderly.

I want to ask you an important question. "During this season, how many times will you fight with your brothers and sisters?" You don't want any such circumstance, but sometimes you get involved and a situation arises. What will you do at that point? You should not allow any fights to happen. You have to avoid creating the circumstances on land before you even go out to the boat. In the morning, while you are fishing, don't let the things inside of you get to you, even if you are burning up inside. On the way home, you can bring something up and try to discuss it then.

Sometimes you will be in the boat and the wind will be blowing, a storm will be coming. This is a very dangerous time and it is very bad to let your feelings out at this time. It is better when you come home and have a hot shower and a good meal. Then, you become generous and you forget the words which might have made you angry. Don't let things bother you while you are out on the water. No matter how someone might agitate you, just ignore him. Think to yourself that it's some neighbor's dog barking at you.

Keep your goal in mind. You didn't come here to fight. You came here to fish for tuna and this is your purpose. Don't get involved in anything that is not the purpose of your coming here. Some days you will dedicate your whole heart and there will be absolutely no result. Then is a good time to repent. You can repent and try to find the area that you missed, that you didn't understand and apply. You have to be so serious. After this training course, you will become an independent person at some time in your life. If you go out on the ocean as your livelihood and cannot catch fish, who is going to help you? Will the government subsidize you? Will God give you money? Probably not. Don't count on my coming to help you. I cannot always do that. Can you do it? Will you come running to me or will you be very serious and do it? Those who can, and will do it, raise your hands. How about the women? What will you do if you cannot catch the fish? The tuna will laugh when they see women coming to catch them. If you want to get quicker results, just listen to the men for once. And then the tuna will say, "Well, even though they are women, they respect the men; we can tolerate them." So you women, don't fight against the men. However, never be outdone by the men in putting your whole heart into it. You can beat the men that way, that is okay.

Do you wonder what I am doing all day long while waiting for tuna? Catching and landing the fish is only about one hour out of the day. What am I doing the rest of the time? I seem to be doing nothing, just sitting there watching the lines in the water, but every moment I am putting my whole heart into the effort. I check the bait on the hooks. Every once in a while, if the fish aren't biting, you have to reel in the line and look at the bait. You should change the bait three times a day, even if the fish don't seem to be around. When I look at the buoy, I can tell if there is bait at the end of the line. I don't know if Gerhard can tell this or not, but Gerhard should be able to. It's a normal thing to know this. If the bait is gone, you have to reel in the line and put new bait on.

The Relationship of Heart With All Things

The human being is actually a very sensitive, knowing creature. You should be able to tell from experience about the current and what it is doing. You should be able to tell how the hook is hanging from the line in the water according to the current. Especially two lines, the seven and a half fathom and the ten fathom line are the ones most likely to catch. You have to be really attuned to your bait and how it goes down the lines. You will also discover many related kinds of phenomena. You may use six or eight lines, but all season long, there is just one line that the tuna will bite. You may think, "Well, that's just the favorite position for the tuna." So you change the line's position, but still the tuna bite that line. How do you explain that by today's science?

The spiritual world is like the dark horse in a race. It may be the most unlikely thing, but it happens. Maybe you pick up an old line that someone else threw away. They caught lots of tuna on that line, but finally they made a new one. And you have all new lines, but you put that old one on. Then suddenly you catch a tuna. How can you explain that? It has happened. That's why I am telling you these things. You have to love your equipment, your hooks and lines. You have to cherish the ones that catch, even bring them to your bed because you never want them out of your sight. That kind of feeling, that kind of love is okay. This love is connected everywhere and it connects in an invisible way, in a most unlikely way.

The Japanese members come around to me and say, "The *New Hope* is becoming an old boat, it's more than thirteen years old now, Father, let's change it." I don't want to hurt their feelings, so I say something like, "Oh, you think so?" Actually, I am wondering, "What are you talking about?" Already, if we were to write the history of how we began this training program, 99% of it would center on the *New Hope*. Even if we got a brand new boat, even if someone donated it to us, we would never write as much about it.

It is like a marriage. If you are married for ten years and your wife gets old, do you try to get rid of her and get a new one? How would the *New Hope* feel if that happened? Would it be happy or sad? It would cry out! Instead, I am thinking of when I give all these things to the next generation I will change the boat and give the new one to them. At that time, I will retire the *New Hope* and put her in a special museum. The *New Hope* will understand because this is normal. The boat knows it cannot live forever and it will agree to a replacement at that time. I truly feel that way. I have that kind of sensitivity to the *New Hope*. This says something to all of us. How are we different from the rest of the world? Through our heart. We are making a heartistic world which is quite different from what most other people are doing. If we are going to ride on the *New Hope* and on the *One Hope* boats, we must really love them.

When you are allocated a boat, don't ever say, "Oh, I want a new boat." Don't ever say that. Just love that boat and eventually that boat will return all the love to you and catch a great deal of fish. Talk to your boat. Say, "I know you worked hard last year. I'm going to take really good care of you this year. Let's get together and be successful."

At the end of the day when you are coming back, clean out the chum area and get rid of the bad smell, take care of the boat and really clean it. Then when you look at the boat, you feel good about it. And the boat looks so good too. Take care of your boat and treat it right. This is your responsibility. In the daytime, you are too busy to keep it clean because you are trying to catch fish; the boat understands this. However, on the ocean, if something goes wrong, even if it is a small thing, you have to take care of that.

After a few weeks of serious experience you will understand how the engine sounds. You will be able to hear when the engine is going over its capacity. You have to slow down at that point. The engine is like the heart of the body. In the ocean, if the engine quits, you will be in a serious situation. In fact, the engine is almost more important than your life. You have to think like that. We should never overwork the engines. Sometimes you cannot help it if the case is an emergency. However, never push your engine for no reason. Love your engine just like a member of your family, like your wife or your husband. Then it will never go out of order.

When the birds are flying around and looking for a boat to land and rest upon, which boat will they pick? We can see this particularly in small villages. There are lots of houses, but always one house has lots of birds that come there to rest. Remarkably, that house is the one which is very prosperous. It's true. The reason for this is that such a house has a great deal of love which has probably accumulated from generation to generation.

We have to bear in mind then, that Moonie boats are to be loved with one's whole heart. Actually, I wondered if you needed me to come and talk to you this year. Then I thought about the *New Hope* and said, "I've been coming to the *New Hope* every year and it will miss me." I couldn't tolerate the thought of that. The *New Hope* has recently been fishing in Montauk and I have been there fishing on it. I asked for it to come back to Gloucester, however, it has just been siting here for several days, so I couldn't help but thinking of coming to Gloucester and visiting it. I wanted to talk to the boat and tell it, "I fished with you all last summer, every day, but this summer I can't fish as much with you. I hope you can understand." I know that the *New Hope* will understand if I am not around so much. I am telling you these things because I want to urge you this year, not to let your loved one, your boat lose its spirit. Don't let it be damaged. Just as you would protect your own body, take care of your boat with all your heart.

Learning to Work Together

I have a reason for bringing you together this summer. Some of you are Ocean Church members and you have already tasted this training experience. Others of you have sold fish, but you never knew how hard it was to catch them. You simply said to the fishermen, "Go out and catch the fish; I will just sell it for you." However, this wasn't right. Those who sell the fish should also understand how hard it is to catch them.

When you have separate channels, when there is just the one who catches and the one who sells, the one who sells always makes demands. He will say, "Oh, I don't like the fish you are catching. You should do this and you should do that." If they have to catch the fish, they will understand and they will not be able to blame the other so easily. At the same time, fish are often wasted after they are caught by bad handling on the boats. They are spoiled in many different ways. Therefore, you have to learn from each other and work together more closely.

Americans can learn a great deal from working with Japanese members. They have an advantage. I have watched them closely for the past several years. The Americans manage boats and they are always sloppy. On the other hand, the Japanese boats are always very tidy. Do you agree that the Japanese are tidy people? They keep everything very neat and orderly. There is very good proof for this: go to New York City and look at the automobiles parked on Fifth avenue. They look really dirty even though they are owned by rich people. However in Tokyo every automobile is spic and span. There is no dirty looking car in the streets of Tokyo. This tells us something about the personality of Japanese people in general.

These are observations. Please keep your boat tidy and up to the Japanese standard. Another point about Oriental people is that they tend to be more frugal with money. Look at the Japanese people, the ones in Happy Group. They are small, they are not so aggressive, but every single one knows how to manage money. Even though you may not like it, you have a lot to learn from them. That is why I am putting you together, so that you learn from each other. The first step is for the Western members to observe the Oriental members.

Let me ask you another question. Do you like me? How come you like me? I am not a Western man. My eyes are slanted and smaller than yours. My skin is brown, not white. I am a Korean man. What if I were to say, "Okay, I'll put someone else in my position. Well, how about Gerhard? He is a very big man. He is seven feet tall and has a big face and big hands. His one foot is larger than both of mine. Maybe I should put him in charge of Unification Church because he is bigger." Do you think that's a good idea? Should Gerhard replace me? You don't think so? Well then, how about Mr. Reagan? Do you think he would fill my shoes? He would never be able to perform as well in my place. I have a capability that cannot be replaced. In the same way, the Japanese are capable of certain things and you cannot replace them. The American leaders and the Japanese leaders are different. In the face of difficulties, the American leader tends to think of a way to retreat. On the other hand, the Japanese leader would never think of retreat. Also, in the religious life, in the life of faith, they are your elder brothers. They were blessed earlier and have pursued this life much longer, so don't complain about them.

I am not favoring the Japanese. Americans may have a better potential, but the Japanese have already proven themselves. Be honest with me. Which one would you take? Once the Japanese have made up their mind to do something, they will do it for the rest of their life. If they get a job in a company, they serve that company for all of their life. How about an American who runs a Japanese restaurant? He hires two cooks, one is American and the other is Japanese. After one year, the American cook gets offered a better salary and without a single regret says "good-bye," and leaves right away. The Japanese would never do that; he would stay with that same restaurant for ten to twenty years. For this reason, the American owner should learn a lesson and hire the Japanese. Once their heart is tied to something, they will never cut from it. You have to become just like this. I have a great deal of hope in you and that is why I have brought you together with the Japanese members.

This begins your training for the summer. Go out and learn from the ocean. I am asking you to be serious and especially have no accidents this year. In tuna fishing, if you don't catch anything for one or two weeks, you begin to lose concentration. You may kick the baskets around and the lines may be on the deck and you just don't care about it, but the tuna strikes without any warning. Your feet must never be standing on any lines. This is very serious. Always pay attention to where you are and where you are moving on the boat.

Keep everything orderly on your boat and this will minimize accidents happening. What will you do if your feet get caught in a line? Be very careful about this point. If you ever get to that point, you would care less about the tuna. It's your safety, your life that is in danger. This summer I am stressing the point that you protect yourself from danger and accidents.

Organize yourselves like a tree. Each ten boats will have a leader, and then, each three boats will have a trinity leader. These three boats should especially be together as a trinity. Look out after each other and help each other. With this kind of organization make sure that no boats are out of order. Take very good care of one another. Three trinities should back up each other and one boat should look out for all three trinities. That is how all boats should be organized for the training courses to come.

Your main concern is not to let your boat get out of order. If your boat goes down, you cannot go out. You should do everything to prevent that. This is the way we shall do it. Today is the beginning. After three more days, we will finish the training on land and we will all go out and begin fishing. Whether I continue to be here or not is not the focus of this training. Don't be concerned about that. I have already done enough tuna fishing. I already know enough about that. Don't worry whether I am fishing or not. Every morning, we will go out at a certain hour. This is our tradition. You have to follow that. However, I am now exploring other kinds of fish, such as striped bass and flounder. Later I will go to Alaska for halibut fishing. Those who make a good record here can go with me. Your concern this season is to become real fishermen. Sleep in the boat and eat in the boat. This summertime is priceless. It is valuable training for you, for the rest of you life. I only want you to put in all of your heart and effort. God bless you.

Tuna Fishing and the
Way of Life

July 5th, 1984 -- Morning Garden

HOW DO YOU FEEL when you look at the ocean? Sometimes it rains and more often the winds blow. Do you have any questions that you would like to ask me? Did you learn how to do things, how to put your bait on the line? Not yet? Did you want to come or did someone tell you to come? Is this is your first time here? The days are long, but you will learn how to go beyond the tiredness.

It takes two or two and one-half hours to go to Provincetown where the fishing grounds are. That means fishing begins at five o'clock in the morning. To get there you have to leave at 3:00 a.m. or even 2:00 a.m. You have to be the first boats there and get ready for the tuna guests. That's courtesy. You are ready for everything. The tuna is already here, but not many fishermen are catching them yet. We have to think about that with our common sense. Why are they here, but cannot be caught?

Patterns of Life Within the Ocean

Sand eels migrate and move according to the season. These sand eels, hordes of them, are coming up from the south. The water temperature is still cold, and the lower you go, the colder it gets, although the temperature stays a little warmer on the surface. The sand eels are beginning to gather; the fish are going after these sand eels, but they are not concentrated yet. They are in the area, but they haven't made their home here yet. These sand eels will settle down when the water temperature goes up.

As the summer goes on, the temperature goes up. Then, they will gather in one area, somewhat like a plateau where the depth is only between seventy to about one hundred and twenty feet. Other depths are 200 or 300 feet and are too deep, too cold. The larger fish know where these tiny sand eels are and they all concentrate in the general area to feed upon them. The whales and tuna stay in the deeper area, but in the morning they come up to eat. One can honestly say it is their breakfast time. That breakfast place is where we are now going out and waiting.

Herring, mackerel and cod are smaller fish which tuna also feed upon. They all come around where the temperature is warm and where there is an abundant amount of sand eels. That is the area we are going to. The tuna, when they come in and out of the feeding area, have a certain approach where they tend to go in and out. That is where we want to place our boats. That is usually on the edge of the area, a ledge. Tuna do not like rough things, just like anything normal. So where there is a cliff, the tuna don't want to come there. Rather, they will come where there is a slope. They prefer a gradual slope and come in and out that way.

First you have to study the charts and see what kind of terrain there is, and then you have to go there and try it out. I spent a lot of time investigating this, scientifically and also intuitively. That is one reason why the *New Hope* has been catching lots of tuna, more than many other boats. Also the boats around *New Hope* have been able to catch a good number of tuna. For this reason, even people who are not Moonies try to fish close to the *New Hope*.

You have to know substantially about these things. You have to have an in-depth perception. You might say, "Well, the ocean is the same everywhere and the fish come here and go there and its a matter of sheer chance." Not so. Not at all. Chance is not involved. Tuna have a manner of doing things, they have habits. We have to understand about their habits. The smaller fish gather together where there is plenty of food, where there is shelter and they can hide and protect themselves.

These small fish move around by schools. You will see some schools that are miles wide and long, and hundreds of feet deep. The tide comes in and out and these schools move around with it. Sometimes the currents are very strong, while other times the currents are weak. The smaller fish go in very large schools for protection, and they are looking for places where they can hide, such as the very big rocks. There are many places like this in certain areas of the ocean and we have to study these kind of things if we are going to catch the kind of fish we want.

For example, we might want to catch striped bass. Sometimes the schools of very small fish are moving too fast because the currents and tides are pulling them, so the fish in front cannot slow down even if they want to. Instead of being able to hide behind a rock, they collide into it. This leaves them somewhat knocked out, dizzy, just like a man would be if he did the same thing to his head. This is where the striped bass hang around. When the small fish hit the rock and swim slowly about in a dazed manner, they are easier to prey upon. You can find striped bass in places like this. You have to think like the striped bass and then figure out the logical place where they will be.

Tuna fishing is the same. You reason everything out; you have to think everything through. Don't just go somewhere and throw your gear into the ocean and just hope the tuna will somehow get hooked. The small fish go with the currents. There are places along the ledge where the currents slow down. This is where the small fish go and where the larger fish come after them to feed. You have to look at the charts and find these places where there is a drop-off and the depths change sharply.

You have to perceive whether the bottom is a sandy, muddy or rocky bottom. There are different types of worms and small creatures. You have to study about that as well. Some live where there is seaweed and others where it is rocky or sandy. If you are going for the smaller fish, you have to understand what the bottom is like. The weight on the tackle is important in rocky areas. If you just throw the hook down there, it will get snagged. Sometimes you might get your gear back, but most often you have to cut your line.

To prevent that, you place your weight about ten feet below your hook and bait. Then, you have to imagine what your tackle will look like down there and be able to feel your weight when it hits the bottom. You have to have some sensitivity about that. And you have to consider the current pulling your hook and bait. If it isn't much, then it won't be ten feet above the weight. It will be more like five feet or just two feet. So, you have to be conscious how your bait will hang on the line and be able to judge from that how high from the bottom it actually is.

In Alaska, where there is halibut, I put my thoughts about this into practice and it worked very well. When I am out tuna fishing, I am always thinking like this, how to do things and what to do next. My mind is never idle. When I went fishing for halibut in Alaska I caught twice as much as the others. They wondered how I did it, but I didn't tell them. However, there isn't much to it. You just have to think, and when your assumption is right, you will catch the fish you are going after. You have to know the habits of the fish, the tendency of the fish and the terrain. The rest is logical reasoning. You think to yourself, "This is so and this must be it." You then try it out and you discover, "that must be it." That is how it works. In the ocean, there are different fish at different layers of the water. Fish live along the bottom and then a few feet above that, and then still above that there are other fish. At different layers and water temperatures, there are different types of fish. Fish are very sensitive. They want to live in the environment which suits them best. They don't live in unfavorable environments like man does. Generally, the differences in depth of water determine the difference in temperature. It tends to get colder as it gets deeper. The difference is only a little, but this difference means quite a bit to fish. Remember, the fish will also go where there is feed. Each different species of fish preys upon fish smaller than themselves. They never prey upon fish that are larger.

Someone may assume that whales and tuna are big fish, so they must be in deeper waters. But don't just assume that. Think of where they would feed. The smaller fish are up in the higher levels. Even if the tuna like to be down deep, they must come up to feed. And sure enough, they do. That's where we catch tuna the most. If you only drop your bait in the deepest waters, you will never catch them. The temperature of the water, the type of feed and the environment, especially where they can be protected, all determine where the fish are going to be. And also, fish spend some of their time playing and resting; that is where the water is still and calm. After they feed, they go to play. The afternoon and early evening are the times when they usually play around.

You have to think about the currents. The small fish don't want to feed in the fast moving currents. Even the large fish find it difficult to feed and swim in strong currents. A lot of this is learned through experience. However, you have to have some idea of things before you also experience them. On the other hand, even if you know the basic theory of something, you don't really know it until you experience it. Think about the moon. There are different phases to the moon. According to what it shows you, quarter moon, half moon or full moon, the tide changes. Every day of the month is not the same. Sometimes the tide moves more strongly. At high tide, the water moves faster. Look at the water mark. You can tell if it is the high tide of the month or the low tide of the month.

It means this. When you know it is high tide, but the water mark is still higher than that, you know that it is the low tide of the month. Do you follow? There is a six hour interval between the high tide and low tide. There is high tide, then mid-tide and then low tide. From low tide it goes back to mid-tide and then high tide. The cycle moves like this and it covers twenty-four hours, two high tides and two low tides.

When you are tuna fishing, you have to consider the tides. You have to think, "What kind of tide is it now, high or low? Is the tide going out or coming in?" You have to ask, "If the tide is going out, what is the tendency of the fish? If it is coming in, what do the fish most likely do?" You have to put all this information together in your mind. And then, you must go out and experience it.

There are fish who eat when the tide is coming in, so when the tide starts to move in, you cast your bait and you can catch a lot. On the other hand, when the tide is moving out, you can even see the fish and yet, no matter how much you cast your bait they do not even touch it. Fish tend to feed at certain times of the day. They feed according to the tides, currents and also the time of the day. This is true of land animals. Did you ever watch the rabbit? There is a certain time the rabbit feeds. There is a very good reason for when they come out to eat. The rabbit does not want to eat in the middle of the day when the hawk is able to spot him clearly. The whole animal kingdom operates like this. They move about at the best times for their protection. For example, the tiger feeds at night. They do this when the small animals are sleeping. They travel up to 100 miles in their excursions. Elephants feed early in the morning when it is not too hot; the rest of the day they look for shade under the trees or they go to the watering hole. This kind of pattern is less and less predictable when it comes to lower animals. The small fish will feed at any time, but the larger fish have a distinct time when they come to feed in full force. Don't over emphasize that fishing is simple. Don't think you can go out anywhere, anytime and just throw out the bait. Don't think it just comes by luck. There is a whole lot more to catching fish than that. You have to study in detail. Then of course, after all that, there is some small element of luck.

Putting Theory into Practice, Practice into Life

I don't expect you to memorize this from one end to the other. You think you understand everything now, but when you get out there in your boat, you won't remember the first thing. However, teaching you in lectures is necessary. Even though you have never put this into practice yet, it is like a seed planted in your mind. By next year, you will begin to realize things and say to yourself, "Oh, what Father said has real meaning; I'm going to put it into practice."

It is like martial arts. The first thing you learn is basic form. However, when you are involved in fighting, you forget all about those forms. You just try to do whatever you can. Later, much later, as you keep using it, you come back to those forms and even use them naturally when you are sparring or fighting. How do you eventually learn anything? Through the practice of it. This is how you learn martial arts. It is not so much the lessons that teach you, but having to fight. In fighting you learn to put together all the lessons. And the one who becomes a champion is the one who challenges to fight again and again, even if he has to fight for twenty-four hours at a time. That kind of commitment eventually makes him the best in his class. It is not the big guy who wins, but the guy who has the most determination and trains the hardest.

It is the same with fishing. The message for us here is that we have to work hard and experience all the aspects of fishing, even twenty-four hours a day. For at least three years, you should fish in these grounds and you explore these areas much more than anyone else. When you become familiar with all these things, you catch more fish in two or three hours than all the others who come and fish the entire day. You must become an expert like this. You just have to start trying things and find out for yourself what works and what doesn't. There is some distance between Provincetown and Gloucester. Also, the fish behave in a different way according to the different tides, currents, depths of water and terrain below. You have to know all about these things.

You have to study about other kinds of fish besides tuna. You have to study the fluke and flounder. In other areas we could catch a lot around twenty feet deep, but in these waters you can't find them at twenty feet at all. So, we have to look for them, perhaps in fifteen feet of water or even less. The *New Hope* is a large boat and it is hard to get into shallow areas. The captain is always worried when I tell him to go anywhere near ten feet of water.

The *One Hope* can go into that depth of water easily. In that sense, it is an all round fishing boat. I designed that boat with the greatest fishing ability in mind. It can truly go fast and it can fit into almost every fishing situation. Some people think the boat is not economical, but if you know where to fish, you can get there quickly and get home quickly. If you don't study and know where you are going, you have to travel all over the place and still not find the fish. In that case, the boat is not so economical. However, if you study and know exactly what kind of fish you want and exactly how you are going to get it, another kind of boat which is slower is less economical. You waste time. You might save on some gas, but you waste the whole day and come back with nothing. What is so economical about that?

The *New Hope* is a slow boat. You cannot fish eight hours and then come back. It takes time to go out and come back. Actually, you don't get a full eight hours of fishing unless you go out very early and come back very late, and that is what we usually do on the *New Hope*. The *One Hope* is much faster; it is much better than the *New Hope* for all kinds of fishing. You have to show that this is the case. I have confidence in you and know that you can do it.

You have to study and then apply the principles which you find. The one who tries the most and also studies the most is the winner. Study the high tide, low tide and mid tide. These are three typical times which you have to try and discover what kind of results you can get. According to the depth and terrain, you go out and fish. You think, "Oh, this is the area where the fish are." And then, when you go out, you catch nothing. Don't just run away. Fish there all day and see what happens at different times of the tide. You have to consider all the factors when you are out fishing.

The striped bass is an extremely difficult fish to catch. I had an experience last year for three hours in the middle of the night when they were in a frenzy. At that time, you can't think of going in for any previous appointment or plan. Just forget about anything else except catching them because when they are eating, when they are biting, that is your opportunity. However, if you planned poorly, you might run out of bait. What will you do then? You cannot run into the store at three o'clock in the morning.

Well, this is what happened to us and we had to find a place at 3:00 a.m. last year. We had to look for bait. Someone had to go and do that. They had to knock on the door above the bait shop where the owner lived. Since the owner was a pro fisherman himself, he understood why we had to do that. But what if you don't have a place to go to and get more bait? I had already caught a lot of striped bass that day. Most people would have given up at that time and said, "It's been a good day and we caught more than anybody else, so let's go in." However, I didn't do that and after we got more bait around 4:00 a.m., we kept fishing and I caught still more striped bass.

Setting a record is very important. It is important for yourself and it is meaningful for the people in that area. When you set a record for striped bass in some area, people recognize you for what you've done. They respect you. What happens when they respect you? Well, they come to you and discuss where to catch a lot of striped bass. They want to know where you fish too, but you don't have to say as much. They may take you to their best spots, and you can then take them to one of yours. If you can set a record with one fish, you can gain tens of years of fishing experience in just one year by sharing with other fishermen like that. However, if you don't have any kind of record, they will never tell you much of anything. For example, I have an unusual story about fishing in Alaska last year. One man had led us to some far out retreat where there is some very good fishing. I asked him, "Who is the best halibut fisherman out here?" He and some of the other men there pointed to one fellow and said, "This guy is called Red. He caught a 400 pound halibut last year. He is the best fishermen in this area."

Then I replied, "Oh, that's a lie." I said it so seriously that I really agitated the man named Red, and he got so angry that he took me to the best spot on that first day, just to prove that he knew where the good fishing was! I also proved that this man knew a good fishing spot, because I caught a 100 pound halibut on the very first day. After that, I gave him full credit and this put him on cloud nine.

At the same time, I showed him a better way of fishing for the halibut and this really impressed the other fisherman. With my method I caught twice as many as the others did. It had to do with time. I was able to work much quicker and save more time than the others. I didn't reel in the line like the other man, but pulled it in just like a tuna line. And then, when I put the line back out, it went out much faster than the reel as well. By sheer mathematics I caught more halibut.

At the end of the day, they asked me about my method. I tried to explain it to them, but they didn't believe it right away. When I argued with them, they were impressed. They had already tried fishing like that, but the line always snagged on them. I had studied that too, but I had found a way to do it so that the line wouldn't snag. I showed that technique to them and they agreed that I had brought a much better result than they had.

This is why you have to study things. You have to assume something and then try it. That's what keeps you going. Assume something and then prove it. That's what makes you men and women. There are many different kinds of fish, but each fish has different habits. You have to come to know these habits. You have to research and study. Don't just sit there. Study, practice, make effort. You have to put in a lot of time and give a lot of effort. It is like this for everything.

Witnessing is like that. You have to put in a lot of time. That is the first thing. At first, you might not get much result. So then, you have to study what you are saying and who you are talking to. Apply this principle and put in a concentrated effort towards accomplishing your goal. Don't you see that this is just a basic principle that prevails throughout your life? It isn't just for fishing that you learn these things this summer. Once you learn this principle down to your bone, you will never forget it. What you learn here can go with you into anything, anywhere. If you learn something by doing it, you never forget. What about the person who doesn't want to study, research and give serious effort to something? We cannot have much hope for him. You have to remember that what begins small now has a big difference later in your life. If you pick up these habits now in your young years, later on in your life you will become somebody. However, if you keep on living without investing yourself in this way, studying and applying the things you learn, in thirty years time, you will be nothing.

I have lived in an intense way all the time. There is nothing that doesn't interest me. Fishing is just one area for me. I am not just a fisherman am I? Yet, I became one of the best fisherman around. This is because I apply the same principle to everything in life.

Become Worthy to Inherit from the Best

Another thing for you to remember is to get hold of the top person. Get hold of the top fisherman. Don't worry so much with the mediocre ones. You have to have a sufficient interest in fishing in order to approach the best person in your area. Even if you have a great deal of interest, you must also have a solid preparation within yourself before you can invite him over for dinner and talk with him. It's important to connect to the top people if you want to get things done. If you want to influence history, you have to become a quality person and be able to move the high quality people in your area. In order to reach these people, you have to be serious and study and be able to gain success in some area. Then, you can move the minds of people who are making the same kind of effort in their lives.

People who accomplish things in life want to have someone whom they respect to inherit those things. Who can they respect? They will respect the person with these qualities: the one who is serious and willing to study or research, and then make real effort to apply what he learns. This is the one who will gain such respect. You have to become like that.

Around the top person are usually four or five people and you have to study them. Each one has some good characteristics. One of them might work hard, but when his time is up, he's immediately gone. Another one might spend more time, but he doesn't work as hard. A third one might spend less time, but he is so serious and his sincerity tops them all. From them, you can figure out which patterns to follow. You take the best habits from all of them. For three years, don't say anything. Talking just drains your energy and takes away your concentration. Just put things into action. Be silent and learn. You must become one of the people to be missed. When you aren't there, the top man will ask, "Where is he today?" And the others will ask the same question as well. They have to become interested in you and they really have to need you to be around. Everyone should miss you. I look at all of you. I am thinking about someone whose face I want to see. This year I don't see someone's face which I remember from years before and I miss him. If I don't miss you, it's because you are not a needed person for the tuna season. That isn't so good is it? The one who has been fishing for a few years and is eager to teach things to others, is the one who has learned something the difficult way and wants to share with others. That person will have little tricks of how to do things and he will be able to teach about many different aspects of fishing that he found out for himself.

You will see someone who is faithful to his own job, but not so serious about the sake of the whole purpose. Then, you will see another one who doesn't spend so much time on his own job, but is more concerned about the whole group and how everyone else is doing. Some people are very faithful to their own boat and they don't pay attention to what others are doing. Such people think that is the best way of life for them. On the other hand, another person comes around, giving a hand to other boats and giving suggestions on how to improve things. The second person in both examples is the more precious person. The second kind of person never seems to bicker with other boats. He has already done his share on his own boat and with his extra time wants to help other boats. He isn't thinking of just his own boat, so how can he be in conflict with another boat? He is interested in all the boats. This way he keeps clear of all the little arguments that can come up.

All of us must become such a person that other people want to have around helping them. This doesn't mean you don't accomplish your own work. That's not it. It means that after you finish your own work, you are free to help others with theirs. You must learn how to be quick and efficient. I have practiced this since I was very young. As a student I developed these habits. In school, no one wanted to do the cleaning jobs, but I always took those jobs. In my school, I helped the teacher with more cleaning jobs than anyone else.

When I go to the toilet and find some litter I always pick up that litter without anyone seeing me and throw it away. When you make a habit of that, the difference will show up later on. Don't only do your own share, but be interested in others doing as well as you. Then, you will really contribute to the effort of the whole class.

I recently came back to Morning Garden after being gone for four years, and immediately I could tell whether the caretaker of this house had been doing a good job or had been neglecting the small things. In the boat it is the same. I never look at the boats on the first day out. On the first day, everyone is meticulous, but the day you finish is when I go to take a look. Some of the boats are really messy by then. The boat which is as clean on the last day as it is on the first day is the winner.

I have that strong standard of judgement in everything. Recently, I was looking through a machine shop. There were veterans of twenty and thirty years working there. I gave them some very strict comments, but each time, they were humble to what I said because they had only thought so far and not beyond that. They recognized that I had thought way beyond their thinking. This impressed them.

People who build boats think they build pretty good boats, but I go through their shop and pin-point things they had not thought about. Not a single point is a mistake on my part. I apply this kind of serious thought to everything. For example, the *Washington Times* newspaper won twenty awards this year in an international competition. Not just one, but twenty awards, and it's just beginning, just in its first few years of existence. This did not come about by accident. The people at the *Washington Times* know it was my serious attitude which produced this result. They don't think they could have put such a thing together on their own.

Basically, this tuna fishing is not just to go out and get the tuna and make some money. That is not the central point at all. This is good basic training for the rest of your life. If you apply the principles you learn faithfully, you can make a success out of your life. Do you understand? Like anything else you do in your life, you have to put a lot of time in. Study everything, discuss it with others and read it again, then put in concentrated effort.

Actually, I didn't have the time to come here, but I felt so much that I wanted to give you a good start, so I came yesterday and went fishing at four o'clock in the morning. Today I am here with you. Tomorrow I may go out too, but that will be the last day. I cannot stay with you all summer, so please, do your best. The last ten years, I devoted every single day of the season out on the ocean. Rain or shine, I went out. Literally, rain or shine. There were storm warnings and still I went out. One time there was a storm coming and everyone could see it clearly, but in the middle of the night I said, "Let's go." The captain obeyed and we went out. I've gone out in the midst of a frenzied ocean and endured it. And then, in the morning I came back in, having won over that.

While I was in the boat waiting for the tuna to come, I thought over and over again of the providence in America and planned what to do. I thought about the problem of world hunger and planned what to do step by step. I didn't just think one or two years ahead, not like that. Instead, I thought about hundreds of years to come and what to do to prepare for that. I thought about how to farm the tuna and how it could be nurtured and used for millions of pounds of nutritional food in the future. I thought like that all the time. There is nothing that I didn't think of in the long hours while I was waiting for the tuna to come.

Every morning I went out, no matter how early. I was always full of hope and expectation for that day. I came back when the sun was setting, returning with elation that I had done my very best for that day and wondering what the next day had in store for me. I expect you to take pride and to go the same path that I have gone. You are now privileged to tread the very same path that I have walked these past ten years.

Everything you do here is directly involved with me. Many things I have invented myself. I have paved the road and pioneered everything for you. Take that as your pride, and just as every rock along the pathway has witnessed what I have done, so your footsteps will also be recorded. All that we do has a deep religious significance. Don't just go out and catch fish like other fishermen, tie it up and bring it home. Please don't fish like this, not in any way like this.

This is a very precious opportunity. Don't be discouraged. Do you think that in my time of fishing there were moments that were difficult? Sure, there were. There were up times, and down times of doubt and worry. When you are very happy and elated, when you are catching the tuna, think of what kind of experience I had in the same moment. Would I have just thought about getting one more tuna, or would I have been happy because one more aspect of creation, of the world, was coming under the influence of God's love?

You have to relate the experiences you have to how I would have thought and experienced things when I was fishing. The success of your own mission is tied to all the other *One Hope* boats. Not just in this area, but wherever they are, all along the coast, even down into South America. When you are operating the Good Go boat think to yourself, "We made this boat with our own hands. Brothers and sisters made this boat." Also realize that we will make larger boats with our own hands as well. Someday there will be hundreds of ocean-going vessels that we will have made with our own hands.

These dreams all began here. They are realized here. The *New Hope* and the *Flying Phoenix* were the modest beginning of the future fishing fleet which will go all over the world. The first time I put my foot into Gloucester they all rose up against me. In a sense, it was ridiculous because they didn't know me at all. Anyway, in ten years they have seen more of us and they know how hard we are working to make the fishing industry successful in the future. Now, some are thinking, "What if Reverend Moon were to quit now like we once kept telling him to?"

Reviving the Fishing Tradition

In the very beginning, tuna was only ten cents per pound, when I first started. Now it is over $4.00 per pound, going up to $5.00 per pound and someday it will reach $10.00 or $20.00 per pound. You will see that day. If we can farm the fish, hundreds of fishermen can hope to make a good living out of tuna fishing. I have been paying the price for that to happen, literally. Our movement has invested millions of dollars to bring the foundation up to this level. We lost all that money in a real sense. It was just a sacrifice in order to bring things to this point.

The middle men who exploited the whole situation were really angry when I came on the scene. However, the fishermen know a different story and many have come to care about us. Not all of them see what is going on. Many fishermen don't look very far beyond their own boat, but some even love us and look for us to come each year.

The consumer will come to find out about tuna and they will begin to like it very much. Just last year, the price began at $1.25 per pound and it went up to $3.00 per pound. The buyers were upset about that, but you know how hard the fishermen work. They get up so early every morning and face the difficult weather. Did the buyers ever have to work so hard? No. They have never worked like that, yet they get most of the profit. That is why the fishermen really loved what we did. Because we paid more, the other middle men had to pay more too; they lost some of their profit margin. They are the only ones who complained. We wanted more of the margin to go to the ones who worked for it. That was our motivation. Those middle men don't have the right to take what belongs to the fishermen. Someone had to come in and fix that situation.

At one time Gloucester was a great export city for cod and other kinds of fish. When I came here the situation had gone so low that many fishermen didn't leave until the afternoon. They didn't even get up until noon! I really wanted to bring back the spirit of Gloucester. I wanted to change it. So, I started going out very early in the morning, as early as 4:00 a.m., and I would bring back a tuna by 9:00 a.m. This motivated them to start going out earlier.

When I saw they were leaving by 4:00 and 5:00 a.m., I started leaving at 2:00 and 3:00 a.m. When some of them even challenged that, I determined not to even leave the tuna grounds and just stay awake all night long on the boat. However, no one left earlier than 2:00 a.m., and so they gave up in a spiritual sense. Also, they had larger boats and they thought they were better because they had more expensive equipment. We proved it is not the size of the boat which brings success; it is the spirit of the man. We proved that.

After a few years of fishing, something like a morning ritual began to occur. In the early morning there would be a tuna strike and everyone's eyes would go searching to see which boat had dropped anchor. They would look for the red anchor ball and see which boat was moving away. Almost every morning, the first boat was a Moonie boat. We had less boats than all the other boats. Out of proportion to the number of boats we had, and the number of boats in the entire fleet, we came up with the first catch in the morning. This is the tradition which we built up with our own effort. Don't disregard this. I don't want to hear, "Well, Reverend Moon didn't come fishing this year so the Moonie boats are only doing a mediocre job." I don't want to hear that. They are thinking that we will be discouraged because I am going to jail. Why should we do less this year than any other year? Why should we be outdone this season? After ten years, we have built up the standard. Now, we can go way beyond that. Will you keep the standard really tight, or will you be defeated this year? How? How will you keep the standard? You have to catch up with my spirit. Whatever you do, do it in my spirit.

The essence is this: put all your heart into it. Talk to God and talk to the tuna. For the sake of the world, for the sake of God, do everything with all your heart. For ten years, we have fought against injustice. We have fought here in Gloucester and now we are beginning to win. Morning Garden has been returned to us, the fishermen are beginning to understand us and the mayor has apologized for Gloucester's earlier unfair treatment towards us. In all these ways, we have won a victory.

We have fought on all three coastlines. When we started building steel boats in Alabama, 3,000 people came and demonstrated against us. At that time, there were thirty-one other shipyards. Now, what has happened? We are the only ones to survive there and we continue to contribute to the economy there. Can you believe that? It has only been five to six years since we began working there. If we hadn't gone there, no one would have survived the crisis.

It was the same way in Alaska. Everything we try to do, the people come and try to stop us, but they have no real reason to do so. You can imagine how it is for me to hear all the reports coming in from everywhere in the United States. Every report that came in when we first started something was very bad.

I have put so much energy into this country. Our movement has invested so much time and money, bringing so much from all over the world and investing it into the United States. I often thought I should give up everything and go invest in someplace else. However, since God truly wants to use America, I have persevered. Everything I have done in this country began under full opposition. No one tried to understand or help me. Still, I have gained a tremendous foundation to uplift America. And you are Americans. You will inherit all this. No one will oppose you as they have opposed me.

They will welcome you. From now on, people will begin to see our motivation more clearly. We will win every fight. We have that foundation. First, you must save your nation. Second, you have to secure the future of the ocean. There used to be at least forty large fishing vessels working out of Gloucester. Now, there are only a few. There is no hope in this country for the ocean. We are bringing hope to this nation.

You cannot complain about anything. You are inheriting everything. The ocean has a great and wonderful future. I know it. You believe it. Who is that future for? For who? For us? For America. You came here, not because of your leader, but because God was calling you. You are here because of God's calling. You have to know how special it is to be here. Don't complain about being here.

I have already endured this course. I have already invested long and tedious hours. Not for myself. I didn't do it for myself. I did it for you. I know young people will come here every year. I did everything for the sake of the young people of America. You represent those young people. You have to receive and inherit all these things from me. If you complain, you won't be able to get what I am giving to you. I am concerned about this.

The *One Hope* is made with everything equipped to catch a tuna. It was made for you! I don't need all those boats. I designed them with you in mind. Before you came, I was working hour after hour. Will you go this course? Will you do everything that I am asking you to do this summer? Think about the tradition that I laid down here with my own sweat and tears. Everyday, working on the boat, I was thinking about you.

I spent ten years preparing everything for you. From now we really have to go out on the ocean and inherit everything that is there. It is there, waiting for you. If you miss this point, you will miss something great in the future. I have been so serious to make the standard--for you! Please remember this. If you don't make a foundation, then someone else will come and take it from you.

I did not pioneer all these areas for that. I have pioneered Gloucester, the Gulf and now Alaska. Many people already stayed here, but they never thought about my effort. No matter how early, I woke up and worked hard all day. Many young people would never work as hard. If you Americans don't take this from me, I will give it to the Japanese. If they don't want it, I will bring Korean members to inherit everything. If they don't, I will get the blessed children and make them take the inheritance. Do you understand? Are you clear about this point? Do you know what I mean?

From this moment, make up your mind. We start the program from this moment. Each day is a step towards the future. May God bless you.

"True Parents"
and
"Indemnity"

August 1985 -- Berkeley

THOSE WHO haven't seen me for over one year, please raise your hands. Where were you? In San Francisco? You are strange people, yes? [No.] Anyway, I am so happy to see you. You are so young; your face can only be compared to a flower, a blooming flower in the springtime. You have a wonderful face, but here in front of you is an old man. Maybe you don't need me. [No!] Sure, you don't need me. [No.]

Well then, what should I talk about? You are young people with vitality. Whatever you ask me to talk about, I can talk about that. In fact, I can talk about it for hours and hours, even months and months. I can talk about being happy or being miserable. I can talk about being excited or working hard in a sacrificial way. I can talk about being joyful or sorrowful. What would you like for me to talk about? [True love.] I don't know if I should talk about true love today. Maybe you should talk about that to me. How about Danbury? Do you know what it is, what it means? It's a prison. What kind of prison is it? It is an American prison. It is not a Korean prison. Why did I have to go there? You say it's because America didn't understand me. Why didn't America understand me? It isn't that America didn't understand, it is you who didn't understand, all of the members who didn't understand. I planned for thirty thousand members to have joined here in America by 1978. Had we reached that goal, we would have gained very different results. With that many members, we would have built a solid foundation here in

America. Without that, the American people and government held us in low regard. Whose fault is that? Is that the American government's fault? Or, is it our fault? Whoever may be responsible, the government went ahead with its prosecution. However, you belong to the American government, don't you? Therefore, if you say that the government is bad, it means that all of you are bad as well. The fact that I was in prison for thirteen months can never be erased from America's history. For the next tens of thousands of years, they can never erase that. The record which contains the case fills up a truck, but when they realize more clearly who I am, how will they ever be able to explain this case?

In your own mind, how do you feel? Do you feel that I should never have gone to prison, or do you feel that I truly deserved it? I can tell from your faces what you feel. Why then, did this have to happen? One thing is this: the government was afraid of me. There was no reason for it, but they were afraid. Why should they be afraid of me? Do I have horns like a monster? Do I represent some monstrous figure in this world? You look at me and you see nothing unusual about me. The only difference is that you wear long sleeve shirts when you are cold, but I only wear short sleeves. I don't mind this cool evening in San Francisco. I am not so different though.

People my age, when they turn sixty years old, start to think about retirement. However, for me, my work is just beginning. I am ready to go out and fight if necessary. Are you also ready to go out and give it a try? The Unification Church has two incredible terms that no one else has. Those terms are "True Parents" and "indemnity". Those two terms are wonderful. Not everybody likes True Parents. And certainly, the other term, indemnity, is not well liked. That's true, especially in America. Isn't that true? Do you like that other term? [No.] That's okay. No one likes that term, that word, indemnity. I don't like it myself. No one likes indemnity, but we have to have that word right in front of our face and always tread towards it. Why is that so? Those who are blessed, raise your hands. Oh, there are too many of you. If there are that many, I think I shouldn't say nice things anymore. I should say harsh things and scolding things. That's what you need to hear.

Also, why do I find myself standing right in front of all these women? Why aren't the men up here? It's one thing I didn't think about when I first sat down. It's no secret that I don't like American women. That's because American women don't like me. Isn't that so? [No!] What do you mean, "no"? You always blame me for not being democratic and fair to women. You always accuse me about male supremacy. You are just boiling inside about these things towards me. And here I am, sitting right in front of you. You know, I am on the side of all you men. Let's get together and envelop all these women. However, can we do that through power or money? No, we cannot.

Let's go on. You know, my life has always been a fighting life. I am the one who has received the most blame and accusation from everyone around me. I may be the most abused person in history. I have been blamed and accused for everything. You cannot imagine it. There doesn't exist one Korean person who has never said something bad about me, about Reverend Moon. Such a species of person does not exist. There was nothing wrong that I ever did to them. I never robbed or cursed another person. However, I have been cursed again and again and again. The Japanese people are also the same. There isn't one Japanese person who hasn't said something bad about Reverend Moon. That's especially true of the Japanese Communists. They have written my name on placards and demonstrated against me for over twenty years. They have continuously said terrible things about me, with nothing behind it, no facts, no reason.

Unification through Indemnity

In 1975 and 1976, when I came to America and set up the theological seminary in Barrytown, and sent out missionaries to 120 countries, is the time when the American nation and the whole world came against me. I made those missionary teams from three people, if you remember; one American, one German and one Japanese. The reason that I did this is because they represent nations which were fighting each other in World War II. Why did I make the teams this way? They were enemies just one generation ago.

Look at it this way. The Japanese are small, but they are "go-getters". Americans are tall and usually thin; they are like grasshoppers, leaping around and looking for just the good things in life. They are "go happy" and "be lucky" type of people. The Germans are precise like a machine or a robot. These three kinds of people were formed into teams, sent out to a foreign country, and they fought to their hearts' content. People wondered why I didn't select a more harmonious group which would get along together. It was a puzzle to many people, many leaders and members in the church. However, I could see the three points which these nations represented. The Japanese members who went on this mission boasted that they were the oldest member of the movement in the group. They had seniority in other words. That is always a very important point in Japanese culture.

On the other hand, America is the top nation in the world. No one can ever belittle the Americans and they insist on that. The Germans don't respect America, however, because they have better technology than Americans, they are more systematic in accomplishing things. The members formed teams, but because of such backgrounds, they wouldn't yield to each other. We not only had problems with pressure from outside, from persecution, but also we had problems within the teams themselves. The internal disunity was actually the greatest question. Then why would I send representatives from these three nations together? You already know the answer don't you? I did it for the purpose of indemnity. Since indemnity is the key to our work, I had to put such teams together.

The first step was extremely difficult because no one even spoke the same language. If you think about it, life can become quite interesting, quite unusual. If someone wants to say, "Let's have dinner," there is no way to say it with simple words. You have to do it with sign language. If you become harmonious in front of God, that is the highest, most stylish way of life. Not only that, but also none of the three spoke the native language of the country to which they were sent. You can imagine these three people caming to live together and not being able to speak the same language nor even speaking the native language. The resident people must have surely wondered what they doing in the country in the first place.

Each nation experienced almost exactly the very same situation. Then, some of the nations began to talk to each other. They would ask, "How about in your country? Did this Unification Church send someone who could speak your language?" They had to reply, "Well, no. They sent three people who couldn't communicate with each other and they couldn't communicate with us either. But, they are here."

Each country wanted to investigate these strange missionaries, but no one could understand what the other was saying. In some of the countries, they took the missionaries to each of their respective embassies and asked for an interpreter. In this way, they investigated about our church in their nation. They had to go to three different embassies. However, in some small countries, the embassy couldn't afford an interpreter, so it became quite difficult. Even though many of the embassies didn't support Unification Church, nonetheless, they defended their own people. The German embassy defended the German missionary and the Japanese embassy defended the Japanese missionary and so on. In that way, we were able to make relationships in many different nations.

Now, I want to reveal the secret as to why I sent out teams like that. I knew that by sending members out in this way, attention would be brought to these missionaries. Since no one likes the Unification Church, they would try to kick them out of their nation. Each nation tried to investigate the Unification Church, but they had to go through an interpreter from that missionary's embassy. Each embassy had it's own pride and didn't want to persecute it's own people. At least not on foreign soil. The world wanted to come against these missionaries and run them down. However, the embassies provided some resistance to that because they at least wanted to protect their own people. Do you think this was a foolish strategy or, in understanding this time of persecution, was this the best strategy available? While there was an uproar in more than 100 nations against our movement, I somehow had to sow a seed in these countries. The undeveloped countries don't know so much what is going on. They just accept what more developed countries say.

At any rate, I was very, very serious and had to make a foundation. The advanced countries were coming against me at this time. However, I sent missionaries into the less advanced nations so that eventually we could embrace the advanced nations. Is there any developed country in the world today which doesn't know the name of Reverend Moon? It's a household name by now, isn't it?

In the past decade, even though the advanced nations have come against me, we have established a strong foundation in many of the "third world" countries. Many of these nations don't want America to influence them anymore. They are putting up "Yankee Go Home" banners. Maybe we can start a new movement and have an affect upon that. There has been a lot of commotion about me in the developed nations like America and Japan, but, at the same time in many other nations, our foundation is growing.

The American government came against me with all that they had. However, the impact was opposite to their hopes. Thousands and millions of people do not believe that Reverend Moon was wrong and the government was right. While I was in Danbury, large segments of the Christian community, which initially came against the Unification Church, united with us and they united amongst themselves.

While I was in Danbury, I sent a package to every single minister in this country. It contained the Divine Principle book and Divine Principle tapes. We sent over 300,000 copies. Some of these ministers were astonished that we did such a thing, some were upset. In spite of that, many of them were drawn to either read the book or listen to the tapes. You know we have that kind of ability, don't you? People are actually fascinated about us and want to know what keeps us going.

The ministers in Christianity have the most valuable books in the world. They have the Old Testament and the New Testament. However, try as they may, they don't understand what these books are all about. They cannot always make a connection between the two testaments. Not only that, they cannot always make a connection between the Bible and the world as it is today. The Bible exists in many homes as something which decorates the book shelf, but it has no bearing on the events of the world today. It's often a mystery to intelligent people what connection the Bible has to the world today, to the culture at hand and the future towards which we are moving. More and more people no longer look to the Christian church as providing a function which is needed in this society. In this way, without a doubt, Christianity is declining. This alienation is the very point from which Christianity is suffering.

On the other hand, look at the Unification Church. We know the principles through which life unfolds. We know the pattern and timetable of God's providential history. Thus, we know clearly where we come from and where we have to go. When I was about to go into prison, many members cried and repented.

However, I said to them, "Do you know why I am going there? And do you know what is waiting for me when I come out of there? Do you understand the goal and objective of my going to Danbury? I knew there were several crucial things which I had to do while I was in Danbury. I knew that I had to accomplish things which American history could never erase, for however long it lasted. In Danbury, the prison officials were surprised to see many famous people come and visit me. They saw people from the Justice Department and the State Department visit me. They wondered, "How can Reverend Moon have such famous people come and visit him?" They wondered about that. Anyway, I did it.

They thought, "Hey! This is America; this isn't Korea. How can he do that? How come this man is leading so many people in America?" You know, inside our movement, the American members think the same thing. They wonder why I do things the way that I do, why I don't do things in an American style. I don't exactly know what American people outside our movement are like, but I know the ones inside our church very well. I can catch that kind of thinking right away. I know more about you than you know about yourselves. That's one reason why I'm the leader of the Unification movement, not you.

In ten years, in spite of everything, I have accomplished everything in America that I said I would. Some members in the church think, "Well, I've been in the Unification Church for ten years and I don't even have a new dress to show for it. I don't have a family, what will be my future?" You may be complaining inside yourself like that. Have you never complained like that in the past? What will you do, if after ten years, I order you to start fundraising all over again? This time around we should have a more meticulous organization than we had before. You may cry when you go out, but you would still have to go out. I might decide something like that. I know that your situation is a very difficult one. And you, you feel that I'm a strange person.

I'm not making you work so hard. Actually, your ancestors in the spiritual world worked much harder than you for this nation. They are pushing you. You Americans with blue eyes don't know the spiritual world so well. Oriental people have very small eyes. That means they can see deep into the spiritual world, while the big eyes of Western people can only see the external world. For example, when the camera lens is opened wide, it can only see a few feet away. However, the smaller the aperture, the more distant it can see. My eyes are very small and I can look deep into eternity. Also, blue is not a deep color. Black eyes are very deep. I like black eyes. That color is the color of African people. I like that. How about this? I have black eyes and when I ask professors who have blue eyes to come, they come. At the same time, when these world famous, blue-eyed professors ask me to come, I don't go. The thing is, they understand. Why? It is because I know them inside and out, and they know that. Do you know how difficult it is to make a match? I can do it for hundreds of couples in just a few hours. These matches are very good matches. How can I do that in just a few hours time? Can you do that? [No.] So then, you need me. That's true. You Western people need me. [Yes.] Well, I say you don't need me, you don't need me at all. No, no, no! [Yes!] Well then, maybe you do. You young American people like excitement. You like too much excitement. Why am I talking about all these things? It is because no one in this country understands what I am doing. Not even Unification Church members understand what I am doing. You have not understood me for the last ten years. It's a miserable situation. If you don't understand me, how can I ever hope to have the American people understand me? It's not only you, my own family never understood me. My own brothers and sisters didn't understand me. They were so puzzled by me that in a way they acted against me.

America may be a great country and Americans may be great people, but all you think about is your own nation. How can you be so great if you think that way? The problems of the world aren't so important to you. There are situations today in some countries where millions and millions of people are starving. Can you understand that? No, you cannot understand that. What I have to do is connect the better side of this world to the spiritual world. And then, I have to turn my eyes down into the deepest hell and I have to pay attention to the most miserable situations. I have to solve that whole thing.

The outside world wants to measure me with inches, but I am going by miles. There are two different measurements, two different criteria. They don't know what I am doing, or why, but I have a deep responsibility. I have to teach the people who can be responsible in a language they can understand. I have to teach the Christian people what to do. I also have to teach the people in the deep part of hell what they must do, and I have to teach them in a language they understand. It's very complex.

A good example of this is American women. They want to stand at the highest, most respected place in society. However, I have to drop them down into the lowest hell and leave them to work themselves up from there. When they plummet down there, they find that they are still able to survive. They never imagined that they would have to live in such a miserable place, but they are still the same person they were before.

Not only that, I have to move people from one extreme to another. This means the Oriental people have to come all the way to the West and Western people have to go all the way to the Orient. I have to bring people of every extreme together. They can't die when I do things like this to them; they have to keep on living. Then, they find out that they do indeed keep on living. Their eyes start to grow and they find that their outlook on life is changing and getting much larger. In this way, even though they are resisting all the way, they are improving as people.

Before, all they could do was look straight forward. They couldn't look up or down, left or right. Now, their eyes can look in any direction. They can look all around and see the whole world around them. Before, Americans could only see America. Now, they see the world and they notice that it has become so small that they want to put it into their back pocket. Don't you think this is an improvement?

The Value of Indemnity

Look at this frail American woman. She can now look at the world and embrace the entire universe. She has that confidence. In this sense, America has to perish. Not in a bad way, but in a good way. I know about you. Unification members have been in the movement for more than ten years, but they don't own much. However, you have come to possess something that can never be bought for millions of dollars. You have an outlook, a character, a confidence to do anything and go anywhere, which can never be bought for any amount of money.

Within ten years, this small sister has come to possess such confidence and "guts" that she can knock on any door and say whatever she has to say from her heart. She knows that even if 240 million people come against her, she is not wrong. That is some kind of character, that is some kind of greatness. That resembles someone you know about. Who does that resemble? You know what kind of person I am. You are becoming a second Reverend Moon. Is that good or bad?

There is so much more to do and I want to push you even more. You often say, "I don't like hard work and I don't like my central figure," but, you somehow like me. How about if I make you work even more? Will you still like me? Until now, you went out and evangelized, coming home with drooping shoulders, drooping head, drooping eyes. The people persecuted you so much that you felt you were about to collapse, so, I always addressed you with nice words and comforting things. However, the times are changing.

When you go out, many people now welcome you. If you come back and I welcome you as well, it's no good. You would just stand still. When the persecution from outside begins to decline and cease, then it's my turn to persecute you. That's true. That is the only way the good leader can be. I have to be that way towards you. Look at the Roman Empire. It was a mighty empire and at that time, it had worldwide influence. However, look at what happened. They forgot one thing and that was that their greatness was for the sake of the world. They decided to keep it for themselves and from that point onward, they began to decline. Finally, they collapsed.

If you look at America, you can clearly see that it is in the exact same position at this time in history. God has blessed this nation; it is not an ordinary country. Unfortunately, the American people think it is for themselves. If they continue to use the blessings of this nation only for themselves and forget about the rest of the world, they will, without exception, collapse as well. After World War II, if there was a great leader in America who could tell the people that their role was to help the less fortunate nations in the world, the American situation in the world would be far different today. In one phrase, it would not be the country hearing, "Yankee Go Home." From this slogan, America is experiencing its own decline.

I know the patterns and secrets of history, when a nation will flourish or perish. I know what will make this nation prosper. How can I guide this nation in the direction it must go? It is the same way in which I guide you. In the last forty-three days of my Danbury term, the world opinion about me began to change dramatically. If I let you become complacent about that, you would follow the same pattern as the Roman Empire. This is now the time when I will have to chase all of you out, for the sake of the nation and the world.

I will chase you to such an extent that you will no longer want to stay around me or be near me. I will be like a lion towards you. Since you will be afraid of that, you will pack your bags and go to where you cannot feel my gaze. You will have to go to another country and serve that country. I know what makes a nation rise or fall. Knowing this, I understand what is good for this nation; I know what is good for you. How can I act in any other way?

Things go around. The whole law of the universe is simply this. What rises up must also come down. Those who are on the rising side often don't understand that they have to come down at some point. This is the problem and the danger. At this moment, I know that this nation will eventually welcome me. Because of that, my mind is already moving beyond this nation. By the time they welcome me, I will already be working in another part of the world. The time when this nation welcomes me will be the time when I leave this nation. Why?

If I stay here, just enjoying their welcome and becoming complacent, I may be able to help America, but the world will be in peril. You may love me and want me to stay with you here forever, but this is not good for you. You would stop at that point. I will tell you this much, "Okay, if you want to see me, then come to the farthest place on the globe. Come to the most difficult place with me until the last soul on earth is saved." If you still want to be with me, and if you go to wherever I am, doing that kind of work, then you will never decline. That is the one way for the American people to prosper.

Maybe you were expecting that when I came out of Danbury, I would make the Unification Church a nice environment. However, I have become even worse towards you. What do you think? Is it because I met thieves and people like that while I was in prison? Did they affect me and make me more difficult? How do you feel about what I am telling you? Are you thinking, "I never expected Father to be like this"? Or are you saying to yourself, "Father, please chase me out, I want to work even more"? Do you want to stay here or get out?

If you don't like my words, I will chase you out anyway. Those who mind are free to go. That's the easiest and most convenient way. Well, which would you choose? Are you going to go away and choose the easy way, or stay and take the difficult course? Why do you want to stay? You must be crazy! I know why you would want to stay. You know the meaning of the word indemnity. You want to follow the difficult path because you know that will lead you to a better place. You don't mind if I give you a pounding because you know you will improve from it. Why? You know it is triple and ten times indemnity. If I chase you out and you go out to a remote country, it is a sure way to gain God's blessing. You know that, and I know that. That is why I chase you out.

Since I have chased you out, when you finally come back, I will welcome you. I will make a big feast and we will have a great celebration. I will praise you then and tell everyone how wonderful you are. Your ancestors will welcome you and that will be all. That will be our time. Until then, you must live the philosophy of indemnity. What you've done tonight then, is say to me, "Father, please send me out to suffer and I promise you I will bring back the result."

We said earlier that the two most wonderful terms in the Unification movement are "True Parents" and "indemnity". True Parents are the ones who take care of you, who receive you when you need help, who clothe you when you are cold and feed you when you are hungry, who lift you up when you are down. Isn't that the case? If that was all, our life wouldn't be so exciting. However, because of indemnity, our life is made more exciting, more meaningful, more joyful. True Parents are really the ones who teach you how to live the life of indemnity. It is the life that I have lived myself. Because of indemnity, I never do one thing at a time. Instead, I do ten or a hundred or a thousand things at one time.

The government may come and investigate my life as much as they want. While they investigate, I am adding even more things that I am doing. If they made it their business to know everything about me, their job would never be done. They would never catch up. Where does this come from? It is because I have suffered. There has not been any kind of treatment that I did not receive. Because of that, I became a versatile person.

The one who is being chased and persecuted must think more than the complacent person. He has to think more in order to survive. While others are sitting comfortably, I have always been active, thinking and moving quickly ahead. I have learned to plan as I go along. I can do many things all at one time. Do you think I am a capable person or not so capable? Let me ask you American women. Do you want to have a husband such as me?

I speak to everyone with the same intent. When I speak to professors, I make them work harder, but they don't mind. Even while I'm talking to them, speaking strongly to them, they are smiling at me. They love me for doing that to them. It is because of the principle of indemnity. In Korea, for example, they persecuted me from A to Z. In other words, they persecuted me in every way possible. However, when I speak in Korea today, they listen to me. They not only listen, when I command them to go out, they are already on their feet to do it.

In Japan, it is the same thing. America will also be like this. Don't worry, it will happen very soon. There is no exception to this principle. If there is success that has been won in this way, I am one of the few people who have done it. Everyone, without exception who has persecuted me, once they were won over, came back to me and expressed their repentance to me in tears. There is only one way to glory and it is this suffering path that must be trodden with utmost patience.

What is my plan now? It is to make every one of you a victor in this very same manner. How about that? You don't want it do you? You don't like it, do you? The Korean way is to say, "No, I don't like it," even though you do inside. It's very simple. One thing that I wanted to do in America was to reveal this simple secret to you. Because you have known about indemnity, you have been able to go on and on. Because of this, you will win the victory.

You know something that no one else knows in America. What is that? You know the value of indemnity. You know the secret of paying indemnity. While others were running their own race, I retreated and studied, knowing that someday I would have to run a race that no one else could do. Those who have lived close to me did not even know what I had to do. It is still the same with whatever I do, even until today.

There is a very good example of this in recent American history. The situation in Nicaragua is so obvious to people with a righteous mind. There was a proposal in Congress to send the Contras fourteen million dollars in aid. When Congress denied them even that small amount, I knew that something was seriously wrong and if that situation was left alone, America would be in trouble. Congress vetoed the whole thing, but the *Washington Times* spoke out strongly against their policy and after a few weeks, that veto was changed, and the Contras got double the original amount. After that, quite a few people started calling to say that Reverend Moon should stay in America, that he shouldn't go to another part of the world. Those kind of phone calls actually came.

You don't always look at the world in the same way that I do, but you need to do so. That is why I want you to get more education. You have to begin to look at the world with the same eyes as True Parents. You have to understand the world through the principle of indemnity. The term, "True Parents" sounds nicer to us than the word, "indemnity". However, if you want to understand True Parents, you have to understand indemnity. If there wasn't such a thing as indemnity, I would not be where I am today. No one would even know who I am. I know that you don't like indemnity when you begin, but there is no other way to get a true and lasting success. The Christian ministers treated me very badly when I first came to America. However, if I invited all the Christian ministers to come and hear me speak, more of them would show up than members of this church. What do ministers believe in? They believe that if they have "belief," they just go to Heaven. That's almost superstition. And yet they call us heretics without a second thought. Their ideas are somewhat like those of people living in a children's world. It's truly ironic, isn't it?

When I came back from prison, everyone was applauding me. My own family welcomed me, all the members of the church welcomed me and many of those same ministers welcomed me. They all said that I had done the right thing. That's remarkable when you consider I had just stepped out of prison. This is history, and it has to develop in a certain way. How can you stop history? It has now been decided in Heaven and so it will be done on this earth. Even though the Western world has dominated recent history, it will eventually have to follow Reverend Moon's way. How can the Western world stand up against God, once He has decided something? God has now decided to back up Reverend Moon, how can the Western world avoid it? They cannot and eventually they will come this way too. You wait and see. There will be thousands of young Americans who will be fighting to get into the Unification Church.

Now, our course is miserable, but they will come looking for you anyway. Think about that. Your future course as a Moonie is wonderful. All over the country, people will be making noise that "Moonism" is good. The atmosphere all over the country is changing and now there is some excitement in a good way towards Moonies. You are going to go up and up. People will come, asking about you and wanting to know where you are going all the time. They will want to follow you there.

I have a reason then, to be concerned. When the people start coming in, they will come in multitudes. We will have a serious competition at that time. They may even be better members than you. Before that happens, I want to put a seal upon each of you signifying that you have passed the true course. That's why I want you to go out and work even harder.

What will become of you in the future is determined by what you do now. Do you fight all the time with the Korean leaders? You don't want to listen to them do you? What did they do to deserve such a position? It's the law of indemnity. They are like the pillars of a building. Once you build something, you don't go and replace the pillars. You will be pillars of this building as well, because we are expanding. You might be smaller pillars, but you will be in that position nonetheless. When that happens, I will not pull you down and replace you. That is what you are preparing for now.

You wait and see if this is not going to be true. The students from Harvard, Princeton, Yale and Stanford and so forth, are going to come in. That's absolutely true. The professors have already come along, so it is certain that the students will someday follow. The professors understand and respect what I stand for. The students will learn about this as well.

If you have pride, forget it. Some members in our church are so ugly that things, monsters which you are afraid to see in the dark, are afraid of them. But I love them because they have lived in the law of indemnity. This is the great secret about Moonies. No matter how hard my words are towards you, you don't mind because you know that you are going to be elevated.

You have already heard what we are going to do for the next four months, haven't you? I explained to you about the 30,000 member goal, but now the time in the providence has changed. We have to educate 70,000 ministers. If we don't meet this deadline, it will not be easy for us. How can we educate that many ministers in such a short time? We have to bring 7,000 ministers who have come to support us or have learned about us through the Religious Liberty campaign. We can motivate them to bring ten ministers each.

These ministers have heard good things about us and they at least know we are not evil people, that there is nothing wrong with us. They at least can listen to us. It will be great news for America when they move, when they start to help us wake up this nation. When they raise up the banners and shout out to the public, this country will once again be on the rise.

For us, this means that the next four months will be an extraordinary effort, working day in and day out in order to educate the ministers about their role in America, in history. I have good reason to be confident that we will move America in such a way that God will once again want to work through this nation. Let's compare your situation with mine. For thirteen months I worked very hard in Danbury prison, still meeting every day with all the different leaders. Until now, who has had the more difficult life? I know you are working day and night, but I have to think of the entire direction of this nation, of the world and I can never leave these thoughts.

Before I went into Danbury prison, if one minister came around to our church and showed some interest in learning about Divine Principle, the members were overjoyed. Now, there are so many ministers coming to listen and understand our theology that there are not enough members to staff the conferences. That has already happened. There has been a great change. Where did such a change come from?

I have been working in America more than twelve, almost thirteen years. Does it look as if I haven't succeeded? Suddenly, it is quite the opposite. Think about it this way. This is your own country;

you know the language and customs of this nation. I had to come here without knowing the language, and the American people persecuted me so much they are almost my enemy. Who should work hard for this country? You should work hard because it is your nation. The law of indemnity is simple. The one who works the hardest will gain the greatest reward. I want you to have that reward, that recognition from your own nation.

Within two hours, I have explained to you about indemnity and you now realize how great it is. It is the guarantee for victory. So then, you have learned what I should do to you. There is another law or rule which is also simple to observe. For example, if you look at man's body, you will see that there is both hard bone and soft flesh. In a sense, it is a relationship of hard and soft or strong and weak, isn't it? If you have a strong personality, you may have a weak body. On the other hand, if you have a strong body, you may not have such a strong personality, but rather a soft or quiet one.

Likewise, America is a huge nation and a very great one, but it's personality is somewhat weak. The American people are not so patriotic towards their country; they are not so fervent to defend their own nation. In Korea, however, it is very different. It has been a weak nation, pounded by China and Japan throughout its history, but the people are bound to their nation with a deep sense of patriotism.

This law of existence seems to be at work wherever you go. Wherever there is the greatest amount of suffering, it seems that the greatest depth of heart and character emerge. From the abyss of suffering again and again for the sake of the nation come the people willing to do their utmost for the leader who can guide them to victory. Korea is now divided between North and South. They are surrounded by great nations and there is nothing that they can do about it. There is nothing that they can do which stems from their own will; they must always consider what other nations might do. They are miserable and suffering from this situation, but their spirit is high and their determination is very strong. Although the nation is externally weak, its internal character is very, very strong.

It is the same with me. The whole world has come against me. I have had to take everything in. I took the weak position, observing everything and allowing myself to be hit again and again. However, when I speak out to America and speak out against Communism, they will lose ground unless they can understand and accept what I am saying. If they cannot accept the righteous advice that I am giving to them, they will eventually lose. Until now, we have been on the weak side, receiving persecution. Once we gain a firm foundation, we have to become very strong and speak out for the truth and against what is wrong in the world. Can you understand clearly that we must become stronger in the realm of acceptance, not softer? As soon as I came out of Danbury you expected to hear comforting things from me, however, I have done nothing but kick you out and make you work even more than ever before.

In the American school system, you cannot hit the child, but here I am kicking the adults. Will you survive? Will America chase me out because I kick their young adults or will they keep me in? If they keep me, will they do that for a selfish reason? It will be because they understand that they need me. You already understand that. I don't need you, but you need me. Those who welcome me, even though I'm going to kick you out, raise your hands. I can work without you, but you cannot work without me. I am more fierce now since I came out of Danbury than I was before I went in. Perhaps you think I have revenge in my heart. No, but I know how God feels towards America and I am going to give that to you. Do you mind receiving tough treatment? "No!" Then, it is my turn to say, "Thank you." I accept your promise and actually, with that, there is not much more to talk about.

The Ocean is Our Foundation for the Future

Since I came here, I have been fed very well in this house and that wasn't easy to take. In prison, when it was time to eat, you had to eat whether you truly desired to eat or didn't feel like it. You get used to the schedule, but here in San Francisco the food came at all different times of the day.

Anyway, what is your impression so far from this talk? Do you think I still might love Unification members? Maybe? Maybe not? I found the word, "maybe" to be very useful in prison. When I wanted to say "yes," I said "maybe," and when I wanted to say "no," I also said "maybe." It was a very convenient term. While I was in prison, I studied the system very closely and I could not respect that system at all. After a careful look at it, I concluded that it serves no real purpose, it wastes a great deal of time and that it only creates a desire for revenge against the government within the inmates. That's no good.

Many of the inmates wanted to call and visit me when they also get out. Many of them came and asked me if they could do so. I couldn't say "yes" because they don't understand my life and my work so well, and I couldn't say "no," because I didn't want to offend them. So, I had to say "maybe." You understand why I did that, don't you? However, with you, there is no such thing as "maybe." I don't like "maybe" and you should not like it either. With our way of life, it is "yes," or "no." We have to be clear. Now you understand that you are either "yes" men or "no" men, but you are not "maybe" men.

It's truly good to see you, but it's getting cold here. Don't you want to go? It's too cold to stay here, so let's go inside. You are here with me and I think it would be nice to eat together, however, I'm going to have some raw fish, some sushi. I don't think you want to eat that. Let me ask you, would you rather eat it or sell it? We have Ocean Church now in our movement, don't we? When did we start that project? Almost five years ago. Do you know which mission Unification members care least about? The wives tell their husbands, "Don't go to Ocean Church; they have to eat sushi and I don't like that." Well, I don't like that kind of woman.

Do you know how the foundation for Ocean Church was made? I made that foundation. I had to do it by myself; I was completely alone in the beginning. Now, we are catching shrimp, lobster, halibut. Many Americans like that kind of seafood and I knew that, so I pioneered and developed every aspect by myself. Then, I had to convince the members. I watched many of them escape from Ocean Church during these past five years, but I kept going on. Now, we have a lobster pound in Canada and we have fishing in Alaska and shrimping in Alabama. We are developing the fishing on the East Coast as well. No one wanted to do this mission; no one really liked this kind of work. I was the only one working, in a lonely way, building this foundation.

In Alaska, we have an automatic system for processing the fish, otherwise, it would be far too expensive to run. I had to plan for that and even design how the factory should be laid out. No one had any interest in it at first. I had to think about how much fish it could handle at one time; I had to think about every detail. We went into a large debt in order to set up this automatic system. However, I knew that such an investment would someday be successful.

In Seattle, we will have to create a factory that can make surimi out of any kind of fish. From that kind of factory, we can make any kind of seafood. That kind of foundation is very important. In the beginning, I had to tackle this project on my own. Now, you are coming to understand it and you can inherit it. That's why I'm telling you to grab raw fish with both of your hands, grasp the providence of it with all your enthusiasm. Be excited about it because it tastes so good and it's very good for your health.

That's true. Meat is not the best thing to eat all the time. Doctors are now testifying about this point. They are telling people to eat more fish. Americans should eat more fish for their health. That's why we should make Japanese restaurants and a delivery system for fresh fish. Many people will get upset about Moonies doing this kind of work, but we are saving the fishing industry with this effort. They will come to see that.

You know about Gloucester, don't you? When I first went there, the cost of tuna was less than ten cents per pound. Now, one tuna is more than $4.50 per pound. When I came onto the scene, the wholesale people raised their voices against me. I didn't mind. That's good. I raised my voice as well, telling them that they exploited the fishermen. That is exactly the case. The fishermen began to see my true motivation.

After a while, when I went out on the *New Hope*, I heard many calls come over the radio, "Hello Reverend Moon! I don't hate you anymore. Have a good day!" That's true. Fishermen don't make much money at all. They are in a miserable situation. You think about the costs of going out on the ocean. The ocean towns are in a miserable situation. Why? The young people are escaping from those towns and moving inland. They can't make any money working on the ocean. Maybe they tried one time, but the boat went out and was caught in a storm. That's a miserable experience and many people don't want to repeat that, especially if there isn't all that much benefit for them. The young people leave those towns, looking for an easier job inland. Young people are the future. It's as simple as that. For these towns, it means they will eventually decline and perish. It's a serious question for them. I thought about this and asked myself how we could attract young people back into these towns and back into the ocean way of life. That is why I chose tuna fishing. When an American young guy catches a tuna, he will never forget that excitement. After one or two times, he can't escape from the ocean. He will be caught by such experiences on the ocean. That is why I want young people to go out on the ocean for an entire summer season. I want them to have this kind of wonderful experience. I've visited many other fishing towns. Fishermen love to brag about the fish they catch. They say to each other, "I caught this kind of striped bass and it weighed this much," or "I caught a halibut and it fought for twenty minutes and weighed this much," and so on. They talk and make so much noise, too much noise.

However, when a young man walks up and shows them a picture of his bluefin tuna and quietly says, "It only weighed 1,000 pounds," they will go crazy. They won't believe it. They will look at him with open mouths, thinking, "Is that true?" Any young man would want to have that moment of pride. I want young people to feel that kind of pride.

Many fishermen will never tell anyone else where they fish, but after catching one tuna like that, you can invite them to fish with you and they will come. Then, they will want to show you all their places and teach you how to fish for different kinds of fish. Isn't that true? Of course it is. That is how people are. If you have a beautiful boat and invite them to fish with you, they will become your friend. In a small town, if you have a beautiful boat like the *One Hope* and you tell the people that you helped to make it, they will automatically have respect for you. You don't know so much about the *One Hope*, but you will find out about it and you will see what kind of a boat it is. I have done many different kinds of fishing and I have researched many different fishing places. Also, my head isn't so bad. In fact, I'm a fairly smart guy. I see many details and I can connect them together.

With that kind of mind, I designed and developed the *One Hope* boat. Have you members, here on the West Coast, seen the *One Hope* boat? Oh, many of you have never even seen it. Well then, you are just like a country boy, not like a city boy, you don't know about anything that's going on. You should find out and catch up to other members.

I designed that boat and from that boat, I can make any kind of boat. I learned how to design larger and larger boats. Now, there isn't any boat that presents a problem to me. We can make any kind of boat. This also means that we can do any kind of fishing. That's how we have to be. If we can do any kind of fishing, we can also do any kind of fish selling. In New York city there is a huge and famous wholesale organization and they sell fish all over the world. Many of the Japanese members who came here worked very, very hard. For whom did they work so hard? They worked hard for America and for you! It is sad that this nation persecutes them, persecutes Moonies. You have to feel something deep inside you about that, otherwise, who will change it?

I know what you are going through. I know very well. You don't have the kind of responsibility that I do. I am the leader of the Unification Church and my concern is always how to make the foundation for you. I am down in the basement, preparing everything for the house you are going to live in.

Twenty years ago, the Americans used to look at the Japanese and say, "They are just like animals, eating raw fish." After these years, the Americans are changing. Now, they are paying a great deal of money, eating at expensive sushi restaurants. The Japanese restaurants in America will make good amounts of money. When those restaurants first came to America, they couldn't make so much money, but now the times have changed. We can make 1,000 restaurants in the cities of America.

Many other restaurant owners don't like the fact that Moonies are also in this line of work. However, it isn't a problem because if you offer people good food and nice service, they will smile every time they eat. We will have that kind of high standard and the customers will come again and again. It is very difficult to persecute the people who give you such a good experience.

We can teach customers who are truly interested how to make sushi in their own homes. We can offer classes during the off hours. Then, we can make a fresh fish store next to the restaurant. The customers who want to make their own meals can buy their fish there. That's a beautiful way to serve people and make good relationships. We can expand to every coast and to every coastal city in this way. It's good for you, it's good for the American people.

What is power? Power is the ability to be responsible for a situation. If you can truly take care of something, you have authority towards that. I know this point very well. The one who takes responsibility is the one who has authentic authority. You have to become people like that as well. Does America have that kind of authority in the world?

People need high quality protein in order to survive. America has that protein, especially within the 200 mile limit, but it doesn't supply much of that protein to the rest of the world. If America doesn't see the need and doesn't help the world, then I am determined somehow to do it myself. There is a lot of trouble over the 200 mile limit. The rest of the world knows the potential that lies in these waters and they want to fish in them. Their second choice would be to buy from America, but America doesn't even fish the waters it restricts other nations from fishing.

Do you understand what I am talking about? I know the contents of this situation and I know what it's doing to the rest of the world in relationship to America. There hasn't been one young American who thought about this. No American youth have come to help me, rather I am laying the foundation for you, you and you. Now that you see this foundation, you understand clearly what I have been doing all along. Now, you have hope.

For the last five years, I have known about the situation of the American fishing industry. There are many connections to drug dealing as well. It's true. Behind many of the companies on shore and the small boats coming in and out of American harbors, there are many drug dealers. The term for these people is the "mafia". The American government won't do anything to prevent this organization from doing its activities. They often control the importing and exporting, the prices at the dock and many other aspects of American harbors. They gain their control by getting people involved in drug dealing. Then, they can make people do whatever they want in business, as well as the illegal activity. Moonies have to be righteous. We have to correct this whole situation, step by step. The main objective of our organization is to help the fishermen. We have to be open twenty-four hours a day for them and for the restaurants. If any restaurant calls for a certain kind of fish, if we don't have it, we have to call everywhere possible and find that kind of fish for them. Everyone else works just eight hours a day. After that, they shut their doors. They don't have any feeling for what they are doing, they just do it and go home. However, along come the Moonies and they are going to put all their hearts into it. We will always have the freshest fish; it will be our pride. That kind of reputation will spread.

Not only that, we will also cooperate from coast to coast, from nation to nation. If they are catching fish in South America, we will help them sell that fish in Europe. If they are catching fish in Africa, we will help them sell that fish in America and so on. There are fish in rivers and lakes and oceans, fish all over the world. We just have to find all the ways to catch them, farm them, process them and sell them. I thought about making a boat that can also process fish at the same time. When we first started making boats in Alabama, one boat yard after another was closing down. Everyone said it was a terrible time to make another company like that. That's the kind of decline that the fishing industry is in. Why don't the Americans like fish so much? It's because they don't understand how good it is, how to fix it and enjoy it. We have to teach them.

They also do not know how wonderful the fishing way of life can be, so we have to bring the young people out on the ocean and show them how to catch a tuna. Then, they will catch the spirit of it. They will want to live their life in that way. I thought of that years ago. Now, I am telling you. Someday, people will look at Reverend Moon and they will say, "Reverend Moon is truly a good man." That will happen someday.

When you are making the foundation for something, people cannot see what you are doing. Only after you are done, do the people finally understand your purpose and motivation. That is why persecution is almost a natural phenomena. It has to happen. Many people ran away because of persecution, but I know all about it. My whole life has been spent in persecution.What happened by my going into Danbury? I lost four years of work and effort. Four years has been completely lost. My concern is how to make restoration go more quickly. I don't want it to drag on and on. That was on my mind the entire time I spent in Danbury. I thought about how things could speed up in America.

We have several cities on the West Coast. Centering on Alaska, Seattle and San Francisco are part of the providence of the North. Los Angeles and San Diego belong to the providence of South America. Think about that. We have many kinds of foundations and we have to make one in South America. They have a future as well; we have to help them make a good foundation in the world-wide fishing industry.

All the way from the North Pole to the South Pole. In South America there is Chile and Argentina. They are connected to the South Pole. No one is the owner of the South Pole. Someday we should go there. You should think about that. We have to connect all the nations between the North Pole and the South Pole. That is something you have to think about. From now on, you are working to establish that.

What are you going to love most? [Fish.] What? [Fish!] Yes, we have to love fish and more fish. We have to research how to make fish in the best way and in the least expensive way. If we send fish to Japan, they have a very high standard and will look at the fish very closely.

People will persecute you in the beginning, but just keep going. America and Japan actually need each other. They have a future destiny together. That is why you see many matches between Japanese and American members. There is something from each culture which can benefit the other. American brothers who have a Japanese wife can go anywhere in Japan. The wife can introduce her husband and he will be trusted by Japanese people. They will feel some kind of connection to him.

America feels it doesn't need Reverend Moon. However, it cannot be isolated from the rest of the world. Japan and America need each other. It's good to have these marriages, to bring cultures together. Everyone benefits from this kind of thing. You have such a special position in the world because you are part of these international marriages. This is the hope for the future. How about you? Do you have any concern about the ocean, about the fishing industry? Did you ever stop and think how it could bring the world together? How wonderful the ocean providence is. You shouldn't feel that it's bad to go to the ocean, to process fish or sell them. The ocean is our foundation for the future and we will all participate in some way or another in the ocean providence.

We have to make this foundation for the entire world. This is the fastest way to bring people and nations together. I am always thinking how this can be done and that is why I am making a foundation on the ocean. When we make this foundation, our direction towards the future will be straight.

Behind us, whatever foundation we make, is the spiritual world. You may not know so much about that, but this is the case. Some of our members are working in Communist countries, risking their lives, but they are making a foundation for the future there. What protects them? The CIA doesn't protect them, that is for sure. Something else is taking care of them--that is the spiritual world. Those members are always on my mind. You don't think about them, but I am the leader of the Unification movement all over the world. My mind is always thinking about things like that.

The physical world is a very narrow place. The spiritual world is wide; it has no limits. Therefore, as you work in the basement, building the foundation, think about how wide your work will go. Why is that so? Because, behind your work is the spiritual world.

This is why I made the ocean foundation all over this nation, in the midst of persecution, when no one welcomed me and everyone tried their best to get rid of me. So, why don't you work hard now and see the result in the future? I did that much without your even knowing about it.

From now on, you can become a "fish selling father." Who is that? That is a Moonie guy. Who is responsible for San Francisco? Who is that person? You have to lay this new foundation. You don't like the ocean; I know that. You can't catch fish, but you have to learn how. Whenever I come, you have to be ready to go out to sea with me. I've already been here two days and nothing is prepared. And who is the leader of Los Angeles? You have to do the same. The "fish selling mothers" are the Moonie sisters; the "fish selling fathers" are the Moonie men.

This is the foundation. Once you have made the foundation, the future is large. Already, during the past ten years, I have prepared this foundation for you. We have invested so much money and manpower, without receiving a great return. That is to be expected when you are laying the foundation for something big.

Learning the Parents' Language

How old am I? I am already sixty-five years old. What age is that? It's the retirement age for most people isn't it? When they reach that age, they don't do much that is new in their lives. Usually, they settle into the habits that they've already established. It was not easy for me to learn English; it is very difficult for me to compose English in my mind and speak it properly to you.

When I was younger, I had a brain like a computer. I could write down the concise meaning of a lesson and having done that once, never forget it, not even after ten years. However, when I now study English, I write down the meaning of one word in the evening and memorize, but by the time I wake up in the morning, everything is forgotten. After ten times memorizing one word, still I can completely forget it. Think about how difficult it is for me. Yet, I have learned English, in spite of how difficult it has been.

If you listen to people speaking English, they fill their sentences with junk words. They know the language, but they speak the worst words they can find. Many times, I have read the Bible and the *Divine Principle* in English. I don't like English, but I have to learn it in order to understand you and your culture. I am here in America and I am the leader of the Unification Church, so I have to learn it in order to communicate with you.

However, you should learn Korean, you have to learn Korean. Why? Because it is the mother tongue. It is the language from which our faith emerged. You can say it is our "hometown" language. When must you learn Korean? You have to learn it by 1990. After that, I won't use an interpreter. Anyone who wants to come to the leaders' meetings will have to know some Korean or else they won't understand anything. That is why many of the Japanese members are now working hard to learn Korean. You American young people have a longer way to go because English is much further away from Korean than Japanese. Still, you have to learn it because the original language of the Unification faith is Korean. Many scholars are now learning Korean so that they can read the *Divine Principle* in its original language. They understand the value of doing that. The reality is that you lose about 75% of the meaning through interpretation. Any intelligent person knows that they have to learn Korean in order to come close to the original meaning. You have to come close to the source of our faith, the inner portion of our faith.

You need to learn Korean before you go to the spiritual world because your ancestors will be upset with you. I know this reality very well. If you don't believe me, then tonight you can pass away and find out for yourself. I am teaching you very clearly about life in this world and in the spiritual world. Some Americans, those big guys, feel too proud to learn another language. That's their misfortune. It's the same with the small guys, those Japanese members who don't want to learn Korean. In the future, when they come to meetings, they will be miserable. Because I speak in Korean and the translation is in English, the Japanese are already experiencing that kind of misery. Usually, they just fall asleep during the speech. I don't want to see that kind of miserable situation, so please learn Korean by the year 1990. Otherwise, don't come to see me in Korea and don't come to my spiritual world. I spent so much effort to learn English. I started at a very late age, so I had an excuse not to learn English. However, can I speak English or not? Can do, or cannot do? So, I learned English at my age. How old are you? You are just young guys. For you, it's no problem to learn Korean.

At my age, I can do anything. I learned English, I went fishing, I did things that other members never thought of doing and I set a pace that even young members could not keep. You are young! You at least have to keep up with me. If you cannot learn Korean, you haven't even come of age. Do you understand this point? After ten years, many members will read the original Korean *Divine Principle* and be able to listen to me in my original language. If you cannot do that much, you will feel miserable in front of those members who can. Please study the mother language, that is what I am asking you to do. After the Fall, mankind divided into many different languages and cultures. God didn't want that. That's Satan's kind of world. You have to restore the original language. What is the original language? It is the language that the first parents spoke in the beginning time. However, those parents fell, as we know, and the history of restoration has been developing until the True Parents could be established. Now that we have True Parents, what is their original language? We have to learn that language, that mother tongue.

Only the power of God can bring the world together under one language. The *Divine Principle* should be read in Korean by everyone in the world. In this way, a common understanding can emerge. People will never stop fighting each other until they have some kind of common understanding. Mankind is separated now because they speak different languages and have different understandings about life. How complicated this world is due to this situation.

Think about God. Every night people are praying to him in thousands of different languages. Actually, it's painful to His ears. That's true. It's very complicated for God to deal with. Someone is praying to "God", while another one is praying to "Kami", while yet another one is praying to "Allah". You have to restore one language for God's sake. Think about how miserable God is in this situation. You don't know how difficult it has been for me in America. It's the same situation with God and so I know how miserable God is. God desires one language, one heart, one common understanding between His children. That is why I am teaching this clearly to you.

The ministers who visited Korea understood this point very well. Many of them came back from Korea saying, "I have to learn Korean in order to understand Reverend Moon and the Unification movement." If they understand this reality, why don't you? If other people can think like that on their own, why don't you? They are not Moonies, but you are. You are the ones closest to me, so you have to know what I'm saying.

By 1990, which is coming in five years, you have to learn Korean. I said this in 1981, but no one paid any attention to me because they said to themselves, "that's nine years away." Now, it's only five years away. Soon, it will only be four years away. Korean will not be easy for you to learn. It's completely opposite to English. There is only one easy way to learn it and that is to memorize it. You have to absorb it as if your mind were a computer. Will you study it? Will you do it? You are always promising things to me, but I am not sure about you sometimes. After 1990, wherever I go, I will only speak in Korean. If I go to Europe, I will only speak in Korean, and those who don't understand me will have to tape record me and find an interpreter afterwards, but I may not allow them to do even that.

I learned English so that you would learn Korean. I just said in Korean, "Those who understand me, please raise your hands," and none of you here did that, so you know what you have to do. Korean is very difficult for you to pronounce. Wherever Koreans go, they learn to speak the language very quickly. You hear the difference between the Japanese members and the Korean members who speak in English. The Koreans learn the language more quickly and their ability to pronounce it is much, much better. Wherever they go, France, Germany, Africa or South America, this is the case. That's because the Korean language carries such a wide variety of sounds, it almost covers any sound in any other language. Those who would like to learn Korean, raise your hands. Your government doesn't like Moonies, but you still want to learn Korean?

Your government doesn't like the fact that I came here and didn't Americanize myself, but instead, "Moonized" you American young people. They didn't like that at all, so they called it "brainwashing" and tried to make it sound evil. That's not a Unification word, that's their word. What are we doing that makes them say things like that about us? Compare your life to what it was before. Are you better or worse? You know how much you have changed, you don't have to say anything to anybody. Soon, they will understand you and recognize how good you are.

From now on, we will work even harder, won't we? There are only 2,500 ministers in this area and that's too small a number for us. You don't understand now why I am pushing you and why I am in such haste, however, in the near future, you will see the reasons more clearly. I trust that you will work hard. My plane was to leave over an hour ago, but I have been speaking to you and could not stop. I will catch another plane later.

Before I came here, I was fishing in Alaska. From early in the morning to late at night, I was on the boat fishing and didn't stop once to rest. As soon as I came here, I began speaking to you and haven't stopped to rest either. So, don't be envious of me, rather be sympathetic if you want. Imagine how the fishermen will be grateful that I once came here, fishing in the different ports up and down this coast, exploring all the possibilities in order to make the fishing industry prosperous in the future.

Not only fishing, but also all of the other projects in which I've invested so much time and effort will remain as the historical record of my work in this nation, long after I am gone. Envision this much: the thought of Unification will embrace the world in years to come. White people, black people and yellow people will all be grateful to know Unification Thought in the future. In the future, there will be poetry and literature coming from those who miss me and long to follow in my tracks; black and white and yellow people will write such things. Even the people from Danbury will have such feelings and express them. This is also true for you. We are not living for the sake of today, but for the sake of the future. I am determined that my course, which started from suffering, will end in success. That same situation must hold for you as well. If I decide something like that, can you go a different course? This is the tradition of True Parents and I am leaving it behind for you and you should tread this way, all the way, until the last of the world is saved. You cannot go any other way until this is accomplished. We call this the greatest way of life and actually, for you, it is the greatest way of life.

In your own mind, you can never erase the memories you have of me. This even includes ex-Moonies. Many of them are now anxious to come back and they are finding some way to come back into the church. Even though they left the church, they can never forget their experiences with me. This situation is a very sad and miserable one. The first time I went into prison, everyone was suffering and I look back at those times and feel the weight of it. However, this time, as I came out of prison, people everywhere were welcoming me.

When I think of members who left, I know that when they see you working out on the streets, they have to look sideways and they cannot come up to you so easily. Who made that miserable situation for them? I didn't. I never want to see people in that position. They made that miserable situation for themselves. It's a very sad thing, and I understand it very clearly. In Korea, there are ex-members like that and they cannot get beyond the suffering they experience in missing this way of life.

This is the only way I have lived my life and I can never leave this way of life, even though so many people have left it while working with me. This is the only way of life for you and you will never regret it when you look back in history. Everyone in the spiritual world knows that this way is the righteous way, the only way. I know that you will work as hard as you can. May God bless you. Amen.

The Heart and Spirit
of Fishing

July 3rd, 1986 -- Morning Garden

IS THERE ANYONE here who is seeing me for the first time tonight? Are you new members? If you are a new member here, I am sure you have not experienced tuna fishing before. What did you do before you joined the church? Are you at least eighteen years old? Even though you are all in your early twenties, you are too young. Those who are here for tuna fishing for the first time, please raise your hands. Don't worry about your result this season. I understand that most of you are inexperienced. You have learned much during these ten days of education and training. However, when you look at the difference between these few days of classes and actual fishing itself, this training is nothing. It is like a speck of dust compared to the reality. The most difficult kind of fishing, amongst all the various kinds which you can learn, is tuna fishing.

Giant tuna are such difficult fish to catch. They can be found all over the world, in five different seas. Because they travel such great distances, they need speed. When you finally see an actual tuna, you will see that the side and back fins fold in so that the tuna moves just like a torpedo. Their top speed is around 100 knots and they average about thirty knots. Think about the life of the giant tuna. They have lived in the ocean for ten to fifteen, some of them more than twenty years. They have gone through so many risks, dangers and difficulties and are still alive. In that sense, some of their brains may work better than ours. For example, when the tuna seiner comes, the tuna don't just pass by the boat casually. They turn sideways and look very carefully. We are here to catch that very smart kind of fish.

271

Some of the largest tuna weigh over 1,000 pounds. They are larger than a big bull, but they don't have bones like the bull. In this sense, God has prepared the tuna as a gift for mankind and we are here to receive that gift. However, in general, American people have been ignorant of how good tuna taste, but the Japanese people have known about it for a long time. The tuna is extremely tasty. A professor in Japan who has been developing and managing a tuna farm expressed concern that if Americans acquired a taste for tuna there would be none left for the Japanese. Fortunately, Americans don't know so much about tuna yet. However, when they find out the Japanese people are in trouble.

Let's compare something. If we say that whales are the kings and queens of the ocean, then tunas are the most handsome princes and beautiful princesses. We are here to catch this handsome and beautiful prince and princess of a fish. How beautiful and handsome are they? Let us suppose you have been on the ocean for days and days and then you catch one. You look at it and then immediately you go and kiss that tuna. Many people have been inspired like that.

You can think like this, "I'm here to catch this tuna, but my skinny and rough Japanese hands are too ugly to even touch such a beautiful and handsome fish." You can certainly think like that. You must have lots of curiosity about catching tuna. I myself started fishing fourteen years ago. When I brought the *New Hope* here for the first time, the entire country knew about it. When I first came here, I didn't know anything about tuna fishing. I didn't know what kind of hook to use or how to make the lines or anything at all about it. However, I had more confidence than anyone else that within three years I would be the master of tuna fishing.

Father's Foundation in Tuna Fishing

When I first came here there were lots of tuna, maybe more than there are now. On the average day, it was not unusual for a boat to go out and catch at least one fish a day, and many times they would catch two fish. Thinking about those early days, I want to share a deep experience with you. In the beginning, I went out time after time and hooked up a fish, but then I would lose it. All the fishermen who had caught their fish would come back and say, "Another day where Reverend Moon hooked up a fish, but lost it."

I was not able to catch the fish and bring it up to the boat. This happened almost every day. And so, this became their daily gossip, whether I could actually bring home a fish or not. You will see that there are many large and luxurious boats which go out tuna fishing. Some of them bring their children and wives. I experienced them telling their families day after day, "Oh, Reverend Moon lost another fish today."

How many times in a row did I hook up but fail to catch? Not once, not twice, not even three times. Not until the sixteenth fish did I finally succeed. That was the first time in twenty-one days that I was finally able to bring one up to the boat. Mr. Ohnuki is a living witness to this history and he should stand up tonight so that you can see who he is. Think about those twenty days that we went out and the fifteen fish which we couldn't bring up to the boat. When we got that sixteenth fish, Mr. Ohnuki was in tears at that moment. Think about the conviction that we had to have to get that first fish.

In my mind was the thought, "I must train the youth of America to be able to catch at least one fish a day." Think about having that thought during those twenty days. My focus was on the way to hook the fish and not lose it. I was constantly studying this point. Another way of looking at it is to consider the money that is spent tuna fishing. Think about spending so much money day after day and not being able to catch even one tuna. I became a desperate person.

You must understand why I started fishing for tuna in the first place. You must know why I designed this type of training. There are four major fishing areas in the world. One is in Norway and the other three are around the American shoreline. There are other fishing areas of course, but the major ones are right here. In other words, no matter what kind of fish you are looking for, you can find it in the waters around America and you can find it usually in great quantity.

The tragedy is that in general Americans don't appreciate fish and don't eat them. The fish go through a cycle, they are born and then die. In a way, it is a real waste to just die. Those fish are there to be eaten, either by a larger fish or by man. Fish are a high source of protein and nutrition. If we don't eat them, if we just let them die and go to the bottom, it is a real waste.

Furthermore, about six or seven years ago, America declared their fishing borders and foreign boats cannot cross over them. This declaration has become a political issue. Nations which really depend on fishing as part of their economy such as Japan, Italy or Germany have been protesting this boundary. At the same time, the American people do not care much for fish, so there is no one to initiate anything new in the fishing industry. Out of concern for the future, I began many of our educational projects and business ventures centered on the ocean. On the land, if you farm, it takes about twenty years to establish your foundation. However, if you begin an enterprise on the ocean, you can begin to see results after just five or six years. Better than gold, the ocean is waiting to be used by man. The problem is that people do not know or care so much about it. One of the reasons that Americans do not care for the fishing industry is the nature of fishing itself. When the large fishing vessels go out, they stay out fishing for three to six months. Many of the fishermen's wives stay at home with nothing to do and often they finally just leave with someone else.

Therefore, young people who are growing up in ocean towns don't think about getting involved in fishing at all. Instead they run to the larger cities where they can get a nice job in an office. For example, this city of Gloucester used to be very busy, before the 200 mile limit was set. Many foreign ships were coming in and out, buying supplies, loading and unloading, so the young people of this town could find jobs and work here. Gloucester was very busy indeed and at that time it was growing. However, after the declaration, many young people ran away and Gloucester became somewhat of a ghost town.

Without the boats coming in and out, without the young people staying to work here, who is the master of this town? Well, the Moonies appeared just a few years ago. When we first came here, people thought, "Moonies are the worst of the worst people." They looked at Reverend Moon as some kind of scary spirit and tried to kick him and all the Moonies out. Actually, Moonies are trying to be the best of the best people. Now their attitude has begun to change from being so nasty to more warm and welcoming.

Many people brought their luxury boats here. They sat on the deck with their big bellies showing from beneath their shirts and shouted at us, "Hey! Who are you? What are you doing here?" They said things with a very nasty feeling behind it. At first, none of us knew anything about tuna fishing. We had to go around buying different kinds of hooks and things. Some of the members went with me, but they didn't know anything either. Then, people would whisper in the stores, "Oh, that must be Reverend Moon." In some cases, a store would close its door when I came and they would say, "You cannot come in." Then, I said right back, "Open the door."

In the beginning, I would ask for some kind of fishing gear which I knew the store owner had, but they didn't want to show it to me. They would show me some equipment which was not as good as what I had asked for. I had to keep going on with endurance and patience, facing all these things. I didn't do it because I wanted to make my own profit; I kept going because I wanted to make these ocean cities alive again.

The Vision Behind Tuna Fishing

My goal is to develop once again the ocean cities in America so that fish and fish products can be exported to feed people all over the world. Some of you may be wondering why you have been called to Gloucester, such a small and insignificant town. You must inherit my spirit which overcomes persecution and difficult situations, because I have a vision of how to save the world and even provide food for the entire world.

The boats you are riding on were designed by me and built by the members. After nine years of experience, I developed the Good Go boat. When I first started building these boats, no one had any expertise. Mr. Kamiyama was at a total loss when he first heard my plan for the boats. He looked completely shocked and said, "What, we are going to build fishing boats?" He truly hoped that I wouldn't tell him to build those boats, but I said, "Build 150 boats in the first year."

Think about it. With so much money invested in such an expensive boat, each one was given to completely inexperienced members who didn't know anything about its value. With these boats, they were trained how to fish for tuna. With each boat that we produced, there was a tremendous amount of tears and sweat and prayer involved. You may not be able to see that, but that kind of spirit is built into each boat. If you truly understand this, you must shed tears when you ride on that boat. When I took my first ride on a Good Go, did I cry or did I just laugh without much serious thought? What do you think? Therefore, you must pray to have the proper attitude and inherit the spiritual and international connection to these boats. Each country around the world sent their members to help build these boats, and they put their tears and sweat into these boats. No one understood anything. We started virtually from scratch. No one knew what kind of material to buy or how to begin the first step. I know the value of each boat will be worth more than 100 thousand or a million dollars in the future. Why? Because people will say, "This is a boat built by Reverend Moon." For this reason, I instructed the members to buy the best quality of materials that they could find; they had to build the boat with the highest standards, not just so-so.

I know that in the future sometime, in each of the fifty states, even if they have to sell their capitol building in order to buy one of these boats, they will do that. But now, some Unification members feel like they don't even want to look at those boats, that they want to run away from their boat. I see that kind of thing. My goal and desire and hope is built into this boat, but the young American members don't understand this and sometimes, they try to run away from this boat.

If you read the speech from when I began Ocean Church, you will see how serious and how important that message was. However, even after I gave that kind of explanation, many of them since that time went away from this Ocean Church activity. It's a shame, but I cannot give up. Even though I wanted to give this to American young people, they didn't catch their opportunity, so I had to bring young Japanese members to do the job. In order for you to find the most valuable and precious treasure, you have to go the most difficult path. That's true.

American members who are here this summer, did you come voluntarily or did you come because you were sent? Do you really want to be here? I don't believe you, yet. You will have to show me. I have watched so many American members leave and run away from this Ocean Church activity, even though there might have been good reason for some to go. I stood by and just watched their coming and going. In the meantime, I never changed my goal and my spirit for this Ocean Church endeavor. Why? Simply because I know the value of it.

If you American young men go out fishing, who will point a finger at you? No one. However, everyone pointed at me because I was a Korean man. You must understand that with everything you go through, every difficult situation and every persecution, I have already gone through this course before you. Do you understand? I never retreat, but always move forward. People might have said this year, "Well, Reverend Moon was in Danbury prison last year and now he is out. His movement must have declined a little since he was there. Well, they had twenty or so boats last year, so maybe this year we will see only ten or so boats." Instead I went right ahead and ordered seventy boats to go out this year! Do you have the same spirit?

I think you are just like any other young American out there. You are the same type. You are shouting "No!", but I think you are the same type. What do you think? Is this true or not? I cannot trust you. You have to show me! When you bring result, then I can see you are different. From now, we are going the difficult way. Can you do it? Raise your hands. Can you do it? Those Japanese members who didn't understand my talk missed the chance to raise your hands. Please do not forget that the boats you are riding in are the best of the best fishing boats in the world and they are made by Reverend Moon. We built this boat, Moonie spirit built this boat. Not because we wanted to make money, but because we wanted to make the spirit of America alive again.

Until this city of Gloucester itself disappears, we will come here every year. We will take care of this town; we will take care of this ocean. We have about 200 people here tonight. Everyone has a similar situation don't they? You have two hands and two eyes and all your limbs intact. I may indeed have the same features as you, but when it comes to the ability to lead people, to having a fighting spirit, to being able to go on, I have more ability than all 200 of you together. The difference is in my determination and dedication, in my spirit.

The Kind of Men and Women We Must Become

Even when I went to Danbury, I was not defeated by this country, but fought against the injustice. When I came out, I was acknowledged for my fight. We need guts. We must stand tall and say, "No matter how fierce the wind blows, no matter how much the storm comes, I will stand here and never stop." Several years ago, there was a storm warning in Gloucester and the radio announcer told everyone to stay at home. Then, at 1:00 a.m., I said, "Let's go." The wind was blowing so hard that everyone knew the danger involved. In spite of that, I said, "March." And out into that storm we went.

I like that kind of man. Any kind of woman likes that kind of man. How about you? Do you like that kind of man? Or, do you just like a disco dancing man? What kind of man are you? Are you a Reverend Moon style of man? I am a very tough man. At the same time, I must follow the spiritual direction. Do you know what I mean? This is the kind of spirit we must have, saying, "Until I have finally closed my eyes, no one will open my fist. I will grab this way as strong as I can and never let go."

In general, the American people do not have a strong tradition, only 200 years of history. A small country like Korea has almost 5,000 years of history. This means you only have 1/25 of the time on earth as Korea. In comparison, you have very little tradition. Americans tend to follow the wind. If it blows east, you go east. If it blows west, you go west. For example, because you lack tradition here, men are saying, "Well, I don't need women. I will just live with other men." The women are saying, "We don't need men either, we will just love each other." If this kind of phenomena continues for another century, the American people will simply disappear.

Think about it. Maybe the Black people and the native Indian people are saying, "Well, you White people just keep on going like that. In another hundred years, we can have our country back; we can take care of this nation without you." It's really a shameful thing. Young people in this nation do not have the concept of shame. They think that free sex is just natural, but Moonies must be different from these kind of people, not just in quantity, but in quality. Your quality must be such that even if someone wanted to trade the entire population of America, 240 million people, for your spiritual life, you would not be swayed by that.

If there are two types of people living together, the stronger of the two will survive. Whoever puts more effort into something will become the subject and whoever works less will become the object. For example, Japanese people work almost twenty-four hours a day and they work seven days a week. On the other hand, American people work only a few hours a day and just part of the week. Who will be the owner in the future? Who comes out ahead? The hard worker or the easy going worker? Yes, the hard worker.

That's why, when I came to America, I looked around and found who was working hard. I said, "If you are working ten hours a day, I will work twenty hours. If you take twenty years to lay the foundation, I will take only ten years." That was my determination and it remains my determination. Those who don't want to inherit that spirit from me can raise your hands. It's easy to hear and understand these words, but if you try to practice this and apply it in your daily life, you will turn your head from it and say, "I can't go on."

Here you are getting up at four o'clock in the morning and there is no light. I can hear you saying, "Oh, this Moonie tradition, I don't like it at all. There's too much to do all the time. This is a problem for me." No! This is a problem for ME! For me, that kind of person presents a problem. Our situation is that we are in a difficult world. As we progress, it gets more difficult. You think about our ideology. We can unify the world. That is our concept; that is our possibility. How will we do it? How difficult has it been for you? From now on it becomes even more difficult. This is our conclusion.

Early in the morning you think, "Oh, this is crazy to live like this. This is Oriental tradition, this is a Korean system. I don't like this!" I know this point. Do you think I am just a Korean guy? For forty years, since the end of World War II, I always took the different way. Even in Korea they said, "This is a crazy guy, something is wrong with his brain." I did everything the difficult way. Not even in Korea did they want to do it this way. This is not the Korean way, not the oriental way! Why were they against Reverend Moon in Korea? Why were they against me in Japan? Why were they against me in this country? Because this way of life is God's way. God knows what I have done. I have done everything the way that God instructed. God doesn't go the way of the handsome guy, the easy way. No! God's way is the most difficult way. I have always compared two ways and gone the more difficult one, no matter what.

Why? Because I am so concerned how to make the shortest course possible. I want to go the distance in the quickest way. No one wants to go that kind of way. However, God insisted I go that way, so I have always gone that way. Now, the spiritual world and the Unification world has to go that way. This way is different from America's way of doing things. That is why the young Moonie doesn't like the Unification way of doing things. Your concepts make it difficult for you, not the way itself. Do you understand this point?

Who can represent the Unification way? You? Or you? I have always thought about the future, about the entire world. You never thought about that so much. Why do you cling to doing things the American way? You say, "Oh, America is the number one country, the leading nation of the world, the champion of the free world. We are the first in everything." And you wonder, "Why should we follow this Oriental system from Reverend Moon?" Either go this way or don't. The Bible says, "Be cold or hot." God doesn't like someone in between. Even Satan doesn't like that kind of person. How about you? You are hot to go this way? Hot water or hot Moonie? What are you? Those who consider yourselves different from the people I just described, raise your hands. What do you think of my response? Am I giving you a good smile or a suspicious smile? Make a new determination in yourself. With your stomach, with your guts make a new determination. This is why I came to speak to you today. It is my sole reason. Let me ask you one more time. Do you want to follow this way?

Father's Heart for Fishing

Okay then, let's return to my story. Sometimes, when you are speaking, you have to clean out the room before you set the table. Isn't that true? That's the meaning of leadership. Now I am sure that you have the kind of spirit that says, "No matter how much the storm comes, I will go out." Do you have that spirit? Good. That's the difference. Now you feel confident and I feel happy to talk to you as well.

You've been given responsibility for these new and clean boats. After seventy days of tuna fishing you must be able to return these boats just as clean. This is how you not only love your boats, but you also love the country. Once you are out in the ocean, which is more important, your body or your boat? No, no, no! Your body is more important! Okay, you insist that the boat is more important. This time, I will agree with you because it is true when you go out on the water. On the water, your boat is how you survive.

Therefore, you must love your boat more than you love your body. No matter how famous you might be, no matter how many people are on the boat, the boat is of more value than they are when you are on the water. Without the boat, you cannot exist. Think about the people who clean their hands when they have grease on them, but don't bother to clean the boat when it has some dirt on the side. That is not the spirit that I have been talking about today.

If we have such an attitude out on the ocean, the boat will hate you and even the ocean will hate you. However, if you love the boat with all your heart, even the ocean will embrace you. Only when the boat returns love to you and the ocean embraces you can you stand and be truly happy. How wonderful it is if you can ask your boat, "Are you proud to be with me?" and your boat replies, "Yes, that's true." If you feel that from your boat, if you feel that from the ocean, how wonderful it is.

Furthermore, you have to love and take care of the equipment on the boat. The engine and the boat are protecting your life. Your lines and hooks, you must love more than your own clothes. When you love someone or something, you never hurt them. And it comes back in the same way. If you love your boat and all the things on that boat, they will not hurt you. They will even protect you.

This is the kind of attitude you must have. If you have such an attitude, there will be no accidents. On the boat, the most important thing is the engine. Without the engine you cannot move, so it is like the heart of the boat. No matter how good your boat may be, if there is a storm and your engine is not operating properly, you will not be able to move. Also, you must learn how to steer the boat correctly. You shouldn't make sudden movements which are dangerous. Don't play on the boats. In the first nine years of fishing, I never went down to the bottom deck and slept. After that period of time, I had a terrible headache one day and had to take a rest. The owner or master of the boat must keep a high spirit and take care of the boat. That is the spirit we must have.

I have seen so many members who just go to sleep all day. They lean over the side of the boat and show their backside to me. It's quite a view. Well, do you know how old I am now? I am almost sixty-seven years old. At my age some men depend on their canes. However, here I am at this age standing straight and I am the one who has to push you, you young American people. I look at you now and see your spirit. Tonight, you have the spirit of a general who wants to take over the entire world. I really wonder how long you will keep that spirit. Forever? I've heard that before! At least for the tuna season? Who said that? That's a good answer. It is the first step.

Please remember the main point. Love your boat. In Gloucester, we have people who have been tuna fishing seriously for many,

many years. They are studying my method and trying to copy it. I came up with the system myself. One aspect of it is that you don't ever have to cut any of the lines. You can untie and re-tie the lines. One tuna line costs about $1,500. Whatever you do, don't lose the line by having to cut it. I have used a line for more than five years without ever losing or cutting it. If you lose a line, even if you catch a tuna, already one fourth of the price is gone.

My method is very organized and economical, therefore, it's superior to any other. The training session you have just gone through is not adopted from somewhere else; it is from my tradition. The original training session is from my heart. You must understand what kind of difficulty and agony others went through until I could come up with this method. With this method and training, you can go out and on your first day on the ocean, you can hook a fish and bring it up. There is a fisherman out there who has tried for three years to catch a tuna and in those years he only caught one. That is how hard it is to catch them, but if you use this method that you have learned, as soon as you go out, you can catch a tuna.

New Hope has a record of thirty-five fish in one season. I am giving you the direction for each boat. You should each catch at least five fish this season. You might think, "Why should I have to catch five fish? I don't like that." You are big and strong American men and you are thinking to yourselves, "Father, you just said that *New Hope* caught thirty-five fish and I just have to catch only five." You may want to catch more, but I am saying to you that it will take hard prayer and work to reach the goal of five fish. You may have to overcome many obstacles and difficulties on the boat. You may feel so discouraged that you will even want to cry on the boat. There may be times when you don't catch a tuna for so long that you will return to the land almost in tears thinking, "Oh, God doesn't love me." It takes that kind of effort, heart and desire. Even when you are tired, when you are ready to drop over, you will see the tuna going by your boat, not biting. Then, you have to wake up and shout with full force, "Hey, you have to come back here and take this line!" You have to have that kind of spirit.

Even in your dreams, or your nightmares, you have to see this happening and make the same effort. Suppose you go in the mountain and try to catch a tiger. How dangerous and difficult that task would be. Catching a tuna is much the same. When you catch a 1,000 pound tuna we are talking about something worth $7,000 or maybe even $10,000. Can you catch a bull or an ox which is worth that kind of money? There is no comparison.

We are going after that kind of treasure. The reality is such that if you catch one tuna like that, you and your family, even three families, could at least eat for one year without using any other source of money. How precious one fish is. If you just go out and sit on the boat, swaying back and forth and say, "Tuna, come to me," you are simply a thief or robber from the other fishermen. You've got to be serious.

I have spiritual sense. Sometimes, I know that within five minutes the tuna will come and strike. And many times, at that exact moment, the tuna does indeed take the line. I have experienced being extremely tired, but when the tuna strikes I am suddenly refreshed--fresh like a cucumber! Think about the excitement of that moment. Sometimes a battle is going on, sometimes it lasts for more than an hour, but I am working and sweating so hard that it seems like just one or two minutes. One time, I was waiting with such anticipation all day long. I couldn't think of anything at all because I knew the tuna was coming. I waited and waited so anxiously that I didn't even think of going to the bathroom. Then, just as I thought of doing that, the tuna struck the line. There was so much excitement at that moment that I completely forgot about going to the bathroom; the fight was the only thing on my mind. Only after the fight did I realize that my pants were wet. However, because we had caught the tuna, I didn't even mind about that. That's the first time I've ever shared this experience. Now, can you imagine the kind of excitement that I felt? You should also have a significant memory such as this one for yourself. Don't just wait for the tuna. You have to spiritually call the tuna to you. They have to feel your anxious heart.

Therefore, the number one rule on the boat is no fighting, no shouting. If you have to give a direction on the boat, give it firmly, but calmly. Many people don't like to chum. Those of you with experience know about this. The smell is bad and it looks so bad that no one can describe it. You just try to pass the job around, don't you? However, when you cut the chum, you have to have my heart. Just say to the others, "It's okay, you rest. I will take care of this job." When you start your boat, don't just push the gears and take off. First, look around and make sure everything is in order. When you are coming back, don't just pack up and leave. Really be thankful for the day.

Serious Points About Tuna Fishing

Up to this point, we have learned what kind of significance there is in tuna fishing. We know there is a great future in the ocean and in ocean businesses. We have learned what kind of position and attitude we should have on the boat when we go out. We know there is a great providence behind tuna fishing. You know now how to take care of your boat and your equipment. Now you know how to really concentrate and attract the tuna to your boat, how to cut the chum and offer it.

When the spiritual world looks down on you, which one will they want to help? The one who puts all his sweat and prayer into whatever he is doing, or the one who just takes it easy? So now, let us look at the time when the tuna strikes and is pulling out the line. This is the time when you must be extremely careful. For the beginners especially, remember this: when the tuna strikes and pulls your line out, put the buoy on it and throw the line in the ocean so the tuna can take it away. That way, you can save your other lines from getting tangled and you save yourself from the risk of getting caught in the line as well. Once the tuna has taken out the line and you have pulled in your other lines, you should call in someone from your trinity who has experience. Then, you can go and pick up the ball and fight the fish. That's the safest way.

We will have a competition between the trinity groups. Please remember, when you have the tuna on your line, you have to pull the line in and put it in the basket. You must never step on that line. Don't ever stand on it. If you get that line wrapped around you and the tuna suddenly pulls, you will go into the ocean and you cannot get out. At that point, there is no escape for you. Please be serious about these points.

Whenever you are pulling the line, someone else has to stand close by and put it neatly away. And never wrap that line around your hand. Just hold on to it, plainly and openly with you hand. Don't twist it. Never bend it 90 degrees. Just let it go through your hand naturally. The quota is usually one fish a day, so once you have the fish on your line, don't panic, don't hurry. Just hold it firmly on the line and let the next person put the extra line neatly away.

You can fight as long as you need to, for two or three hours if you need to. I have one idea about giving some prize money for the fish caught which took the longest and safest amount of time. Maybe you can get $5,000. Whoever takes the longest time and does it the safest way can receive that money. You can share it with everyone on your boat, or in your trinity. This doesn't mean that you hook the fish early in the morning and play with it all day. Some people might pull the fish up to the boat and let it hang there all day long, almost dead, going round and round and they will just sleep. Don't do that. You must live with your conscience. When your tuna comes close enough, you have to harpoon it. If you don't do that, the tuna will say to you, "You swindler, you are not trying to catch me!" And, that would be true. I would really like to give this prize money. I'm also thinking it should go to a sister's boat. How about that? Is that the right way? Let's see what happens.

This is a historical year for catching tuna. Here amongst you are some of the second generation of blessed children. They were recently blessed in marriage and the tuna will come out of curiosity just to look at their face. You may not understand the significance of fishing with these blessed children, but I want you to understand this. You should think, "I must do better than these blessed children and catch more tuna." On the other hand, those blessed children might think, "Heavenly Father, you've got to help us."

They have made the determination to become the expert tuna fishermen this summer, but I don't want you to get behind them. I already told them to have the goal of catching a minimum of five fish per person, not per boat. I want to know what your goal is. Have you made a serious determination as of yet? If you haven't, that is no good. Don't speak out loud, just put it into your stomach and say, "At least I will catch more than five, that is for sure."

Have you made up your mind? I want to conclude by saying that we have to be really careful this year. This summer is especially dangerous. If we follow everything that I have said tonight, there should be no accidents. However, if we don't unite and do well, someone might get hurt. It might not even be one of us, but someone who just comes out to tuna fish without knowing the significance of it. Please be very, very careful. Please pray hard and put all of your effort into it.

Conclusion

Don't worry if I am here or not. These are dangerous and difficult times. There are people in the world who are very serious and they know who I am and they are aiming at me. For this reason, the boat is not the best place for me to be. I am fully aware of the tactics that Communists and terrorists use. I have already experienced them before. Don't be concerned about my schedule. Actually, it is not easy to meet with me like this. You may just take it for granted, but many people ask to see me, especially in these times. Presidential candidates and former prime ministers, people like this are requesting to see me, but I don't answer all their requests. Now is not the time. You should consider yourself like a buffer zone surrounding me.

There is a providential war going on. Who is the commander of that war? I am the one who really understands the details of what is going on. No one in America may think so, but America needs me. In order to unite this world and begin a new world, I must be here. No one else knows how it has to be done. I am aware of this because I recognize where we are in history. The time is that serious. My hope for you tonight is that you can inherit my spirit and the purpose and goal which I have told you about. Then, you must apply that in your daily life. At the end of ten, twenty years you must become successful. Then, in thirty, forty years from now, after I've gone to spirit world, you can say, "I remember that day forty years ago in Morning Garden when Father spoke to me and that is why I have become so successful today." I am hoping and praying that many of you will become the person I've just described. Those who are more than determined to become that successful man or woman who inherits my spirit, please raise your hand.

You have given your determination in front of me tonight, so don't think about complaining this summer. If you have complaints, there can be one day when you bring all your complaints to me and I will take them. Do you want to have such a day? No? Well, then, that is even better. Is it true? You really don't want such a day? Really true? Your answer is strong and clear. Then, I trust you. I am counting on you. May God bless you.

The Way of
the Ocean

August 28th, 1986 -- Morning Garden

WHO ARE YOU? What are you doing here? Where are you heading, where will you go? The purpose or the destination must be clear, otherwise you will end up on a march to nowhere. If you met God and asked him, "Where are you going, Mister God," what do you think God would answer? God knows where He is going and He knows what He desires. He has an absolutely clear-cut desire, goal and purpose.

Is that purpose for one small village or town, city or nation, or for the universe? Of course, the small matter is part of the larger concern, but the important thing is that no matter how small or large, everything is connected to the ultimate goal and purpose. What is that ultimate goal? In one word, it is one world--a peaceful world, a world of ideals and a world of perfection.

That is not only the goal here on earth, it is also the goal of the spiritual world. So that is the purpose, one (spiritual and physical) world. Can God fulfill this purpose by Himself alone, or does God need anything else? Because you know the Divine Principle, you know the answer. Divine Principle teaches us that God cannot fulfill the purpose alone. God needs man absolutely.

The important thing is this: God knows how to bring about such a world; He knows the structure of it. However, the problem is this: Man himself doesn't understand the plan. Thus, God has had to announce his plan in advance in order to prepare man. That is, at the proper time, He will send the messiah to lead the way and let mankind know how to live so that he does not remain in ignorance.

Throughout history, man has pursued value, but has interpreted that value in his own way. In other words, man has pursued his own idea of happiness. For example, Japan has a goal that is centered on Japan. In Red China the people thought that Marxism-Leninism would be good for their country, but they found out that it led to failure. Here in the United States people think that democracy is best for their nation. Every respective country has devised some goal, but struggles today in failure.

The Ultimate Goal for Which We are Headed

Let us think, "What is nearest to me and most valuable?" People are looking all over for this kind of thing, but they look too far. They look way beyond themselves. What is very, very close to you and also extremely valuable? You say, "True love." Okay, but how can that love be ignited? What is the essence or origin of that love?

How does true love begin? Does it begin among brothers or friends? The origin of true love comes from God. Therefore, the fundamental and basic relationship of mankind is to be united with God. God and man. However, when you say mankind, you mean both men and women. The most dynamic relationship happens between men and women. When that relationship is centered upon God, that is the trinity of true love. God, man and woman. This is the basic and most essential relationship which fulfills all mankind's needs.

What is God's position to men and women? Teacher? What kind of teacher? Somehow, teacher doesn't quite describe the relationship of true love. It must be something better than teacher. What about master? Master and servant? It doesn't sound quite right either. It somehow doesn't fully connect to true love. So then, we come to the concept which fits most closely to true love. Only parents can encompass that kind of love. Well, if the first human beings, Adam and Eve were the parents, where does that leave God? What was God? How should we address God properly if we call Adam and Eve the parents?

Fortunately, man has what we call the spirit; he has a spiritual part of his being. There are two aspects of man, spiritual and physical. For this reason we can have both spiritual as well as physical parents. God can dwell in the spirit of man and in this way we would have God as our spiritual parents and our parents as physical parents. Centered on true love, God dwells in oneness with the parents on earth. Unless this standard is born, there is no way to bring the spiritual world and the physical world together. This is the focus and central point to which God has been trying to awaken mankind. When we know this goal, this relation between God and man, we know who we are and where we are going. We are to be the embodiment of true love, both spiritually and physically. We are to be in the image of God. The ultimate direction in which we are heading is to be the image of true love in the fullest extension. Therefore, God is always with the people who are going towards this standard of truth, this embodiment of love. God shall always be with them.

When you grasp your parents, and within them God is existing, you are holding onto true love. How does God dwell within us? Centering on true love alone, God dwells within mankind. This is the highest ideal which humanity has been pursuing throughout all of history. Who are you then? Who are the Moonies? We are the ones who will propagate and fulfill this ideal, making it reality.

If you ever cut yourself, what was inside? No matter how many different places you might cut, you would find more of the same inside. More Moonie, more Moonie, more Moonie. Your body is just one chunk of Moonie. The real and genuine Moonie cannot be digested by Satan. That Moonie is the personification of the spirit of true love, the embodiment of true love. Therefore, the genuine Moonie is like real gold, containing the true spirit of God. Satan cannot make any claim for that person.

You have measurements over here. You measure by pounds and inches. You have one inch and one pound for which you have an original standard. Do you have two different standards or just one? Every factory and home in America has measuring tools which use inches and pounds. Something is long or short, heavy or light according to how many inches or pounds it is. However, an inch is always an inch and a pound is always a pound wherever you go. What is the first, original inch of the Unification Church?

Well, you immediately said, "Father," so I can only concede that you are not so dumb. Then what happens? You, looking at what kind of material you are, measure up to me and then you find out just how you measure up. You see that and say, "Oh, I'm a little short," or "I'm a little bit too light." Do you have this kind of scale, this ability to measure? Show me where it is. The amazing thing is that each one of you have this scale, in your mind you know it. You have the ability to detect and measure where you are inside.

Why did you come here first of all? You came here simply because of me. Without me no one would have come here. You see that I am starting some kind of ocean venture, that I have some kind of vision for the ocean and you say to yourself, "If Father is interested in this, I've got to be interested in it too." That's why you came.

Those who graduated from the seminary, raise your hands. When you came to Gloucester, were you thinking, "Oh gee, I have to go there and fish," or were your thoughts instead filled with bubbling enthusiasm and burning desire to go out? Which one? After so many days have now passed, and you've experienced the ocean and heard me talk, you should not have a cool mind about it. If you do, something is wrong. By now you should feel something like a magnet is pulling you along; you should feel like I do. Maybe some of you said, "Well, I've tasted this for the first time and its enough. Enough is enough. I will never return here." Some of you might be thinking like that. Those who think like that, raise your hands. No one? I don't believe you. Sometimes you want to be with me forever, sometimes you are changing. Adam and Eve wanted to be with God forever, but they were changing too. I'm looking at you and some of your faces are saying, "Oh, the wind is about twenty-five knots tomorrow and Father won't let us go out if the waves are over eight feet high, so I hope it's goes up to eight feet." You know that normal weather creates waves from two to six feet, so some of you might think each night, "I hope it's bad weather tomorrow and we can stay in." Others of you might be praying for a typhoon every day. Those kind of people are just wasting their time and energy. They are going on a forward march to nowhere.

I am still a puzzle and a mystery to many people. Actually, I am a simple man, coming here and going fishing, but in the meantime, the highest possible leaders in America are being moved and world leaders are moving too. When do I have the time to do all these things? Do you think I accomplish this by just sitting and doing nothing, just letting my head drop and go to sleep? Does everything happen like this? There are 240 million people living in this country. Those people cannot save this country. They would have done so by now, don't you think? They cannot save it. Only one man can save this country. Do you know why? Only Reverend Moon is saving this nation. With what?

American people are proud. They are proud of their country, but now, this country is crumbling down. How can we permit this situation? We cannot let this happen. It's a serious situation and all Americans know about it, but no one will stand up. Only one man came here and said, "I will save America." With what? What power do I have?

America has scientific power, political power, economic power, military power. It is number one in so many areas. How can only one person stand up and save this nation? What can save this country? Only God's love. Without God there is no hope. This is the problem. American people don't know about this. They don't know about the true love of God. They don't know the purpose of God. Therefore, they don't know the purpose of America and cannot reach the goal.

I came to teach clearly, "This is God and this is God's love." I have a clear understanding of these two points. The American people don't have these points clear in their minds. This is the problem. That is why I am teaching you. Centered on love, God can dwell on earth. In the spiritual world we have God and here on earth we have True Parents. Centered on love we can become one, and we can do anything. We can have dominion of true love over anything.

Many people think, "Oh, Unification Church, it's just one little church. We don't have to think about it." If they continue like that, they will never find out. Our teaching is not just for Unification Church. You have to know and be able to say, "True Parents are my parents." No matter how powerful our opponents may be they can never overcome us. We have been persecuted from all four corners of the world, but we have never been pushed out. How about you? Do you now understand this point? Where are you standing? Where have you been going until now? You have to take a strong stand. There are powerful countries in this world. You have to think about it seriously. How can you overcome the evil in this world? Only with truth. Only with love. Do you now understand? Who is God to you? You have to be able to say, "My parent." You should be able to stand up and proudly say, "God is not just the parent of True Parents, but also my parent." And, on this earth, you can declare, "True Parents are my parents." With this, we will go marching on. This is the most important thing for us to know.

Therefore, whatever we tackle, whether it is Ocean Church or an ocean business, it is not out of a sense of duty. No! Whatever you are doing you must understand is yours. You must be able to look at what you are doing and proudly say, "That's mine." Look at the *One Hope* boat. Who made that boat? I initiated it and Mr. Kamiyama organized it, but whose boat is it? It is yours.

Although Ocean Church owns the boats, you cannot think that someone else will take responsibility. You have to know that when you take a boat out, it is truly your responsibility. And the fishing gear, who designed it? I did. However, when you take that equipment and use it, to whom does it belong? To you. This way you have direct attachment and responsibility.

What is the center of our moving forward? Only true love. With true love, your accomplishments will go on for eternity. With true love, what you accomplish will never disappear, never go away, but will remain for eternity. What about the contents of your mind? If you think, "I am too far away from the standard," then this is the time to think again.

I am sure that when some of the members finished their training this summer and went back to school, you started thinking, "Oh, they are going back to their respective places. I wish it was my turn to go." Even though you are only staying a few more days or weeks, you are already thinking like that. If you don't think that way, my idea about you and my own experience is wrong. However, I am seldom wrong. How about the rest of you? Well, the rest of you have the mission of not going back anywhere because you haven't caught any tuna yet. So, you have to follow the tuna, follow them all the way until you catch them. Follow them all the way to the north pole.

You only say "all right" because you heard me talk tonight, but you should have been thinking "all right" from the very beginning. You might also think, "Oh Father, you are the True Parent. You are supposed to be loving me. Why do you always push me down to do the impossible task?" Some of you might think that. However, the people who always complain are the ones who always lose.

The Price of Laying the Foundation

Many of you have never heard the kind of report before that Colonel Pak gave tonight of the media tour of Asia. Some of you may wonder, "When did Father do all of this? How come all of these things are happening?" Without any of the hard work, just by listening to it tonight, you are inheriting all of it. However, it isn't that simple. It is like this: when you finally receive the PhD from Harvard, everyone will give you praise and tribute, but none of them will ever understand the suffering and hardship you have gone through. Maybe it took twenty years or only one year. Certainly, whoever went through the course more quickly, suffered more.

In fourteen years, since I came to the United States, I have accomplished unprecedented things in history. No one has even imagined accomplishing these things in American history. You cannot understand what kind of hardship, suffering and agony has gone on behind it. All by myself, alone. No one welcomed my coming. No one welcomed my suffering. No one wanted to go to Danbury. I worked hard and paid the sacrifice in order to achieve the goal. Anyone just trying to receive the fruit from that effort has a mind like a thief. You cannot get the priceless treasure without paying the price deserving of it.

The American people have been very skeptical. Especially the young people have been skeptical about my goal and my way of doing things. They have been 50/50, not 100% behind me. Now they realize that they were wrong, that this has been a sure thing, that I have been right all along. At that moment, they want to grab the result, grab the achievement, but it's not fair. It's not even possible.

You are not ready to receive; your container is not ready to receive what I want to give. The treasure is ready, but the container is not ready, so you have to leave the treasure behind and make the container ready. In the meantime, someone else who has been working hard may come and take the treasure. I don't like that. I want you to have that treasure. That is why I am pushing you along the road of suffering and difficulty so that you are able to contain the treasures that are waiting for you.

Seven years ago, sixty-one Japanese members were invited to New York. They were each given a $100 bill and told, "You are the pioneers of the fishing business, the seafood business. Go forward, pioneer the way and bring back prosperity." This year that same group came back and reported that without a doubt they have made the strongest of foundations in the fishing industry. That kind of foundation is spreading throughout the country, so the seafood people are noticing that Moonies are everywhere. Some of them think, "The only place where the Moonies aren't pushing any further is the Pacific ocean itself. If I am to escape them, I'll have to jump in." Why are these Japanese brothers winning? Because they think, "I am responsible for this business. This isn't anyone else's business. It is my business. It is my Heavenly Father's business." With that thought in their minds and hearts, they work harder and faster.

When they go forward like this, totally united in their soul and mind with the purpose of God, the blessing of God is always with them. The result is that their business is simply growing by leaps and bounds. Based upon that, we are going to pioneer in the same way with several hundred more members. Each one will be just like a seed. They will be given the same amount of money to start with. I know that if they follow exactly the same course as the first pioneers they will succeed without a doubt. Just become a clone of these older members. You have that capacity and potential. You can double and triple their result.

The Divine Providence Awaiting Us

America has that capacity. What do you think? When Americans start to learn to like the taste of fish, should the amount of money they spend on fish be more, or should they spend more money on drugs? Several years ago, I heard the statistic that in one year Americans spend more than 40 billion dollars on drugs. That must be more than doubled by now. Someone said tonight that they had heard as much as 200 billion has been spent on drugs. At least fish is a good and nutritious food for Americans; at least fish should be sold up to triple the amount of 200 billion dollars each year. That means Americans should spend 600 billion dollars on fish. Don't you think that should happen? Maybe there will be too much money and no one will know what to do with it. Maybe we will go out to the ocean and give that money as bait to the fish. You know, I might say, "So many fish died to feed this country and they paid a lot of indemnity. Go ahead and spread out some of the cash to them." What if we put some of that money into the ocean and the ocean waves carried it to South America? And then, what if the fishermen down there would come up with a big net of dollars? Instead of fishing for fish, they would fish for dollars! Eventually they would pay the international debt. Isn't that a good idea? What do you think? This fish business and ocean providence is truly something for Moonies to do. Nobody else can do what we do. It takes guts and drive to do it. What will become of it in twenty years? These pioneers will accomplish even more things than they already have. Where will you be in twenty years? Don't be like a grasshopper, idle today and subordinate to others in the future.

You should think about where this movement started from. Forty years ago I was all by myself. There were no friends, no house, no money, no organization. I was completely alone. There were no brothers, no family, no parents. They didn't understand. My parents worried about me. They thought, "Oh, our son was a very capable man, but he is going in a strange direction." Who then was the only ally that I had? Sometimes I was at the point where I cried out, "Even by myself, I will never give up." Then, God became my sole ally and only God was with me. That was the beginning point.

Today, if you consider that God is your only ally, then don't worry about your future. God will guide you and protect you. That is the key, that is the most important thing. You can compete with God saying, "God, if you are going to get up at four o'clock in the morning, I will get up at three o'clock. I will beat you by an hour." And you can say, "God, if you want to sweat, then I want to shed tears and sweat, not just sweat." You know the story about the Gloucester campaign. When I was going out at four o'clock in the morning, some of the fishermen started to go out earlier. Then, I went out even earlier until finally I was leaving at one o'clock in the morning, and staying out all night. Then, they couldn't compete anymore. We won Gloucester that way, we won their respect in that way.

The parent is always the one who works later, works harder and begins earlier. It is the parent's heart which wants the children to rest while the parent wants to do more and prepare for the next thing. The parental heart always wants to take care and watch over everything until the last moment. You thought that you were getting up early, but I tell you, before you got up, God was already there ahead of you. When you realize that God is always one step ahead of you, you cannot get tired. You cannot just give up. You always feel, "I want to comfort God," but God is already there giving you comfort. With this understanding you just want to make every effort to alleviate God's heart. With this kind of heart and mind, you will march forward and you will never fail.

This is the testimony which I am giving to you. I have been living this testimony throughout my entire life, over and over. I still have the goal that I want to grab this nation, turn it and bring it back to God. It is like a dream, but this dream will come true. To those graduates of the seminary, if I give you this dream, would you accomplish it? You may get tired, but I will never get tired. You may get tired and stay behind and become a drop-out. But, I will never do that. I will ultimately achieve that goal, win that goal and then, a few steps ahead of you, wait for your return. Don't come to me then with shame. Don't be sons and daughters of shame.

Those who promise, "Father, I will never become a son or daughter of shame," raise your hands and repeat, "I promise." This is the true hope of America and the world will become a better world than we could ever think. Wherever you go you must look for the difficult task. Think, "Whatever is the most difficult task, I will do." If you go to the most difficult task, you will already find the parents there. Parents always go to the most difficult task. You will truly find God there.

The typhoon may be blowing, but if you say, "No typhoon will ever stop my *One Hope*," then God will be there. God will say, "My son, my daughter. You are truly my children. Welcome." That is the secret of my daily life. It is my daily credo. Everyone look at the clock. When you look at the clock and see that it is already midnight, you think, "Uh, oh, it's too late." However, your thinking is late. If you think that God is starting to maneuver at three o'clock in the morning, then you will say, "Oh, it's only midnight. It's early." That's the way to think.

You have to look forward to being embraced by God. In order to do that, you have to begin by at least three o'clock in the morning. In that state, you are tired and start to doze in the car for just a moment. At that time, God will come to you and give you a revelation. If you just wake up happy in the morning with eight hours of sleep and say, "Oh let's go for another picnic today," then you will never receive any revelation. You will never meet God there.

You have to select the route where Satan cannot go. It must be so extreme that Satan will say, "Oh no, I could never go that way. You go without me." That is the course you must select. There, God alone will be waiting. And you solely will have the opportunity to meet with God.

You might think, "I've been working so hard and I'm bored with this, it's monotonous. There's no joy in this." You've got to be different. You have to look forward to tomorrow. You have to expect something exciting to happen tomorrow, the next day and for the next ten, twenty years. You must always feel excited for life and never get tired. That is Reverend Moon's kind of Moonie. I will always bless this kind of person with the blessing of God.

Today is a special opportunity so that you can rediscover yourself. It is historical and it is your honor to have listened to me tonight. Each one of you shall go on to your mission. Go with strength, fortitude and determination. I will always be with you. Ocean Church and the ocean businesses are a divine providence. I have declared it many times before and I declare it again tonight. These are providential missions. Therefore, anyone who is devoted to this direction will receive God's blessing and protection and shall eventually prosper. Someday, some of you will become national leaders, lawmakers, congressmen, senators. I am a mysterious person. American people think that I am only famous in America, but when they go to Asia they find out that I am even more famous there. It is the same in South America and Africa. Being here with me tonight is a rare opportunity. It is very rare. The reason that I meet with you face to face and talk to you is because you at least follow me and are trying to be one with me.

If I had not been able to establish the True Parents, who else would give a clear vision for the world today? Who else is really giving clear guidance and direction? I have had to work in the most adverse conditions, but the veil of that opposition is leaving and the world will soon be able to see who I am. Truly, we are going to be very unique people indeed. We are going to have an exciting future ahead of us. Please, look forward to and work hard for that day. May God bless you.

Excerpts from
Published Speeches

1974 — 1983

You should know, in order to be a qualified leader, you absolutely need more training. You have to know how to speak out and persuade others. Everyday, I go fishing out in the Freeport, Long Island area. Some of the people think, "Oh, Reverend Moon is a world renowned preacher. Why does he have any connection with fishing? He should forget it"

To Belvedere Trainees
August 29, 1974

I am leaving again today for Boston, and again I have an important mission. I will go out to sea, not for pleasure, but to lay a foundation for the future economy of the Unification Church. That's my goal. There is no way we can exceed the advances in industry and technology, except in the one virtually untapped area of the sea and sea products. The international law has recently been changed and America can soon claim jurisdiction over the waters extending 200 miles out from shore. There will be much more territory to cope with, and the American people do not pay very much attention to the sea, nor invest very much in marine industries. Thus, the treasure of the sea surrounding America is virtually untapped. I feel that the future economic foundation of the Unification Church lies in this area. Some time ago, I promised that in three years I would start exploring the treasures of the sea.

I have to train you. People criticize me and say that Reverend Moon is taking it easy on a yacht out in the Atlantic Ocean, enjoying himself. Nothing could be further from the truth. I don't think very many of you will inherit large fortunes from your own parents, so I am responsible for you. I must begin to plan how you can support yourselves. You will be blessed in marriage, and God will bless your marriages with children, whom you must be able to support. While you're going down to Washington to fight this battle, I am looking more than ten years ahead and going to sea to prepare our future economic foundation. Going out to sea is the most wearying and tiresome task I have ever done, but I am determined to do more and to endure more physical hardship than any one of you.

Since we have developed a worldwide system of organization, our movement can grow rapidly in this new industry. Even in this area I want to play the role of a forefather, a pioneer.

Past and Future Generations
August 1, 1976

Do you want to participate in the creation of the economy that will restore this world? I am now starting our fishing industry and with that purpose in mind, I experimented with the tuna trade this summer. No matter what time of day or night or what type of weather there was, I went out to sea. If the sea was rough the captain of the *New Hope* used to ask whether we were going out, but now he knows I will go out no matter what the circumstances.

The members who finished at the Seminary and now have their Master's diplomas may work at sea. The captains of our boats may have Ph.D's. Don't laugh. It is that kind of condescending attitude that has caused the decline of America's fishing industry. Unless I resurrect it, the fishing industry in this country will die. I will contribute to America by restoring the dying marine industry. We are now negotiating to buy a mother ship, but it is not for a pleasure cruise to the Caribbean. It is to catch the treasures of the sea. I don't like the smell of fish, but we can create a great economic foundation for God's work. Catching fish is not our goal, but the liberation of the communist world is. That is why we must advance. If you unmarried women don't want to be blessed to fishermen, you should leave now. If you don't want to marry a sailor then you will have to marry someone outside our church.

There is a vast treasure lying in the sea, waiting to be harvested by our hands, but right now the American fishing industry is dying because American young people do not like the hard work of going out to sea. When they go out to sea for three months, they return to find that their wives have left them and their money has been squandered and they never want to go out to sea again. If they are not married, they are still not interested in going out because sometimes the weather is so brutal. You women who marry fishermen must be proud of them for working for God and mankind.

I have experienced how the sea will make a man more reverent. At sea, you need faith in God because you must totally rely on Him. Furthermore, when the men go out to sea they will not forget their families. In my own experience, I thought of Mother and my children more at sea than at home because at sea I never knew what would happen in the next moment. At sea, I love and pray for my wife and children more than anywhere else. When the *New Hope* docks, and Mother and the children are waiting and waving to me, I feel as though I have met God at that moment. The women who can love their husbands when they return from harsh work at sea will be the most superb, exemplary wives in the sight of God.

Perfection and Gratitude
October 3, 1976

You should not just know these things, but take up the responsibility for them. Even more than I, you have got to go and awaken these people and turn this nation back to God. I am determined to train young people to become responsible for this country. For example, I am now training the seminarians; they are making up a new fishing net now, and I have had them fishing in the icy water of the Hudson River to see what kind of young men and women they are. They are not making nets and fishing for the sake of making money, but to build their own iron will and to become determined young leaders who cannot be stopped by anything.

I do not only deliver sermons to you. When I get down to action, I can do anything, and do it better than anyone. Those seminarians are really rediscovering me, finding out that I do not just have theories, but that I have the kind of knowledge which can only come from experience. I have studied fishing and designed several patented tools for fishing. For instance, sometimes the hook gets caught in the fish's mouth, and the fishermen have an awful time getting the hook out. I have invented a small tool to push the barb through and get the hook out easily.

One member saw me cutting the metal to make this tool myself, and he said, "Father, why do you work so hard? Why don't you just go to a tackle shop and buy one?" I told him, "America doesn't have such a tool; if I could buy this kind of tool, then why should I make it?" I invented a new net at Barrytown, one you have never seen. It is a one-way-street net and once the fish goes into the net, there is no way it can turn around.

Yesterday, I had an appointment with the Belvedere people, but I had a new inspiration for the net and got caught up in directing the seminarians about how to make it. We worked very hard all night, and I could not get there on time.

Twenty-third Anniversary of the Unification Church
May 1, 1977

I frequently go out to sea because the future economy of the world will depend upon the vast resources of the sea. The future will belong to the person who pays more attention to the oceans of the world. In addition, many people throughout history have died at sea in war or tragic accidents, and I want to comfort those people and pay indemnity for them. Sometimes, when I hear that a dangerous storm is coming, I purposely go out to sea.

Many people think I go out only for pleasure, but going out in such weather is a desperate battle, not a pleasure. I must do these things to liberate the many people who died under such circumstances. In 1975, I had a special ceremony at sea with Mother and one of our daughters, for the sake of people who died at sea. Even my own captain did not know what kind of ceremony was being held at that time.

Things That Belong to God and to Man
May 15, 1977

In leading the fishing expeditions at Barrytown, where many hundreds of carp were caught, I thought very much about the universal principle of creation being killed to become food for man. Six big turtles lost their home as we dredged the Barrytown lake to accommodate more carp. I felt sorry for them and had them put in the Hudson River, thinking, "You turtles go and live in the wide world."

When I go fishing, I send the first fish back to its home. Even a lowly creature like a carp appreciates love, and when someone appreciates their purpose for being what they are, they even want to die for that person. In that sense, the carp are not a sacrifice as they give themselves for the person who loves them. This was God's idea for creation. By being loved and appreciated by the Unification Church members, all these creatures will be thankful and proud of living and dying for the purpose for which they were created.

Love is supreme. Living for love and dying in love always brings happiness. When the moment of your death comes, you will be smiling as you think about your love, and it will be your joy at that moment to be embraced by the one you love.

Suppose someone said, "I understand that Reverend Moon caught a lot of carp in the Hudson River. I'm sure those fish just curse him as they die." How would you answer? Before hearing my explanation, I'm sure you would have been confused, but now you know how carp have a perfected life if they can die for the sake of God's purpose, becoming the flesh and blood of God-centered people. Is there any more precious cause carp could pursue? There is the difference of heaven and earth in your actions, depending on how you are motivated.

This principle applies the same way both to a carp and to a man. The ultimate question we have to ask ourselves then is, "Am I ready to die for the love of God?" What is your answer? If your answer is "yes", then your death is not death. Your flesh and your spirit become the spirit and flesh of all mankind and of all the universe. When you center your life on the higher level, you will live for eternity.

Let Us Thank God
May 29, 1977

Yesterday, I saw a member who has a Masters degree scrubbing the floors in the Manhattan Center. Do you hate to do such jobs, or do you do any work with appreciation? I am never ashamed of anything I am doing. At Barrytown, I taught the students how to make fishing nets. Even our professors were amazed. At that time, a theologian's conference was going on and the visiting scholars never expected to see me at Barrytown. They sneaked in to take a look at what I was doing with the students and were amazed and impressed to see me doing such humble, menial work. You have no excuses to make to me because I have done everything before you, even the most humble labor.

God Depends on Us Alone
June 1, 1977

I have been going out to sea in a boat called *New Hope*. The public may think I just go yachting for pleasure, but every day I am collecting more material. God has hidden unlimited resources underneath the sea, and the oceans will be the key to future development in the world.

I know very well that in the course of developing sea industries, we may sometimes suffer some sacrifice. Eventually, we will have hundreds of fishing boats, and some of them may be lost at sea. Even losing husbands and brothers will not deter our pioneering zeal because that work will be for the sake of humanity.

We want to become masters of the sea. The ocean surface is twice as big as the surface of the land. Furthermore, there are vast resources beneath the sea. Any nation which can overcome the difficulties will conquer the sea. We first learned to have dominion on the land, and with the same pioneering spirit we can conquer the sea as well.

Our battle is now being waged on the land, and we must be victorious here, being tested and seasoned by a hurricane of persecution. Then, when real storms come at sea, we can welcome them. The Pilgrims who came to America were pioneering people, otherwise, they would not have crossed the Atlantic Ocean, especially during the stormy months. They realized that an uncertain destiny lay ahead of them, and that they had no guarantee for their lives. Few before had ever safely arrived in the New World, but they started anyway. They overcame by their hope and faith in God. Now, in the 20th century, we also are forging ahead, like a boat in a rough ocean, with faith in God. Whatever the persecution and blowing winds, we have faith in God.

I look at the vast ocean resources as God's blessing waiting for the Unification Church. I have promised to God, "Give me twenty years' time and we will conquer the sea, taking dominion over it and returning the glory to You." That is how I think every time I go out. Later, we will establish a great foundation, and even the Ford or Rockefeller Foundations will look like peanuts in comparison. That is the way we must realistically feel.

All these things are our pride in the Unification Church. The fisherman's life is a hard, dirty, even crude life and fishermen have to be very rugged. Furthermore, fishermen have often been known as thieves and liars. Why should I have us get into the kind of business which is known as a living hell? I go down to the bottom of hell, and by revolutionizing such a place, by bringing heaven there, I can hasten the Kingdom of Heaven on earth.

Our Pride
June 5, 1977

The characteristics of beauty include contrast, like the combination of blonde hair, blue eyes and white teeth. At sea, there is nothing but blue water for miles and miles, and after awhile the blue color becomes boring. If suddenly, you see a black ship approaching from far away, that black dot attracts your entire attention. When the black ship raises its white sails, it becomes more exciting and dramatic to watch. If the black ship raises a multi-colored flag, it becomes absolutely gorgeous. Since everything else around is blue, you become content to watch only the black ship with white sails and multi-colored flag. That is what I call dramatic.

I am causing a lot of controversy because the white culture is like a vast ocean in which a yellow dot has suddenly appeared, and is attracting attention. Some Americans are not welcoming me, but God has been sailing vast oceans and is bored with man's present culture. All of a sudden, I have appeared like the black ship. God is focusing His entire attention upon me. I will not only raise white sails, but also the multi-colored flags of all the nations. Put yourself in God's position and look down on the little ship, raising white sails and waving multi-colored flags. It is a very dramatic sight to behold.

You are the sailors on that ship which is attracting so much attention. White, black, yellow, red and brown people are waving to the nations. There is a great deal of excitement and action on our boat!

The Desire of God
June 19, 1977

You must have the faith and conviction that you are a lighthouse lighting a dark world. The lighthouse will shine forth even in the worst kind of weather because that is the time ships need the lighthouse most. When you are surrounded by the thickest fog, you must shine forth all the more. The more adversity, the greater must be your light.

I have become a legend in the Gloucester area; the newspaper there wrote several articles about our fishing and we have been a topic of conversation for the whole town. Hundreds of boats come every year from all over to fish in that particular area. When the *New Hope* put out to sea and dropped anchor, many other boats would follow and anchor in the vicinity. When we had a tuna strike, other fishermen would bring out their binoculars to watch what I was doing. At first, the negative people would want the tuna to break loose and escape, but after a few days of successful catches, they began to change their thinking and the rumor began that I have something good working for me.

I was always the first one out to sea. Some of the seasoned professional fishermen would go out early to outdo me, but no matter how early they got out, the *New Hope* was already there. The fishermen were not inspired by this, but when they tried to compete with me, they had to work so hard that they had no time for their usual drinking or laziness. By the end of the summer a rumor was going around that declining town that I was the only one who could save Gloucester.

Without any exception, I got up every day at 3:00 a.m. The *New Hope* went out in the moonlight and in many cases returned home with the stars and moon shining. Do you like to get up early in the morning? The staff members working on the boat were never told what time to get up, but since I arose at three o'clock every morning, they followed me, no matter how sleepy they were.

This has been my tradition for four years in America. It is not easy to follow me because no one can outwork me. My crew knows what I would do, and if I tell them to be out by 1:30 a.m. on the Atlantic, they get up and go out with no grumbling. I have even set the tradition of staying out and working all night.

This summer, I did not earn much in terms of money, but in terms of tradition, I earned billions of dollars worth. By following that tradition, the fishing industry in our movement will blossom and contribute much to America's entire fishing industry in days to come. Because I have now set the fishing tradition, no one will hesitate to go out to sea, even the women. If I were a coward, then no one would go seriously, but now people will be eager to go. There is a record of when and where I caught each fish and how big it was. In the future, fishermen will try to challenge that record.

Even though fishing is incredibly hard work, I wanted to give myself without any reservation to set the tradition for the posterity of the Unification Church. That has been my work for the last seventy days.

The Heart of Reunion
September 11, 1977

Two weeks ago, I was in Alabama, which is known as the shipbuilding capital of the United States, looking around to buy a shipyard so we can build our own vessels. Would you want our factory to be mediocre or number one? That is easy to say, but not to fulfill. We have to work harder than anyone in order to be number one. It is going to be a tough job, but I will push you. There were no women working in the Alabama shipyards, and I thought that this is one way we can make history. We will have women shipyard workers. If you women become welders, your fingers and faces will get marked up, but is that all right? Now, at 7:42 a.m., on 1 November 1977, the women have pledged that they want to be welders at the shipyard in Alabama. All you men are out of jobs today! If the women are willing to do that much, then you men have to work harder, even into the night.

I knew years ago that unless I intervened in the shipbuilding and fishing industries with my own resolve and determination, this nation could have no hope for those two industries to survive. I met two wonderful individuals in Alabama, a father and son who have spent their lifetimes in the business. They said that the boat-building business is in a boom period, with many people going out to sea. I answered, "That may be true, but what about a few years in the future?" They replied thoughtfully, "Reverend Moon, we didn't think about that, but you are absolutely right. The men have no deep motivation and American women just cannot wait patiently for their husbands to come home from the sea."

Often in the past, the wives of fishermen have betrayed their husbands. What shall we do in order to reverse the trend? I will make you welders and fishing captains, and our fishermen won't have to worry about their wives running off. If the Moonies are doing that, the rest of America will not want to face being defeated and having to give everything up to us. Once they decide to compete with us, the marine industries will be revived. I am determined to give vision and hope to the American young people so they will be motivated to go out to sea. The oceans are a vast, untapped area waiting to be utilized by courageous men and women, and we want to initiate that. There is a chance for America to become great by conquering the sea, but if your countrymen ignore the sea and only want to lead complacent lives, then America has no hope to lead the world. America is blind to this.

I am leading the way in this field and the Unification Church will follow through. I would truly like to see you beautiful sisters become fishing captains and go out to sea, being so knowledgeable and dedicated that men won't mind taking orders from you. Then, people will recognize Moonie power. I want to make our women the presidents of many companies so that the employees who just graduated from Harvard and Yale will all have to listen to you. You may look tiny and weak, but when the men on the ship are scared to death, you women will take command and give orders to rectify the situation. You might even take your own babies with you! I am very excited about this idea. I was planning to travel around and look at businesses in Alabama, for instance. Mother was somewhat hesitant and said, "Father, you know that's a man's job, so you go and I will stay home." However, I told her she should come along anyway.

I will establish a system in which you women will be the captains and your husbands the first mates. You men will have to say, "Yes, ma'am," when the captain gives orders, even though she may be your wife. Do you men feel good or bad about that? If you are a seasoned captain, then whether you are man or woman doesn't make any difference; the crew has to obey.

We are not seeking millions of dollars for ourselves by starting businesses; we are looking at the world and this nation and preparing to spearhead change. Imagine the time when we have thousands of vessels and I can say to the American government, "There are so many farmers sitting idle and receiving government subsidies for doing nothing. What kind of ridiculous system is that? You pay them for not growing crops, but in the meantime millions of people are starving in other parts of the world. Let the farmers grow their crops and let us transport that food all over the world to feed the poor. We have the boats to do it."

Fishing has seasons and doesn't last twelve months a year, so why shouldn't we transport things all over the world in between seasons? How would you feel being the captain of a boat loaded with grain and headed for a nation where many people are starving? I would select the tiniest of all women to the captain of such a boat and have her wear a special hat with official decorations. We must all have a dream to live for. I have more dreams than anyone else, but the difference is that my dreams become reality.

Our Newborn Selves
November 1, 1977

I was fishing for tuna at that time, but just catching fish was not my purpose. My mind was totally concentrated on Washington Monument and I thought of nothing else.

Anniversary of Washington Monument
September 18, 1978

We did not start our fishing businesses only to make money, but to start rebuilding America's economy. For five years, I have worked every day to set the tradition and find the best way. Now, some officials in the government have heard what I am doing and they remark at what a perceptive man I am to see that America cannot afford to abandon her fishing industry. For fifty years, that industry in America has been desolate, but in time it will feed America. I have started far in advance of everyone else. In the last three years, our investment of millions of dollars has not made a penny, but do you think we should give up?

Our Position
January 2, 1979

If I go to the farm I am a good farmer. When I go into the fishing business I become one of the fishermen. I can eat raw fish and even their guts out of my hand. There is nothing I can't do. If I go to a mine, I will dig day after day just as if it were my vocation. I can go to the slums and talk to the people and win their hearts. Without doing all these things, how can you know what your objective is?

Eternal Happiness
February 25, 1979

Although the Unification Church was founded in Korea, it was not begun for a local purpose, but with a religious meaning for the worldwide dispensation. A drop of water can originate deep in the mountains and trickle down the hillside, gathering with others and becoming a brook, then a river, finally to join the ocean, and in that way travel around the world.

Cultures mix and mingle, and out of this can come something good which will advance and elevate all people. This also happens in religious development. At first a few people gather, like drops from different mountains. Then, more will come together and a river will form, flowing down to the ocean, all the time enhancing man's standard.

If I go tuna fishing this summer, who will volunteer to go with me? What about the women? I have one boat and there is a limit to how many can get on it, so I will have more boats built for all of you to get on and we'll have an armada. We will have women as captains. Then, you women would like your future husbands to be captains too, right? Does that mean you want to marry fishermen?

Jesus told Peter he would be a fisherman; being a fisherman is not bad at all. Often American women are somewhat stronger than men, so I think the 200 mile limit was reserved by God for American women. I don't just believe that, I know it! When you have a full boatload of fish, I will recognize and accept you.

Did you know we recently acquired new property for a ship building industry? What would you do to become rich? Fishermen in this nation are some of the poorest-paid professionals, so we will create the best schools and best living standards for fishermen. Now, people visit the seashore for fun, but someday soon, they will come to the sea to work and go to the mountains instead for recreation. If that trend doesn't appear automatically, I will create it.

Twenty-fifth Anniversary of the Unification Church
May 1, 1979

Recently, I invited some elder ministers to travel the world and examine Unification Church activities. They were amazed at the tremendous variety of things I am doing around the world and they said, "There is nothing Reverend Moon cannot do, and nothing that he does not do." I was going to go to sea today, but the weather did not permit it. Some people might say I should rest on the Sabbath, but since the Sabbath is still a workday for God, going to sea and catching many fish for needy people is in accord with God's own standard. In our concept, a holy day is not one for just sitting around. It is far better to go out and bring reconciliation to people who are fighting.

The Trust Placed in Us
January 3, 1979

How many years will it take for you to win the marathon? Three? Ten? Even for the unbeatable Reverend Moon it took sixty years to cover the course and still I have not finished the race. Last night after graduation at the seminary, I took all the leaders fishing. It was in the midst of a thunderstorm and we were cramped in a little boat. Even though they didn't say this, inside they were probably thinking, "What kind of father are you? Can't you have even one day to rest?"

When a person occupies love, he occupies all other authority and dignity as well. The record-setter is the kind of person God and history are looking at. God is expecting you to become one who sets the record, so this is a one-in-a-million opportunity. I am now investing much energy in the fishing industry and I am determined to make it successful. When you see my desire, you should put your shoulders to the job to be a champion in that arena. I would like to see all the seminarians and church leaders go for sea duty for one and a half years. At this time, there is no master or host who is claiming or leading the American fishing industry because this is one arena God carved out and saved for the heavenly dispensation.

What if I supply sufficient fish and say that Unification Church members will eat nothing else for six months, not even bread? We will give all the good fish to the trade and eat the leftovers ourselves. Will God say we shouldn't eat just the leftovers, or will He be touched? Who do we suffer for? For God and humanity. By doing this, we are covering God with an invisible net, making Him our prisoner. All you have to do then, is pull that net and God will have to follow you.

Record-Setter of History
July 1, 1979

Are you the kind of people who can rebound from pressure like a rubber ball, or will you be shattered by it? We need people who are not only elastic, but who are also tough and can endure. American religion is like a ship caught in a hurricane and the government is helpless and has no anchor. When the water is rough and the wind is strong and your ship is pitching and rocking out of control, what will happen? That is the kind of perilous situation we are living in today.

Do we in the Unification Church have an anchor? God is our anchor and I am the rope. That means all you have to do to survive is hold onto the rope; you don't even have to grip the anchor directly. The anchor is always deep in the water, so what you have to do is grab the rope and hang on. Other churches may be offering people a beautiful rope of gold, but there is no anchor at the bottom. The Unification Church rope is plain, but there is an anchor down below. Those people who advertise their beautiful rope criticize ours; even the government boasts how big its rope is and how fish-smelling the Unification Church is. However, the difference is that we have an anchor and they don't.

Historical View of the Dispensation
September 18, 1979

America is surrounded by the sea, but has not conquered it. I initiated our fishing business to revitalize American fishing and seaports. This is certainly our pride. The ocean contains tremendous resources, but no one has received them. We are inheriting it from God and all we have to do is tap it.

To the MFT
January 2, 1980

You may think you have been working a great deal, but by my standard you have been relaxing too much. When I was out fishing all day, not for one moment was I relaxing or napping. Every moment my mind was busy. When I watch the vast horizon on the ocean, I see a peaceful new world dawning and the whole responsibility is on my shoulders. How could I spend one idle moment?

I will not be indebted to anyone, not the thirty-six couples or anyone else, so I receive the credit for what has been done. In the fishing industry, for example, I laid a pioneering path for seven years. You know who won our first international tuna tournament; my boat caught the most tuna. I don't want to be second even in catching tuna. In every field and competition I have been second to none.

Every day I go out to the ocean at 2:00 or 3:00 a.m., and come back at midnight. So far, tuna fishing has been a pleasure sport, but when I started fighting, it became a battle. Usually, fishermen go out at 9:00 or 10:00 a.m., but if they want to beat me, they have to go out much earlier. I am already out when they come at 5:00 a.m.! When I started, the price of tuna was ten cents per pound, but now we have pushed it up to $2.50, and eventually it will go up to $5.00 per pound. This is how I will bring prosperity to tuna fishermen, who in the past only made a meager living. Those who have opposed me in the past for no reason are now realizing that I am helping the fishermen and reviving the local economy.

The European leaders really worked hard when they came this time. We are building many boats, not only small ones, but thirty and forty foot boats. Professional tuna boats are 150 ft long and carry a crew of twenty-five people. I will build many of those in the future. Then, I will designate national leaders as captains of those boats, or even just to be fishermen. They will have no time to look left or right, but will just go.

Total Self Re-Evaluation
September 14, 1980

We have also started an Ocean Church. It is a simple fact that the world is one-third land and two-thirds ocean. Man can eat everything that lives in the ocean, including the plants that grow there. Can you eat everything that grows on land? The ocean has whatever the land has, and even more. There are thousands of kinds of fish. Americans prefer to eat the meat grown on land, but they never learned to eat the meat grown in the ocean. Recently, Americans have learned that fish is better protein than red meat, and they think of it as natural food which is uncontaminated. Now they are becoming interested in eating fish, so that they can live longer.

In Wyoming, a cattleman told me that cattle could be bought from twenty to seventy dollars a head if bought in quantity. In New York, beef is much more expensive, more like $400 a head. One big tuna costs $3.50 per pound, and sometimes they are over one thousand pounds. If you caught one big tuna a year, that would be almost $4,000 income. A tuna lays 1.5 million eggs in spawning season, but what about a cow? She has one calf a year, or two at the most.

Would it be more advantageous to raise cattle and take care of them all year, or go out on the ocean and catch one tuna? I really like the name "tuna" better than the name "cow!" If you catch one tuna a year, you can support yourself. You can ask your husband why he bothers holding down a regular job where his superiors just give him headaches, and advise him to catch just two tuna to support his family for one year. When you are confident you can catch two tuna, you won't worry about not having enough money any more.

The fishing ports in America are declining because young people don't want to fish, so the citizens are anxious to see their towns revived. They know there is a good future in the oceans. Our leaders were told to go talk to the city fathers in the towns I have picked and tell them why we are there and what we will do with our own money and what kind of center activities we will have. When they know we are committed to making the fishing business prosper once more, there will be some support groups which will want to help train our ocean-going crews.

We will offer a program to any young men who are interested in working at sea and show them what we are about. If they like our way of worshipping God, we will take them as candidates. . .As soon as a five-man crew is assembled, it will be assigned one boat. The thirty centers will compete to see who brings the better quality people.

Which will have more results--Ocean Church or the present system in the state centers? As the work expands, each small boat will have ten more boats under it, and soon we will have (with 30 centers) 300 boats plus 30 big boats around the American coastline.

Would you unmatched members like to be matched with people from the land church or Ocean Church? It's up to you; you have to live with that person, not me. When this Ocean Church is really underway, people will cherish it as a monument to the revival of their towns. America has three of the four best fishing grounds in the entire world, but America is not utilizing them because there is no substantial market for fish here. The beauty of our organization is that we will make our own boats, catch our own fish and sell them in our own stores.

America's fishing industry is declining, first of all because the ocean-going way of life is harder than life on land. Young people don't want a hard life. Second, fish don't sell well here; wholesalers sometimes pay only five cents per pound for fish, which is ridiculous. Third, the husbands are away at sea often, and their families start to break up. In this situation, who will go out to the ocean? Only Unification Church members! We pass the test in all areas.

Technology has made boat operation simple by the development of automatic pilots. You tell the machine which direction to go and the boat will follow that course automatically. Now, even a frail young woman can sit in the seat that used to be occupied by husky, burly captains. How fascinated God will be to see her, even when she dozes off because the automatic pilot is driving the boat and she has nothing to do. I like that! How beautiful she would be.

Will you women become captains one day? You should not forget there are sharks in the water. If even the women want to go, how can the men back away? You have to kick any such man. We have people who want to go, so that's the first problem taken care of. Second, is selling any problem for us? The women say it is no problem. Third, would you wives leave your husbands because they are away at sea so much? Even if they are out for six years? This ocean business is truly reserved for Unification Church members.

Our Duty, Our Mission
October 5, 1980

In the Unification Church we have five different colors of skin coming from all different parts of the world. Our goal is to unite them into one family of man. Furthermore, Unification Church life is complex. It involves not only Sunday morning service, but all kinds of things, including boat building and catching fish. There are even more fantastic things coming in the future.

The same principle is being applied to boat-making. Our people are making the best boat under the sun, but making it the least expensive. The only way they can do that is by sacrificially giving themselves. Through this process the most beautiful boat is created, and no one else has a boat that can compete. With the same spirit we can make a society, a nation. If we Moonies make the best kind of nation for the cheapest price, there won't be room for communism to creep in.

In the fishing industry, for example, I am working on such a scale that no competitor can outdo me. Once I proclaim something, it will echo through the entire country and the entire world. People cannot help but listen. I operate on a simple principle and I have a plan.

Things that are Important to You
February 1, 1981

My activities are not just religious; this is why people say I am an industrialist, a scholar, a movie-maker, etc. I deal with every facet of life with the same principle of love. Even if I go fishing, it is never to enjoy myself. I am never apart from my fundamental mission. That is why even tuna are attracted to me.

I am always living most naturally in two worlds, both high and low, moving back and forth between them. When Colonel Pak was in South America last summer, he met and was entertained by presidents of seven nations. He was given a great deal of honor because he was my aide . . . but when he came to report to me in Morning Garden, he couldn't find me in the house. Finally he found me at the bottom of the back yard, working with several members to fix a rope for fishing. In my life, I have embraced both extremes of high and low. God's will is to bring these two extremes into harmony, and only God's power can do this. A true Moonie is the personification of the life-power of love, so we can bring the two worlds together.

The Two Worlds of Good and Evil
February 15, 1981

I will probably be fishing in Gloucester again this summer, living in fisherman's clothes instead of suits. Even if you are wearing smelly fisherman's clothes, the righteous side is still the same, and it is always going up; you cannot come down lower than where you are now. Though we may find ourselves in the beggar's position, we will never go down, but will go up. I live here in order to leave the right tradition. When young people in the future learn about my experiences in jail, it will set their minds on fire. I never minded having to endure prison life, knowing that it would leave a strong tradition for the future.

Our Identity
April 1, 1981

Perhaps you might think when you are out fundraising, "Here I am on this hot day and Father is on his yacht somewhere." However, when I go out to sea, I do not do it as a pleasant diversion for one day or one week. I go out for many weeks, every day, rain or shine. I created Ocean Church for the sake of mankind; I had to establish the tradition for the future. There is no one else who can do it.

I have spoken extensively about Ocean Church and some of you American members may think, "I don't want to hear any more about Ocean Church," but who can take responsibility for the ocean in America? No matter how difficult, I will take that responsibility--

that is my own determination. No matter how much you hate to go to the ocean, I will continue to do it for the sake of this country. After making that kind of foundation, I know American young people will get the message. You might say, "I like what Father says, but I don't like the things he does!" I can sort out among you those who like what I do and those who don't like what I do. How about you American young men? Do you like Ocean Church? Are you faithful only with your mouth?

During the tuna season this summer, we will spend half a million dollars--every year we have lost money on tuna fishing, but we must do it anyway. Nobody else is doing it. The tuna season is only during the summer, so all the rest of the year is unproductive. I have an overall plan to supplement tuna fishing with other fish--fluke, flounder, bluefish, etc.--according to their own seasons. We must establish the standard for successful businesses and use all the different fish throughout the year.

Once you get out on the ocean, you come to love it, but until you do, the ocean is a stranger. Do you think I was born an expert on tuna fishing? No, I had to learn it from scratch. I kept on working day after day and established the tradition. Now, I am known as an expert among the other tuna fishermen. I developed the plan, putting in seven or eight seasons faithfully, until I learned how to catch tuna. Such a thing cannot be accomplished as a hobby or by someone who just enjoys the ocean.

I spoke yesterday at the seventh graduation of the seminary. Afterwards, with all the parents and professors around, I changed into my fishing clothes and went out on the boat again. The waves were rough in the Hudson, but I went out anyway. Those people might have thought me eccentric, but they don't understand what our goal is. Even though my feet swell up from standing all day, I reprimand them and command them to continue working. I certainly don't do this because it is enjoyable. I am very serious in this work.

As a religious leader, I certainly do not enjoy killing tuna. When they are bleeding and staining the water all around, I cannot enjoy such a sight. I am in deep prayer, apologizing to those tuna and begging them to understand. I tell them, "You must give yourselves for the sake of the people of America because they are much more important to God and the universe than you. I need you as a sacrifice to offer for all mankind; I beg you to give yourselves." Since God and the universe know that, they are helping us and our ocean businesses are prospering. You must have a clear understanding of this.

For the sake of mankind, it is righteous to go out to the ocean. From this perspective, who is the noble, righteous American who wants to follow my tradition? I have been looking for those Americans for over ten years. Probably, I must bring people from Japan to set the standard here and then Americans can inherit it. If the Japanese do not succeed, I will use the Korean people. If they fail, I will send my own sons and daughters to make the right tradition. That is why I have been taking all the Blessed children out on the boats this summer. This is the first time I have done such a thing, but we must accomplish our objective on the ocean.

America will lose its chance to take advantage of the resources of the ocean because it is not taking any initiative in that direction. Many other nations are taking the ocean away from them. I have followed the Divine Principle in setting the Ocean Church tradition. I waited and tried to give every chance to Americans, encouraging you to participate in ocean fishing. If you still do not respond, what else can I do? The one who loves the ocean the most will become its master. I am trying to love the ocean the most.

You should not dismiss this thinking of mine. It is very important. All the other shipbuilding companies in the South have gone bankrupt except the Master Marine Company. Even though we were losing money for a while too, we did not stop our business . . . The businesses of our church members are based on love. If you truly put your heart into a business, it cannot fail because God and the universe will support you.

Our Ideal Home (Part Two)
June 26, 1983

Look at how dark my skin is. I did not lie in the sun on a relaxing vacation. I am fighting on the ocean and enduring every day, leading Ocean Church. There has been no master, no caretaker of the ocean; no hope in the ocean. I want to harness the ocean and bring young people to the ocean so that its resources can be harvested. The ocean has been abandoned. Look at what is happening in South America, in Central America. All the countries there have become isolated, with the ocean being given away.

Look at the American seashores, east, west and south. Those sea coast towns and ocean ports have become desolate ghost towns. All have been given away to the refugees from South America with many becoming routes of Communist infiltration. Those people are harnessing the resources from the ocean. They use them as a staging area for drugs as, for example, with the Mafia who use those ports to bring in drugs that are corrupting American youth. The Coast Guard and police alone become helpless unless each citizen is willing to participate in a great crusade in order to prevent America from being turned over to communism. Somebody must defend this country. No one is really doing it; no one is risking their life to do it. While I am doing it, the local governments persecute me instead of helping me. No tuna fishing season is a fun time, but a war time. I knew the experience of catching a giant tuna would be one that members could not forget for the rest of their lives. Everybody is looking for an opportunity to fish for tuna; they look forward to it, hoping I will invite them again. In order to make American young people pay attention to the ocean, I studied how tuna fishing could be made more interesting and exciting. I am a champion of tuna fishing around the world. I discovered the "Reverend Moon" system. People observed my way of doing it and now they try to imitate me. In fact, one fishing shop sells "Moonie" fishing gear. Whatever I use, they want to buy. Everybody is following me.

Usually, during the tuna season, rich people would go out at ten in the morning and come back at two or three in the afternoon. I changed that tradition; I left at two in the morning and came back ten at night. Now, everybody who fishes for tuna in Provincetown knows that when the tuna season comes, they have to get up at two in the morning. No one can deny that Reverend Moon is the pace setter.

You think fishing is where you spend hours and hours doing nothing. No, you must always be alert. It is a master technique which I cannot explain (you must experience it). It's the black belt technique. For example, when a fish is coming, I know without looking directly at the fish, that the fish is ready to bite. There is a teasing game; if you pull in too wildly, you lose the moment. You just need to pull, pull a little bit, then the fish is so interested, coming at you and ready to bite. At that moment, you pull hard, double level, second level, two levels pulling. Who knows such things? Who even bothers to figure out such timing? I am researching and studying all things. You have to go through certain levels of instruction: level one, two, three--even more levels to go. If it's raining, do you think we should stop and go back? Mother always thinks that I should come back a little early, that it's not good for my health to stay out so late. However, I must go on; I must finish! I am just intoxicated in teaching the members. I have to study more. How can I come in early? The future economy of the world, the food problem of the world, the survival of mankind will be solved by the ocean. This time of study can determine the future life or death of mankind.

In the future seafood industry, Reverend Moon and his determination, his world view and ideology of fishing will go on. When I am suntanned to an incredible degree, is it a shame or pride? By doing the most incredible work for the sake of humanity and the future of this country, I am going to develop catching different species of fish. Each fish requires special treatment and a special secret to catch it. I develop techniques and at the same time, I can teach those techniques. When you apply those techniques, you become an economically viable fisherman. Then, you will think about moving into higher level fishing.

This nation of America is God's blessed nation. Abundant material blessing has been given, but this belongs to God. We are the custodians or stewards of this property. No matter what, we have to do it. Organize! We have to win over all the God-given blessings. I laid the foundation. I will set the tradition in America. If you succeed in following that tradition, you can inherit the rest of the world. That is what you will do.

This is a new chapter, a new era, a new history. You are the master of this new history. In order to do that, you must have determination. Without that determination, you will not even get near it. With the determination to give up your life, you can separate yourself from Satan; Satan will have no business with you anymore. Don't try to survive. Go to the land of death. That means that God will take your sacrifice, and God will never let you die. That is the Principle. That is my life exactly! I have always been ready to die. This tradition goes down from me to you, from you to all others. As long as you are alive, as long as you are breathing, you cannot complain because you have already made that resolution; you are ready to die, but you have not died yet. You can say, "I am still alive! I have to go on, more and more. I am not yet dying, that means I can still go further. Thank God!"

My leg is not just muscle, it is always swollen for some reason. Even with the overuse of my legs from standing on the deck so long, I say, "Thank God! I have not yet died; I am still breathing. God, I can go on." One night there was an accident and I collapsed in the bathroom. Mother does not know, but I fainted. I got up and the first words I spoke were, "Thank God, I have not died. I can go on and on and on." That is the kind of tradition I laid in the Unification Church. How can we complain? If we disregard this tradition, America will become a very dismal and tragic country. When you inherit this tradition, America will be glorious and prosperous. Everlasting blessings will come if you inherit this.

Leaders' Conference
June 27, 1983

There are so many varieties of activities and different projects in our movement, but when the summer comes, the most important of all is Ocean Church.

As you know, only one third of the surface of the globe is land; two thirds are ocean. Therefore, without knowing the ocean we can never have dominion over the entire globe. So every one of you, every member of the Unification Church, is required to take a basic training in Ocean Church, including navigation, repairing and so forth.

It is just incredible to think that the ocean is not dead! It is alive and moving; not only moving by itself, but moving in conjunction with the land masses and the solar system's sun and moon. It's so wonderful to know the beauties and wonders that are hidden within the ocean. More than anything else in all of God's creation, the ocean is most sensitive to all the movements of the universe and the weather.

Once you understand the sensitivity of the ocean, have dialogue with it, and cope with it, you'll understand the most intricate of God's creation. By doing so, you can understand about land masses in no time.

The ocean is not only sensitive, but is also very changeable. Therefore, to know how to cope with this changeable situation provides us the best understanding of ourselves and nature. In order for us to mold our God-centered character we must know how to deal with the ocean, how to become subject over it, and how to have dominion over God-given creation.

Since God is presiding over the whole realm of dominion, God presides over all the changing and moving sensitivity of the entire creation. This is God's character, so we have to mold ourselves into resemblance of that character, particularly the American youth, because this nation is surrounded on three sides by the vast ocean. Generally, an American's interest is focused in one narrow direction, but that is not the way God likes. You must open yourself up to all four directions, and the ocean is presenting you such a training ground. American young people have had very little interest in the ocean. Without this interest you might find it alright just for the present time, but as to a future vision, without an interest in the ocean you will never be a leader.

Many people say the space age has arrived, but you cannot dwell in space. From the ocean, however, you can draw resources, you can make a living from it. For this reason I founded and created Ocean Church. I feel in the future, the Ocean Church foundation can be greater than the land church. So far we've been living in the land church era, but from now on we'll be living in the Ocean Church era.

Becoming Flexible

Another important point is that when you deal with the ocean, you cannot be stubborn, cannot be inflexible -- there's no way that you could survive on the ocean. The ocean-going person must be flexible, and understanding of all situations.

For example, land people work during the day and rest at night. There's no such thing on the ocean; you work day and night because the tidal waters are moving and all the fish groups move accordingly. When certain tidal waters and the fish come at night, then you've got to work at night.

Furthermore, even if you have a perfect schedule, when a typhoon comes, you absolutely have to abandon that schedule. You cannot go by your own will; you have to adapt to your surroundings and accomodate to others. So in ocean life, you have to make harmony with nature, particularly the ocean's nature. On land you can mostly plan and set your goals, but on the ocean you cannot do so. While on the land, man confronts and tries to dominate nature. However, the ocean nature doesn't allow it so easily; therefore, men must learn how to live with the environment and how to be flexible. Instead of confronting nature, the ocean-going man must try to harmonize with it.

Training for Hopeless People

Some people have an inherent difficulty with the ocean because they have seasickness. Father sees that those guys have very poor ancestors! (Laughter)

In the long run, it is true that there was something wrong with their ancestors; either they had ulcers, or some kind of physical problem, some kind of deficiency -- you cannot deny that.

Unification Church members can be classified into three different groups. One is the *champions* of the ocean. You know we favor them, and the second class would be the *mediocre*: they're not so bad on the ocean but not so good either. Finally the third category is the *hopeless* group.

The Ocean Church mission is to use this hopeless group and make it into champions. This is true with any country that a nation is declining not beceause there are no strong people, but because there are so many hopeless or weak people. So the nation's well-being is assured by making the hopeless people strong, then the safety of the nation is assured. To transform hopeless people to hopeful people, that is the challenge of the Unification Church, particularly the mission of the Ocean Church. That means that the hopeless people will go to Ocean Church first, because they need the most training. So I have to tackle those people first.

Exposing Human Nature

I know how to train the hopeless people: take them and kick them into the ocean for three months. As long as they survive there . . . initially they look miserable, throwing up, looking pale like a green apple, and from every hole in their body there's some kind of mucous coming out.

But without hesitation, I say, "Kick 'em in." One by one people come out. Seasick people don't need any hospital you just leave them on the land for a while. There they get their appetite back, and restore themselves -- this is the best hospital. When their health is restored we kick them into the ocean again and repeat the same cycle. Then, after coming out again -- almost dead, let them recuperate, and then for the third time, kick them out again.

This three time repetiton will make everyone who is hopeless into a champion. To make hopeless people hopeful again, that's the true challenge for Ocean Church and it is just as true for the nation.

Also, those healthy people who have aptitude for the ocean are ready to go. Tyler just completed his Ph.D., but he never dreamed that he would be assigned to Ocean Church, yet I kicked him into the ocean. I'm sure he thought he'd make a good professor at the Unification Theological Seminary, or he could write a book, or go to other universities and teach. I'm sure he thought about those things. Tyler Hendricks is like a real gentleman-type. He's very suave, very cordial. But once someone goes to the ocean . . . there is no bathroom, not even on the *New Hope.*

This summer I gave a boat to the sisters and a boat to the brothers, working side by side. When bathroom time comes, what do you do? You've got to do something! You have to get yourself relieved! Whether there are sisters around, or brothers, it doesn't make any difference. Then you need guts. You have to attend to your relieving mission. The men face such situations and deal with it naturally without any panic. They have to have guts to deal with it. When a sister goes to the ocean, there's not such a thing as always being polite and looking nice; she's got to be like a man and survive and deal with the ocean. She's got to expose her hip sometimes. But she doesn't even mind; she just thinks, "Well, my hip is somehow exposed, but I know all the brothers will close their eyes, so I don't even have to shield myself too much."

She needs that kind of guts, and when the man is doing his "business" he knows that all the sisters will close their eyes. No problem. That's the way it goes, and if anybody doesn't close their eyes, they will suffer the consequences.

Ocean training occurs at a crude, raw level of experience; therefore it will show the basic human nature. It exposes everything: you cannot hide on the ocean, so when you go out, you have to expose yourself. You can learn about yourself, about others and how to harmonize with others.

Another point: when you live on the land, you don't worry about record breaking or setting new records, but anyone who goes on the ocean always thinks about setting a record and breaking the record. These people are always goal-oriented.

In this life, it's so complicated, so sophisticated, it's virtually impossible to try to stand up or find a place to make a stand. But when you go to the ocean you have a chance. Everybody is at the starting point. You go down to the zero point and start from there to rise up and win all over again. When you men and women go out to the ocean, try to be the champion, set a new record. That kind of goal-oriented life, I like very much.

Leaders' Conference
August 26, 1983

Christianity, Judaism, and all great religions had some connection to the mountains. Moses went to the mountains to pray for forty days, Jesus prayed and fasted on the mountain, and Buddha spent six years in the mountains searching spiritually. The Unification Church has experienced those sorts of things, but we don't stop there. We move on and create "Ocean Church" for the first time in history.

Why did Father Create it?

When you look at the globe, two-thirds of the surface is water. So where, do you think, would there be the greater quantity of living things, in the ocean or on the land? In the water. The population of the earth is estimated as four billion people, but how many hundreds of billions of living things are there in the sea! One more difference between the sea and the land is that tall the oceans connect, so that you can go from one ocean into another. Land masses are also connected, but the oceans are all moving into each other as one harmonious whole. The ocean is living and moving accordingly; it's not dead. Because the waters covering this planet earth are alive, we can see that the planet is alive.

So far the ocean has been used for transportation -- but people haven't begun digging in the ocean to find its hidden resources. In recent years, some nations have claimed a 200-mile limit as "territorial waters." More and more, the competition for ocean resources is sharply dividing the nations. Will the 200-mile limit still have meaning if there are no more fish to catch?

When people begin to discover resources in the oceans, maybe they'll begin to claim 300 miles, or even 1,000 miles as their nation's territory, and then the question will arise, "Who is the true master of the ocean? Who will be the true host?"

Suppose all of a sudden a gigantic land mass emerged -- an island in the middle of the ocean. Who could claim that land? Volcanic eruptions can happen anywhere. Nature follows nature's laws.

While God is looking over His creation saying, "I created the ocean; who shall be the host?" what is He searching for? He is looking for men of vision and courage. Actually God is looking for a group of people who are organized and committed to meeting that challenge of the ocean. If such a committed group of ocean-loving people can be found, God will give the blessing to them. Those people finally become candidates for lordship over the ocean. They must be thinking with the Creator's mind. As such courageous people from around the world come together and unite in one common goal, one ideal, that vision must transcend all national and racial boundaries. Once such an international group is set up, it will be very difficult for any single nation to challenge it, for it will truly have a global perspective.

What will Ocean Church do in the future? What is its purpose? It is to teach how to love the ocean, to utilise it under the concept of the Creator's ideal, and have dominion over it according to the Principle of Creation.

The dividing line between ocean and land is the coastline, so the coast represents the link to both worlds. Eventually the coastline will become most important. Coastline property will become most valuable of all.

Ocean Beauty

The ocean encompasses an incredible variety of moods. The calm sea is like a beautiful woman, and the beach sand is like silk --

dazzling beauty and peace. But that is not all the ocean presents to you -- a little breeze and the water starts to dance -- just a little bit. No matter what kind of a ballerina or dancer you may find, you can never compare her/him to the dancing of the ocean! The dancer is on a small, limited stage, but the ocean dances without limit. There is no end to its stage.

Sea birds fly around, coming and going, landing and taking off, all with different shapes, but all with harmony. Seagulls come, they sing and present beautiful harmonious motion. Sometimes this beautiful scene is changed dramatically by the sudden volcanic explosion of a huge whale jumping out of the water. The splashing water shines, reflecting the light -- just incredible beauty. So much variety and change!

When the ocean gets mad it definitely shows its dignity and power as if it's saying, "Anyone who comes at me -- I will swallow you." Indeed, the ocean can swallow anything riding on it.

Normally, a high-speed boat runs beautifully on calm water just like on a silky highway, but once those waters get mad, splashing with high waves, that boat becomes helpless. When the waves go up, the boat answers, "Yes sir, yes sir!" When the waves suddenly drop down the boat can only obey because there nature is the most powerful and the ocean says, "You listen to me. Here I am!" For that reason, men and women who love the sea cannot be boastful, cannot be arrogant. They must know how to humble themselves to the overpowering strength of nature.

On the land you see green. Sometimes you see butterflies or birds flying around, but everything is stationary. In the ocean, however, the varieties of fish are moving in all kinds of ways and from one place to another, demonstrating their own beauty. So is there greater beauty and incredible mystery on land or in the ocean? [Ocean]

When you put yourself in God's position and ask, "Why did God make the ocean?" we might say, "It 's because God would be bored with the land in just a few days, but the ocean is never boring. The sea and the ocean represent the future vision, the future dream." Therefore, anyone linked to a futuristic vision must be interested in the ocean. In this way, he is bound to become a visionary person.

Great Literature

What kind of people are found on the ocean? Courageous men following other courageous men. What about women?

If the husband got very bad diarrhea, lying flat on his back, would his wife beg him to stay at home and postpone the journey, or would she stand up and say, "Well, come on. I'll take over. I'll continue the mission." If she has that much determination then even the boat's steering wheel will wake up and be happy to find a woman's soft hands on the wheel after being handled by so many men's rough hands. When you women take charge of the mission, then even the ocean waters will feel sorry for you. They don't want to be rough on such beautiful women; they want to be nice to you. Even the ocean spray raining down is smiling, and saying, "I want to cling onto your skirt!"

It's so poetic isn't it? That's the way great literature and great poetry were born. When I start speaking about the ocean, there are many stories, legends, and myths to be told. Sometimes I speak to the birds and sometimes it's as if the birds are obeying whatever I am thinking, flying this way, or landing over there. Then when I think, "Now go away," the birds will suddenly depart.

Literature is written in that form, expressing such communication with nature. Creation says to man, "If you leave me yet still love me, I will go away from you." Man and the creation are just longing for each other, like the love between man and woman.

If a man and a woman have a date on top of the Empire State Building, 102 stories above the ground, it's very romantic. But why is such a date considered romantic? Because such a tall building is unique, and the two people are getting together at one of the highest points on the land. Even though no one notices, they feel they're coming together as a king and queen, meeting on the top of the world.

Say a man and a woman meet at the South Pole. There's no one around. It's all ice and snow. That's where only penguins are kissing each other. Even just imagining it is a romantic moment! In order to have some incredible stimulating experiences, you have to go through what some normal people would not do -- something unique, challenging, something special. Without it, you cannot derive that kind of intoxication and beauty of stimulation.

Alaska

Recently I have traveled to Alaska two times. Alaska is a mysterious virgin land with hardly any people living there. It's a land of bears and wild animals. Most people think of it as snow-covered, with glaciers, rugged coast, and white whales, sea lions, and seals. One day I went to a small island and encountered some sea lions. As soon as they saw me, they began giving their welcoming rally, "Arrh, arrh, arrh, arrh, arrh!" They started all at once, sounding incredibly unique! But there were two kinds of sound to distinguish: one was a male sound and the other a female sound. United in harmony, they built a resounding chorus.

There were also whales, and halibut, which are flat-fish like flounder, and grow up to 300 pounds. Maybe there are many people who don't know about the halibut, and God is thinking, "You poor people. I created such an incredible creature, and gave it to you. All you have to do is come and claim it and use it for your benefit, but you never even bother to come. You never even look at my creation and try to enjoy it. You poor people!"

God is interested in courageous people. God Himself is adventurous, and He also made us that way.

American Women

Having all these special experiences, I was thinking about how American women should be. In Alaska, I met a certain couple. The man lived there all his life, and I was interested in why this couple lived there. "Why do you live here?" I asked. "Because we love the freedom -- total freedom." They explained that in New York and other places, even if you're just trying to walk in order to get somewhere, you always bump into someone. Or else you're always stepping onto somebody's territory and they're telling you, "No, no, don't touch it." But in Alaska, they said, you keep running year after year, and you bother no one. "We are totally free," they said. Doesn't it sound good? So even though Alaska legally belongs to the United States, men and women living like this couple in Alaska virtually have no nationality.

When I looked at the woman, I saw that she was so tiny and skinny. But this particular American woman had guts. She had a vision, and she had a universal mind. She had confidence and conviction, so that even if she went bear hunting, she could knock down the bear! So I thought, "That's the kind of woman's spirit that impelled the westward-bound Americans toward their new horzon. This was the Frontier Spirit."

So how did she come to meet and marry a man like that? She revealed to me that she'd traveled all around the world. So she'd met all kinds of men, including civilized and educated men. Then she came to Alaska and met simple and unassuming men. The ones who went to the ocean were fishermen, and those who went to the mountains were hunters. Here was the hunter-fisherman combination. This one man completely captured her attention by his rugged simplicity and his very natural and unassuming nature. She married him and remained living in that environment where whatever they were doing, they were just as they are -- very real, very truthful. So when they met their neighbors, or even a stranger, they gave everything, and they loved these people much more than they'd love even their own brothers and sisters.

The man told his wife that he would show her the most beautiful places and he took her to where there was an abundance of wealth from the ocean, and when they went to the mountain they saw the hunting grounds with an abundance of wild game.

Normally when a fisherman has a good fishing ground, he keeps the secret for himself, but this man said, "this is the fishing heaven -- you can catch even bigger ones." This man was really trying to be helpful and of service to others. When I was there, he prepared bait and tackle for others, and he tried to have my party catch a big fish. He really wanted me to catch the big ones.

On that day, a lot of fish were caught, and I was truly appreciative, so at the end of the day, I wanted to give him a little token of appreciation, some gift. But the man said, "No, not at all. It's my privilege, it's my honor. If you give that to me, you are taking away my honor." I sent a representative trying to persuade him to please receive this gift but the man was adamant in refusing. Finally, though, that humble man gave in and said he would accept a gift, since he saw the Reverend Moon's beautiful heart. So I thought, "After many long years, I met the True American!"

Salmon

Upon examination, I decided that the salmon shall be the fish of the Moonies, that the salmon symbolizes the Moon spirit. The male and female salmon go swimming together side by side up the streams to the spawning grounds. The purpose for going all the way on such a journey is to lay eggs. The couple starts digging in the sandy bottom for a place to lay eggs. The male swims protectively around the female. Their skin color and their muscles change, and after their egg-laying mission is accomplished, they give up their lives and die. Their bodies decompose and become fertilizer for the feed for their babies.

This is their destiny of death, to succeed in reproduction by the laying of eggs, it is for love. Without fear, they go toward that destiny side by side. It's a beautiful thing to behold. I saw the image of the ideal couple in those salmon.

When all mankind is living like salmon, surely the dwelling of God will be with men, and God will be happy among men. Why did God create salmon? To educate men, to present the example to people in order that they can follow.

Let me draw a conclusion. Ocean Church has been created in order to teach the ideal of God. His creation of the ocean, so that we gain true love for, and true dominion over, the ocean. Each person can become a co-creator with God, anticipating and participating in God's great task of creation, and understanding it as a friend.

Vision and Providence in Ocean Church
August 28, 1983